# Singing with Sai Baba

# Conflict and Social Change Series

## Series Editors
## Scott Whiteford and William Derman
*Michigan State University*

*Singing with Sai Baba: The Politics of Revitalization in Trinidad,* Morton Klass

*The Spiral Road: Change in a Chinese Village Through the Eyes of a Communist Party Leader,* Huang Shu-min

*Struggling for Survival: Workers, Women, and Class on a Nicaraguan State Farm,* Gary Ruchwarger

*Kilowatts and Crisis: Hydroelectric Power and Social Dislocation in Eastern Panama,* Alaka Wali

*Deep Water: Development and Change in Pacific Village Fisheries,* Margaret Critchlow Rodman

### Forthcoming

*The Bushman Myth and the Making of a Namibian Underclass,* Robert J. Gordon

*Surviving Drought and Development: The Ariaal of Northern Kenya,* Elliot M. Fratkin

*Harvest of Want: Hunger and Food Security in Central America and Mexico,* edited by Scott Whiteford and Anne Ferguson

*The Myth of the Male Breadwinner: Women, Industrialization, and State Policy in the Caribbean,* Helen I. Safa

*Reform Without Change in El Salvador: The Political War in the Countryside,* Martin Diskin

*Literacy and People's Power in a Mozambican Factory,* Judith Marshall

# Singing with Sai Baba

## The Politics of Revitalization in Trinidad

Morton Klass

**Westview Press**

BOULDER • SAN FRANCISCO • OXFORD

*Conflict and Social Change Series*

This Westview softcover edition is printed on acid-free paper and bound in library-quality, coated covers that carry the highest rating of the National Association of State Textbook Administrators, in consultation with the Association of American Publishers and the Book Manufacturers' Institute.

The extract from "The Caribbean Man" by Leroy Calliste (the Black Stalin) on p. 66 is reprinted by permission of the Copyright Organisation of Trinidad and Tobago Ltd.

Copyright © 1991 by Westview Press, Inc.

Published in 1991 in the United States of America by Westview Press, Inc., 5500 Central Avenue, Boulder, Colorado 80301, and in the United Kingdom by Westview Press, 36 Lonsdale Road, Summertown, Oxford OX2 7EW

Library of Congress Cataloging-in-Publication Data
Klass, Morton. 1927–
  Singing with Sai Baba : the politics of revitalization in Trinidad
/ Morton Klass.
    p. cm.—(Conflict and social change series)
  ISBN 0-8133-7969-5
  1. Hinduism—Trinidad and Tobago—History—20th century.
  2. Sathya Sai Baba, 1926–    . 3. East Indians—Trinidad and Tobago—
Religion.  4. Trinidad and Tobago—Religion.  I. Title.
II. Series.
BL1168.T753K42  1991
306.6′945′0972983—dc20                                        90–12014
                                                                  CIP

Printed and bound in the United States of America

The paper used in this publication meets the requirements
of the American National Standard for Permanence of Paper
for Printed Library Materials Z39.48-1984.

10   9   8   7   6   5   4   3   2

*For Fran*

*More than a sister,*
*less than a lambchop,*
*with much affection*

# Contents

# Preface and Acknowledgments

In the summer of 1985 my wife and I returned to Trinidad and Tobago for the first time in twenty-seven years. The immediate reason for the visit was my desire to learn about the growing "Sai Movement" in that country, the account of which makes up most of the following text. But I would be dissembling if I did not note that we had other reasons for returning to that island nation. For one thing, the study would bring us back among the people of South Asian descent who make up a large segment of the Trinidad and Tobago population. The teachings—and the person—of the Indian holy man known as Sai Baba have a particular attraction for many Indo-Trinidadians, and the Indo-Trinidadians, in turn, have a particular attraction for me.

My professional career began in a village in rural Trinidad in 1957. I was one of a group of nascent social scientists led by Dr. Vera Rubin, the Director of the Research Institute for the Study of Man, and advised by Professor Charles Wagley of Columbia University and Dr. Lloyd Braithwaite of the University College of the West Indies. Our group was among the forerunners of a generation of scholars, at first from the United States and other countries and then from Trinidad itself, that would study and debate the changes that were taking place in the West Indies in general, and in Trinidad in particular.

For a year, my wife and I lived in the village of "Amity" (a protectively fictitious name) and wrestled with the question of the extent to which the villagers exhibited "Indian" or "West Indian" culture (or both). We made lasting friends, who helped us with our research and who taught us about life and friendship and much more. We studied them while they studied us, and during the year we lived in Amity our first child was born. It was one of the most wonderful years of our lives.

My doctoral dissertation (see Klass 1959) became a book eventually (see Klass 1961) and took its place among the growing and disputatious literature on ethnicity and change in the Caribbean. Meanwhile, my own academic interests shifted to South Asia proper and to other (though not unrelated) issues of anthropological theory and substance (Klass 1978, 1980a, etc.).

I wanted, therefore, to revisit the village I named "Amity." That is, really, I wanted to see how socioeconomic problems and prospects had worked themselves out in the island nation composed of two major and very different ethnic groups (and many smaller groups); I wanted to renew old friendships throughout the island and to meet scholars who had come to the fore in Trinidad since my first visit; and I wanted to view the East Indian dimension of Trinidad, as of 1985, from the perspective of a scholar who had first visited the island in 1957.

Trinidad, as we shall see in the text, has changed—in some ways out of all recognition, and in some ways (I shall argue) hardly at all. "Change" has always presented a challenge to the ethnographer, who usually studies a community *in vivo*—at a moment in the present—on the basis of which he or she must attempt to penetrate both past and future. In the case of the village of Amity in Trinidad, as it happens, *two* ethnographers have contemplated the community at widely spaced intervals, both using the "ethnographic present" tense.

To compound the problem, theoretical interests and conventions also change over time, making comparative analysis a tricky and chancy business. There is in fact no end to the changes to which one must adjust when one attempts an overview of events taking place in more than a quarter of a century. The very terms people use for themselves undergo modification and even substitution. In the 1950s, for example, the descendants of immigrants from South Asia who were living in the then British colony of Trinidad preferred to be called "East Indians" (in preference to the earlier and pejorative term "Coolies"), particularly because it distinguished them from what they perceived as the African-derived "West Indians."

Now—at the moment this book is being written—the political scene is very different. Most of the British West Indian colonies have become sovereign states: British Guiana, for example, is now Guyana. Trinidad and Tobago, of course, is now an independent nation. All the citizens are Trinidadians (some prefer to call themselves Trinbagonians), and most of those with African—and some with Indian—ancestors consider themselves to be "black." Many Trinidadians of South Asian descent, however, (as we shall see) perceive "black" to be a politically imperialistic, or hegemonic, category, and while agreeing that all are "West Indians" together, prefer to distinguish themselves from those they refer to as "Africans" or "Negroes" by calling themselves "Indians."

In Trinidadian academic writings, there are signs of a mutually acceptable distinction between "Afro-Trinidadians" and "Indo-Trini-dadians," but it is difficult to assess the use of these terms by the population at large. I shall explore some aspects and implications of all this in much greater detail in later chapters. I propose, however, to use the term "Indians" for the ethnic group (as the one in most common use by all segments of the present population)—except, of course, where context demands something else.

Currency has changed, too, over the years, and the reader who wishes to evaluate the significance of changes in people's income requires some guidance. British currency (pre-decimal pounds, shillings, and pence) was used in Trinidad during the nineteenth and early twentieth centuries and was only beginning to be replaced (school arithmetic problems were still in terms of pounds and shillings) in 1957 by the decimal "BWI (British West Indian) dollar." One "BWI dollar" (usually represented as BWI$1.00) was worth about US$.68 in 1957. In 1985, the national currency was the "TT (Trinidad & Tobago) dollar," equivalent in that year to approximately US$.41. The interested reader is now left the task of estimating the significance of changes in the relative buying power of all the currencies concerned.

Orthography does not so much change as remain stubbornly different. We (scholars and typesetters) continue to suffer because the British and American users of the same English language cannot agree on one consistent spelling for "color" ("colour"?) or "apologize" ("apologise"?)—and in this study I have had to distinguish between "Centers" in the United States and "Centres" where British English is spoken and written.

The knottiest problems, however, have arisen from the need to render into English orthography words of South Asian derivation—from ancient Sanskrit, and from Hindi and other contemporary languages. I suppose I could be stubborn about it: adopt one orthographic convention and force all South Asian terms to conform to it. Such a procedure would not be advisable in a work such as this—for one thing, in a direct citation I am bound to spell the word as the original author does, and the spelling conventions in the works I will draw upon are astonishingly varied.

I propose the following, therefore:

(a) In my own text, I will adhere to the conventional English spelling for a term, where there is one (e.g., Krishna). If the term lacks a common English spelling, I will use the more scholarly transliteration. Italicization is always a problem: I propose to italicize only terms deriving directly from Sanskrit or Hindi and not generally familiar to Western readers, and which, further, are of major religious significance. This requires difficult judgment calls on my part: I do not italicize "guru" and "avatar"—but I do italicize *karma, moksha* and *Rama*. Finally, I have decided to dispense with the various diacritical marks as unnecessarily distracting for those readers who are not Sanskritists:

the intricacies of Indian languages are not of primary concern for this work.

(b) In citations from the works of others I will of course render terms as in the original texts. Thus, for terms that relate to, and most particularly derive from, the religion of Sai Baba, I will use the orthography to be found in the publications of that movement. Where those publications exhibit inconsistencies, and they do (e.g., "Satya" and "Sathya" are used in almost free alternation), I will make my own choice (e.g., Sathya)—except, of course, in citations where an alternate form is used. After much uncertainty, I have decided to give the text of prayers used in Sai Baba services exactly as they are rendered in the publications of that movement, even though such renditions may depart sharply from what scholars of South Asian languages would consider acceptable orthography (or, for that matter, translation).

(c) Names—most particularly the names of Trinidad Indians (e.g., Rooplalsingh, Marajh)—will be spelled as their owners appear to wish. Other Trinidad Indian terms will also conform to the practices and conventions of that nation (e.g., *Chuttri,* which for Sanskritists would be *kshatriya,* second highest of the four *varnas,* or caste groupings).

And, if here and there I am found to be in violation of the rules I have just set forth, I beg forbearance: as you can imagine, it hasn't been easy!

But it has been fun, and many people have gone out of their way to make the research enjoyable as well as productive. The list of those to whom I am deeply grateful is long, and inevitably incomplete.

Professor Judith Johnston of Adelphi University is entitled to head the list: she first made me aware of the emergence of the Sai Baba movement in Trinidad and urged me to conduct a study. Her recommendations—people to contact, places to stay, things to do—amply demonstrated her deep and continuing attachment to the nation and its people.

I am grateful to Barnard College for the Faculty Research Grant that made it possible for me to go to Trinidad in 1985 and to complete the study from which this book derives.

Professor Lambros Comitas of the Research Institute for the Study of Man (and of Teachers College, Columbia University) gave me much good advice before I set out. In doing so, he was continuing the tradition of the founder of the RISM, the late Dr. Vera Rubin, who counseled many a young scholar—myself included—off to conduct research in the West Indies.

The list of Trinidadians who went out of their way to be helpful is long indeed. Professor Lloyd Braithwaite, my guide and mentor in 1957, resumed the office as if hardly a month had intervened—to my great good fortune, for his insights into Trinidad, and West Indian, social structure stand sharply alone.

Director Jack Harewood of the Institute for Social and Economic Research, University of the West Indies, and Mrs. Walters, his assistant, were most kind and helpful. I am grateful to them and to so many others at UWI who gave us time, advice, and much-needed assistance: the Chief Librarian, Mrs. Jordan, and Mr. Bal Persaud of her staff; Mrs. De Lima of the Housing Office; the faculty and staff of the Sociology Department, and others whose names I neglected to write down but whose kindnesses will not be forgotten.

Professor R. K. Jain and his wife, Dr. Shobitha Jain; Dr. Bruce Godsave; Dr. T. K. Haraksingh; Dr. Brinsley Samaroo; Dr. Colin Clarke; Dr. Kenneth Ramchand were among the many new friends we made and to whom we are indebted for both scholarly and personal support and counsel. I thank them all for making our stay so pleasant. Steven Vertovec took time from his own busy research schedule (see Vertovec 1987) to instruct me on the complexities and subtleties of current religious practices among rural Trinidad Indians.

In my first book about Trinidad, I acknowledged my enormous debt to Dr. Michael and Rita Reesal. We have remained close friends for the past quarter-century, and the debt has grown ever larger. Though no longer resident in Trinidad, they have guided and advised from a distance, and again—and again inadequately—I express my deep gratitude. There is apparently a family tradition of hospitality: on this visit we were fortunate enough to be befriended by their cousins, Doyle and Mollie Seunarine.

Dr. Surujrattan Rambachan is a busy man, a leader in politics and religion, but he sat with me for hours, patiently answering questions and offering insights. I am grateful to him and to his wife for their hospitality.

Devotees of Sai Baba demonstrated their confidence in their faith, and their belief in kindness and service to others. It is impossible to name all who welcomed us, but I must give special thanks to Mr. Chilo Rooplalsingh, Mr. Ramlochan Nancoo, Mrs. Laksmi Rao, our old friends Mr. and Mrs. Parsuram Ramsundar and Mr. and Mrs. Naipaul Sookdeo, Mr. Rajanand Persad, Dr. Ramnarace, Pandit Jairam Sharma—and all the members of the El Dorado Sai Centre, beginning with the amiable and most patient Chairman, Mr. Chandrasein Dookie.

Our friends in Amity have grown older, as we have, but their capacity for hospitality has not changed. My wife and I offer more than thanks—

we extend our abiding affection to Mr. and Mrs. Solomon Lochan, to Mrs. Sheila Ramsingh and her family, and to all the others who welcomed us again to their homes.

Headmaster Hardeo Ramsingh and Mrs. Ramsingh were their usual hospitable selves, and we thank them for much good food and pleasant conversation. But I want, in addition, to take this opportunity to acknowledge a very special debt: I have had the good fortune, in my research in Trinidad in both 1957 and 1985, to have been the recipient of the knowledge that can accrue only to a life-long resident who is a natural sociologist. Headmaster Hardeo Ramsingh taught me to understand his people and his community during my first visit to Trinidad, and he was there to advise Dr. Joseph Nevadomsky in 1972. When I returned in 1985, I sat again at his feet—and learned. I think it is fair to say that much of what has been written about the changing life of the people of Amity, and indeed about the Indians of Trinidad, derives from the continuous, compassionate, and perceptive observations of this teacher and scholar.

I particularly thank all those who assisted during the writing of this book. Professor Abraham Rosman, as is his wont, cleared away underbrush that was obstructing my view. Shirra Birnbaum and Mia Ahntholtz, Research Assistants extraordinaire, achieved miracles in the dusty stacks of the Columbia libraries. I am grateful to all the students and colleagues who had the fortitude to listen to my accounts of the religion of Sai Baba. They gave me much good advice; and if I am still in error, the fault is unquestionably mine.

And, as I reach the end of the list, I wish to express my most particular gratitude to Aisha Khan—who returned from her own research in Trinidad as I was completing the final draft of this book. Her perceptive comments, wide-ranging knowledge, and imaginative suggestions lightened my task immeasurably. I have cited many of her observations throughout the text, but I want to acknowledge my indebtedness for more than just an occasional reference or clarification: when her own work is completed and sees publication, other scholars will share my enthusiasm and gratitude for her insights.

Sheila Solomon Klass, as I have noted in my earlier books, was there from the beginning. I thank my co-researcher, my best critic, my editor, my colleague . . . my wife.

*Morton Klass*

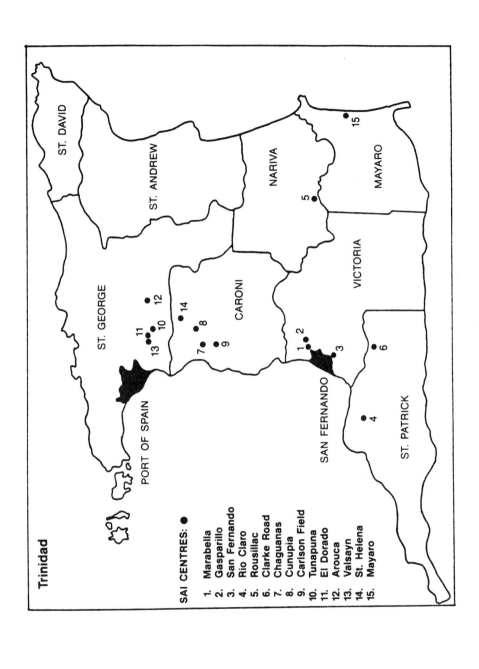

Trinidad

SAI CENTRES: ●

1. Marabella
2. Gasparillo
3. San Fernando
4. Rio Claro
5. Rousillac
6. Clarke Road
7. Chaguanas
8. Cunupia
9. Carlson Field
10. Tunapuna
11. El Dorado
12. Arouca
13. Valsayn
14. St. Helena
15. Mayaro

# 1

# Introduction

This book is offered—at least to begin with—as a contribution to the rapidly accumulating scholarly literature about "Overseas Indians." Specifically, it is a report about the contemporary "Indians" of the West Indian nation of Trinidad and Tobago—but one, I hope, that is seen to encompass a number of other issues given considerable attention by contemporary social scientists. Scholars interested in such issues, however, often derive from different disciplines and sometimes isolated specializations; in this study much disparate scholarship will be drawn upon in an effort to explore unexpected relationships and to offer new hypotheses.

In the late 1950s I studied, and reported on, the round of life in one "East Indian" community; on this occasion I hope to illuminate important aspects of current "Indo-Trinidadian" life by examining the implications of the recent spread throughout that population of a new religious movement, deriving from contemporary South India, constructed around the adoration of a holy man known as Sathya Sai Baba. Happily, however, it is not necessary to restrict myself, in my current account, to my own observations in Trinidad then and now. There is a wealth of literature on the "Indians" of Trinidad, written by both internal and external scholars, and I shall attempt to incorporate some of their findings and views.

But, as I have indicated, it is my hope that this book serves to take the reader beyond the single issue of what is happening today to the "Indians" of Trinidad. Everywhere in the world, and frequently (as in Trinidad and Tobago) as a legacy of colonialism, nations have emerged exhibiting remarkable, and sometimes divisive, ethnic diversity. Who are the "natives" and who—no matter how many generations of residence—the "aliens"? Whose nation is it—who shall rule? Can diversity of language, religion and other aspects of culture be permitted to continue in a modern state? One need only look at the day's newspaper: the strife and the attendant anguish are unabating. Clearly, there is a continuing urgent need to further explore and better understand the boundaries and processes subsumed under the term "ethnicity" and this book is intended as one response to that need.

And, all over the world people are found to be turning to seemingly obscure or out-of-the-mainstream religious leaders. This book will give give close attention to the concerns and perceptions—as expressed in their own words—of the Trinidadian followers of Sathya Sai Baba.[1]

Many scholars have sought to discover what such seekers are searching for—and others have tried to understand what they are turning from. Neither question is an easy one, and the issue is further complicated by the likelihood that people of different societies, different ethnicities, different classes, and different religious backgrounds have very different motivations. There is a growing and important literature on new religious emergences—on what some people call "cults" and on what others term "millenarian" or "revitalization" movements—and it is my hope that this study is seen as a useful contribution to that literature as well.

It is therefore likely that the readers of a book such as this may represent a wide variety of interests, differentially familiar with the various topics under discussion in the pages that follow. I shall endeavor, throughout the work, to provide some of the background information necessary for those who, on the one hand, know little of the interaction between sugar and slavery in the West Indies, and those who, on the other hand, know little of currents and conflicts in contemporary Hinduism. Nevertheless, of course, this is clearly not intended as a definitive work on "slavery" or "Hinduism" as such—but rather as a consideration of the interpenetrating effects on the Indians of Trinidad of such things as the circumstances of West Indian history or the consequences of South Asian theological ferment.

In this chapter, and before I begin my account of what I have concluded are the sources, the events, and the implications of the recent emergence in Trinidad of an influential body of people who believe sincerely in the divinity of Sathya Sai Baba of Puttaparthi, I propose to explore what I perceive to be important, and often related, dimensions of many of these seemingly disparate issues. Some of these issues will be pursued in further detail throughout the work; others, such as the ramifications of "East Indian" ethnicity and the dispute over the meaning of "caste," are provided to clarify my own position on matters of continuing contemporary dispute.

The word "Indian" has caused trouble since ancient times. The Greeks (or maybe the Persians) converted the initial sound of "Sindh" to an "h" and eventually it was lost completely. Columbus, as every schoolchild knows, thought he was in "India" when in fact he had barely reached the Bahamas, and the indigenous inhabitants of the New World have ever since been saddled, to their understandable indignation, with the misleading label of "Indians."

Then, to compound the confusion, Europeans brought in Africans whose descendants came to be known as "West Indians." This was followed by the importation of laborers from South Asia (and even, on occasion, from the "East Indies"!) to the sugar plantations of the New World, as well as to plantations in Africa, Oceania, and elsewhere. As a consequence of all this, territories in and around the Caribbean came to exhibit (in addition to "Red Indians" or "Amerinds" or "Native Americans") a number of local populations of South Asian descent who were called "East Indians" to distinguish them from the "West Indians."

Over the course of time some of these "East Indian" populations increased in size and proportion until in such current nations as Trinidad and Tobago, Guyana, and Suriname they came to constitute a minority so large as to approach—sometimes to reach—numerical majority status. Significantly, and as a response to national independence, such communities are often in the process of a new name change, answering to "Indo-Trinidadians" or "Indo-Guyanese" or to some other hyphenation reflective of their new citizenship.

Whatever name is used for or by them, the members of such populations—let us call them "Indian," at least for the moment—contribute much to the economies, to the popular culture, to the intellectual ferment . . . and occasionally to the political volatility, of the nations of which they are citizens.

The "Indian" community of Trinidad and Tobago, as I have already noted, has fascinated social scientists for a long time. The questions to be posed, and investigated, and debated, were of abiding interest to scholars of many disciplines. Did the "Indians" maintain—*could* they have?—Indian values over the generations they were embedded in that Caribbean melange of European and African cultures? For thirty years, scholars (including myself) have tried to reach agreement on the extent to which the immigrants and their descendants did or did not reconstruct South Asian patterns of family, of community, and of social relationships. There was much dispute and, as we shall see, certainly little consensus.

And, whatever they were, what were they in the process of *becoming*? In 1957—the year in which I began my research on "East Indians" in Trinidad—a distinguished scholar of the Caribbean, Daniel J. Crowley, argued in an article in the *American Anthropologist* (Crowley 1957) that the East Indian population of Trinidad was moving rapidly and perhaps inescapably toward assimilation and the emergence of one amalgamated (or Creole) culture. On the other hand, however, and as a result of my own study of one community (Klass 1961), I concluded that the "East Indians" of at least that village had managed to reconstitute a community exhibiting north Indian forms of social, economic, and ideological structure. It seemed to me at the time that this "persistence" in the midst of change was a crucial component of the East Indian way of life, and so I questioned (Klass 1960) whether the future would in fact see the rapid cultural assimilation projected by Crowley.

I think now that we were both right—and wrong—and that what actually happened during the ensuing quarter-century could not have been predicted by anyone.

In 1985 I returned to find striking changes in the village I had studied almost thirty years before. For one thing, it can no longer meaningfully be considered an isolated community, and so in this account the information from the village I called "Amity" is subsumed within the larger context of the total Trinidad Indian community.

Nevertheless, the ethnographer who moves too far from "little community" runs the risks of overgeneralization and over-simplification. I was particularly fortunate in having Amity as a base, and as a baseline—for another anthropologist had studied it between my two visits. The changes that took place in Amity reflect and derive from the changes that took place in the larger Trinidad Indian community, and indeed throughout the nation of Trinidad and Tobago.

During the course of this work I will review the circumstances of Trinidad Indian life from the earliest days to the present, and I will attempt to show how recent events—such as "oil boom" and subsequent "oil bust"—precipitated profound and unexpected consequences.

Indeed, I am further convinced that "what happened" had a lot to do with the reception ultimately accorded Sathya Sai Baba. I am suggesting, in other words, that an examination of the ways in which Sai Baba's teachings have spread may provide a new illumination of the islands' ethnic diversity and on the changes that are, or are not, taking place.

For example: it is obvious that this is a book about the passage of an "Indian" religion from "India" to a group of "Overseas Indians." True, but there is so much more to the event than that. After all, we shall see that the teachings of Sai Baba are universalistic: not only are they directed to all people, everywhere, of all ethnic identities and faiths, but in addition they assert that all religions are one, and all forms of God are one—and the prospective devotees are assured that they may continue all their traditional religious practices.

If the message of Sai Baba came to Trinidad and Tobago, therefore, did it come only to the "Indian" segment of the population? Were these teachings able to cross the sharp ethnic divide in that West Indian nation between those of putative African descent and those of putative South Asian descent? If not, what happened to the "universalistic" content of the message?

Furthermore, did the message of Sai Baba appeal to all the varieties of "Indians" in Trinidad? As it happens, the "Indian" community is seamless and monolithic only to the unobservant outsider; to those who know it it exhibits many highly important subdivisions and lines of stress. Was Sai Baba's message of equal interest—of *any* interest—to Muslim or Christian "Indo-Trinidadians," or were the Hindus the only ones to respond favorably to the Indian holy man?

Since we must wrestle with questions such as these in the course of this book, we must here pause and resolutely bring the word "ethnic" front and center. What *are* "East Indians"? Are they a "race," "a nationality," an "ethnic enclave," a "minority," just part of the "Third World," or rather just part of the "Black" division of certain "White" dominated societies?

Views held by scholars, as well as by people inside the group and in groups in contact with it, have changed and continue to change— though, of course, there are still those who hold resolutely to the older beliefs. In the nineteenth and early twentieth centuries, most observers saw the South Asian immigrants as a distinct "race": that is, as a group supposedly biologically distinguishable from the "race" variously known as "Black," "African," "Negro," or "Negroid"—as well as from the "race" known as "European," "White," or "Caucasoid"—and from the "race" called "Chinese," or "Mongoloid," and so on.

In Trinidad, in those days, there were obviously a lot of "races" and there were interests sufficiently vested to keep them distinct: "Portuguese" were not "White" (because their ancestors had been indentured laborers) and neither, for other reasons, were East European Jews and Lebanese Christians (who were subsumed together in the census under the intriguing racial category "Syrians"). People of combined European and African descent were considered members of a "mixed," or "coloured," "race"—and thus categorically distinct from either of the two supposedly "pure races" (Klass 1960).

As might be imagined, not all people were happy with their "racial" designations—though they rarely questioned the assumptions underlying such categorizations. In 1958, rural Trinidadians who admitted to some African ancestry, but who were lighter in skin color than their neighbors, or even just a bit wealthier, made a point of informing the visiting anthropologist that they were "Coloured" and not "Negro"—and they were often quick to characterize the "Negro" as "lazy" and "stupid." On the other hand, many East Indians argued that it would be wrong to ascribe "race" solely on the basis of skin color: they pointed to the hair on their heads and argued that the texture of East Indian hair separated the group from "Negroes" (of essentially similar skin color) and placed them firmly in the same "race" ("Caucasian") with Europeans.

As we shall see, this concern with hair as a racial indicator has never completely disappeared among East Indians, and plays a part in the reception of Sathya Sai Baba in Trinidad.

By mid-century, however, many scholars, and anthropologists most of all, were turning away from "race" both as a biologically useful term (for dealing with human variation) and as a meaningful basis for observed differences in behavior or propensities. "Culture" and later "ethnicity" replaced "race" in the scholarly lexicon.

Change in popular perception and usage was of course slower. For many people *ethnic group* remains simply a euphemism for *race:* supposedly a biological category. Nevertheless, once social scientists shifted their attention from biological to cultural heritage members of groups under study had their own reactions to—and developed their own ways of utilizing—the contemporary scholarly perceptions, conclusions and terminology. The Prime Minister of Trinidad and Tobago often insisted publicly, for example, that East Indians had lost most of their "Indian" cultural heritage and were now simply "poor" Trinidadians—while East Indian members of opposition parties introduced anthropological works into public debates to counter the views of the Prime Minister.

There is still much debate about what "ethnicity" means or should mean, about why it persists—or disappears—or re-emerges, and the Caribbean remains an area of particular scholarly interest.[2] In Trinidad and Tobago, as we shall see, ethnic distinction is very much alive and has a role to play in politics, in social relationships—and in the arena of particular concern in this work, that of religion.

But "ethnicity"—crucial though it may be—is not the only factor for us to consider, in our search for answers to the questions posed above. A *religious movement* came to Trinidad, and so it will also be necessary to look closely at Sai Baba and his teachings, and to appreciate relationships, as well as similarities and differences, between Sai Baba's teachings and those of Islam and Christianity. Only then can we hope to deal effectively with the reception accorded his teachings by different Trinidad ethnic groups.

True, the man (or "Godman") known to his followers as Bhagavan Sri Sathya Sai Baba was born a Hindu in a village called Puttaparthi, not far from the city of Bangalore in south India,[3] and his teachings, as we shall see, derive from those of Hinduism. Nevertheless, just as he has proclaimed that he has now transcended his original human birth as a Hindu man to become incarnate and manifest divinity, so his message, he says, both supersedes and encompasses Hinduism along with all the other religions of the world.

Sathya Sai Baba, in other words, claims to represent the universal "Godhood" that underlies all names and forms of divinity among all humans everywhere in the world. His fundamental message is that he has come to usher in a new age of Love and Peace, and that it will begin during his present human lifetime (he was born in 1926), during which the leaders and followers of all religions will acknowledge him as God. After that, he says, he will die and be reborn again to preside over the new age. Meanwhile, it is his task and that of his followers to spread the word, to alleviate suffering, and to help individuals turn toward spiritual improvement and away from material concerns.

His teachings, and the miracles he has performed over the years (materializing sacred and precious substances, healing the sick, etc.), have unquestionably attracted people of other religions, from all over the world. Indeed, his devotees are said to number by the millions in India, and by the thousands in other parts of Asia, in Europe, in Africa, in North and South America. They worship him simply, as he has requested, by singing hymns at devotional gatherings known as "sat-sangs" and by performing acts of charity in his name. Sai Baba does not require that devotees relinquish their wealth—there are no assessments or even dues—or even adopt ascetic practices: a devotee should try to "improve" to the best of his or her ability, and should give to the needy with a full heart.

Given all this, some might want to know why I have limited myself only to the manifestations and permutations of the worship of Sai Baba to be observed in the tiny West Indian nation of Trinidad and Tobago.

Why that, specifically? Why not a study of the religion in India, where it began and where most of the devotees are to be found? Why not focus upon Sathya Sai Baba, himself? The answers lie partly in the areas of my own limitation and expertise, and partly in the need, in a work such as this, to provide sharp boundaries for theoretical interests and topical concerns. Thus, I am a cultural anthropologist interested in the comparative study of religion, but I am not a theologian or professional student of "Religion." I have earlier studied, and written about, community life and village-level religion both in India and among the descendants of emigrants from India who now form half the population of Trinidad and Tobago (Klass 1961, 1978). I have not met with Sai Baba nor visited the myriad communities of his followers in India (though I have read most of the available literature). I have, however, returned to Trinidad where I interviewed Sai Baba devotees at length, and attended satsangs with them at their Sai Centres all over the island.

In other words, I cannot, on the basis of personal on-site research, command all aspects of Sai Baba worship in India and the entire world—but I can report, as a result of the kind of research I have conducted, on this religious movement and its members in one bounded locality with which I have long-term familiarity. I can begin by conveying something of the total matrix—social, economic, political, and religious—of the West Indian nation of Trinidad and Tobago. Within that framework, I will be able to explore how the news of Sai Baba arrived and was received—accepted and rejected, and by whom—and how leadership and formal organization emerged.

Indeed, I think I can do more. Using the available literature, and the insights gained from my own research in India and in Trinidad, I can examine the similarities and differences between orthodox Hinduism and the teachings of Sai Baba—and between the so-called "Western" religions and those of South Asia. Such an examination becomes particularly important in a study such as this, because the "Indians" of Trinidad have long been exposed to the missionary activities of Christian churches, and for the most part have proved remarkably resistant: in that context, what is the attraction of this India-derived religion, and for whom—and how does the message and the proselytizing differ from that of Christianity?

Thus, when we turn our attention specifically to Trinidad Hindus, we can begin to probe aspects of structure as well as belief. How has the Trinidad Hindu leadership responded to the spreading interest in Sathya Sai Baba? Do they recognize him as God? What of those who in various ways had broken away from orthodox Hinduism before Sai Baba's message arrived on the island—what of those who had identified with Arya Samaj or other reformist movements from India? What of those who had moved away from religion entirely—among the doctors and educators and other professionals?

Whatever the local "ethnic" or "racial" ascriptions and assertions, are *we* justified in calling such people "Indians"? Can we really look to Hinduism, to South Asian norms and structural principles, for any explanation or understanding of reactions in this island nation to the teachings of Sathya Sai Baba? I think so, but I admit the issues are quite complex and subject to much dispute. It will be necessary, inevitably, to sift the arguments about whether or not the "Indo-Trinidadians" remain recognizably "Indian."

Unhappily, much of the discussion about change in East Indian institutions has been clouded by serious differences in understanding about the fundamental nature of those institutions. For example, one of the most controversial issues of the earlier debate was whether anything resembling "the caste system" of India had been reconstituted among the overseas Indians in Trinidad. The question seems simple enough at first glance—but the answer depends upon more than accurate field research. Most of all, how do you *define* "caste" and "caste system"?

Do you, to be specific, see "caste" as a phenomenon integral to the "caste system" of South Asia—so that by definition outside that system there can *be* no "caste"? Or, do you define "caste" simply as an endogamous marriage group—so that once there are (unpunished) marriages with members of other groups, the group is no longer endogamous and therefore no longer a "caste"? Or do you see "caste" as an occupationally specialized body, so that once members depart from the "traditional" occupation they cease being members of the "caste"? Is "caste" to you solely a reflection of an ideologial system—one in which people who believe in the rebirth of the soul assume that one's "caste" is divine reward or retribution? Or do you, finally, define "caste" in terms of some combination of all of the above?

As it happens, I subscribe to none of the above definitions and approaches, and in my own writings on the nature of "caste" (Klass 1980a) I have argued that we should begin any consideration of the "caste system of South Asia" by noting that it is the manifestation of an institutionalized socioeconomic arrangement for the production and distribution of food, goods, and services. This system seems to have prevailed in South Asia for centuries, probably millenia—very possibly since rice agriculture and social stratification began to characterize the region.

But there is of course more to the "caste system of South Asia" than that: there is a complex infrastructure of values and beliefs which supports and validates it. These in turn find their expression in Hindu teachings (as in accounts of the "origins" of caste distinctions, or in theories about the relationship between social position and reincarnation) and in many other ramifications of the social and ideological system.

In other words, the structural principles that underlie "caste" are to be observed—*in India*—in such phenomena as the particularistic values of Hinduism, as expressed both in the so-called "Great Tradition" and in the actual village-level religious practices, as well as in other aspects of life that, as in any society, reflect the principles of perception and ordering that govern choice.

What, then, of "Overseas Indians"? Has "caste" disappeared or been retained among the present-day descendants in the West Indies of emigrants from South Asia? I suggest that we can begin by agreeing (a) that the classic economic system of South Asia (whatever it may have been) could never have been transported to the West Indies, and

(b) that traditional caste occupations and internal political structures are also unlikely to have been reconstituted among overseas Indians. Surely, the evidence supports such conclusions, and few would want to contest them.

Those issues behind us, we can address questions of changes in values and social structure, and here there must inevitably be debate, for these are difficult matters to deal with. As we shall see, the ethnographer, returning from the field, can report specifically—even statistically—on marriages and occupations. But how are "values" expressed? Can we ever be sure that the same value is present even when two people make the same choice in the same situation? What of the same choice in different situations? Is it possible that one and the same value may be being expressed by *different* choices in varying circumstances?

Here, I suggest, an analysis of the responses in Trinidad to the teachings of Sai Baba has an important contribution to make. We will find that we must focus directly on values and structural principles as we strive to make sense of what happened—and what did not happen. In such an endeavor, the fact that we are dealing with an emigrant population—an ethnic enclave, or what you will—both complicates and illuminates our inquiry, for it is one thing to analyze a society and its culture as an isolate and a very different thing to try to explore the dizzying interpenetrations of ethnicity.

Louis Dumont (*Homo Hierarchicus,* 1970), for example, has argued that the Hindu (South Asian) social system—as expressed in what we call "the caste system"—reflects the unfolding of a set of values and structural principles which he encapsulates in the term "hierarchy." He contrasts this set schematically with what he (following Tocqueville) considers the set of "egalitarian" values and principles underlying contemporary European and European-derived societies.

This work is not the place for a review of Dumont's work, or of the criticisms and support it has received. I would simply observe that, whatever the difficulties with Dumont's types—whatever the questions that may arise about the nature of "hierarchy" in India or "equality" in the West—it must be immediately apparent that, from the perspective of Dumont's dichotomy, the "Indian" of Trinidad comprises an unusually special case: is he to be considered "Homo hierarchicus" still, after a century and a half in the West, or has he become "Homo aequalis"—or perhaps something else entirely?

This is no sterile academic conundrum, I would argue, for a consideration of this issue will lead us to understand some of the reasons why some Indians in Trinidad are so attracted to Sai Baba—and why some reject him so emphatically.

The seemingly simple questions, we see, take us in many directions. As I have indicated, we have to look closely at Trinidad and Tobago and the "Indian" community, past and present, from many perspectives. We also have to look very closely at the religion offered by Sathya Sai Baba—and therefore at certain aspects of "religion" itself. Do Christians and Muslims of whatever ethnic identity agree with Hindus and Buddhists about the nature and concerns of what they may all label as "religion"?

But before we can even attempt to answer such questions, we find ourselves faced with other, more difficult, ones. What of *us*—the scholars? Do *we* agree on what "religion" is or is not? Consult the literature and you will find little consensus—even in a single discipline, such as anthropology—on the definition and boundaries of the term. Happily or unhappily, in a work such as this we cannot brush such disagreements under the rug, for the subject under consideration necessitates sharp terminological boundaries. Do the teachings of Sathya Sai Baba, for example, indeed constitute a "religion" or has he simply introduced another "cult" onto the world scene?

Opinion, it is hardly necessary to observe, is divided. In the many published volumes of his sermons and speeches, and in the writings of his devotees, his is a "religion" and sometimes a "movement." On the other hand, the two scholars who have written extensively on Sai Baba and his followers in India (Swallow 1976, 1982; Babb 1986) refer to the phenomenon as a "cult."

Does it really matter which term we use? I think it does. Anthropologists have long known that pejorative terminology obstructs understanding. We have resolutely abjured such terms as "primitive," "barbaric," "savage," and "civilized"—not because we are noble, but because such terms are ethnocentric value judgements, the very opposite of scholarly objectivity. In the study of kinship, we long ago broke the restraints imposed by such categories as "descriptive" (European, civilized) and "classificatory" (non-Western, primitive).

Only in the study of religion do we seem to continue to have a problem. We still struggle to find neutral terms like "religious practitioner" to replace "witch doctor" and "medicine man," and we have barely contemplated the difficulties caused by terms, still in use, such as "magic," "myth," and "supernatural." In my view, "cult" is another such pejorative term—implying a belief system not to be accorded the dignity of being called a "religion."

In my discussion of Sai Baba's teachings, therefore, I shall avoid the term "cult" because it requires me to voice an opinion on a matter outside the scope of the investigation—indeed, outside my competence. In a precisely similar vein, I shall avoid any speculation about whether or not Sai Baba is actually divine, or whether he can or cannot perform "real" miracles. I hope to report accurately on what he teaches about himself and about the nature of the universe, and on what his devotees claim to believe, and to have experienced. I have no way of determining whether or not Sai Baba has brought a dead man back to life—but what is important for this work is that many of his devotees tell me that they believe that he has.

It may relieve the reader to know that I do not mean to quarrel with all terms and concepts to be found in the anthropological study of religion. I have raised these matters now only to point up my argument that a study such as this requires us to reflect on the terms we use—and therefore gives us new insights into those very terms and concepts. Thus, I have concluded, as will be seen, that the religion of Sai Baba has become—in Trinidad and Tobago—a "revitalization movement." That label is an important one in contemporary anthropology, but like many other terms in the study of religion it has inevitably precipitated controversy.

Some scholars, for example, prefer the term "millenarian" to "revitalization" in order to distinguish religious movements concerned with effecting change in earthly social conditions from those primarily concerned with salvation, or a better life in the world to come. Others of us, however, do not perceive the two concepts as necessarily mutually exclusive—and, as we shall see, they do not appear to be in the case of the religion taught by Sathya Sai Baba.

I prefer, therefore, to follow the approach to "revitalization" favored by Anthony F. C. Wallace. In societies where there is an "identity dilemma," he proposes; where there are "too many elements" so that "behavior is minimally predictable and approaches randomness," then: "the only possibility for improvement lies in simultaneously simplifying the repertoire and insisting on regularity of performance. Such a procedure, often carried out under the auspices of religion, constitutes a revitalization movement" (Wallace 1966: 212–215).

I expect to experience little difficulty in demonstrating that the "Sai Movement"—*in Trinidad and Tobago*—can be subsumed within Wallace's definition of a revitalization movement. Let us observe, however, that it is not an indigenous development—like the Ghost Dance of the Native Americans or the Cargo Cults of the Melanesians—but is a local manifestation of a determinedly universalistic world-wide religious movement. Should it then be labeled a "revitalization movement" in India—or in other parts of the world?

I don't know. My knowledge of Sathya Sai Baba and his teachings —in India—derives from the writings of others, both impartial scholars and devout devotees. I did attend satsangs at a Center in New York before my departure for Trinidad, however—and these preliminary observations and readings lead me to suspect that the same set of teachings can be received and absorbed in very different ways in different places.

For all these reasons, therefore, I would emphasize that—while I plan to touch on aspects of the "Sai Movement" outside of the West Indies—my primary concern in applying the concept of "revitalization movement" is to illuminate the stresses and complexities within the Indian community of Trinidad and Tobago, together with the relations in that nation between Indians and non-Indians.

### Notes

1. Transcriptions, or segments thereof, of interviews conducted with Sai Baba devotees will be found throughout this work; they are labeled "Interview References," are labeled consecutively, and are italicized to distinguish them from the rest of the text.

2. Glazier (1985) has compiled a collection of contemporary papers on ethnicity in the Caribbean, with overviews by Klass, Glick and Glazier himself.

The literature on "ethnicity" and "ethnic groups" is of course voluminous. My own usage tends to follow that advocated by Fredrik Barth (1969): an "ethnic group" is a form of social organization characterized by either (or both) self-ascription and ascription by others, and usually reflecting assumptions of common origin or background. My concern in this work, obviously, is with ethnic groups within a poly-ethnic system.

3. State boundaries and names have changed in India since Independence. The village, now in the modern state of Andhra Pradesh, was then in the state of Mysore (now for the most part in Karnataka). For many of his followers, and in much of the literature, Sathya Sai Baba is identified primarily with Mysore.

# 2

# Slavery and Indentured Labor

## Europe in the Caribbean

Contemporary Trinidadians of South Asian descent are the primary focus of this study. But why, it may reasonably be asked, *are* there Hindus and Muslims in the contemporary West Indies? What could have possessed their nineteenth century ancestors to travel half-way around the world to the Caribbean island of Trinidad?

Any discussion of current social or political issues in the West Indies must inevitably begin—if it is to be meaningful—with at least a passing reference to the importance there, in the past, of the cultivation of sugar and the concomitant of that activity—the institution of slavery. As Eric Williams, the distinguished scholar and political leader, once wrote: "Sugar meant labor—at times that labor has been slave, at times nominally free; at times black, at other times white or brown or yellow" (Williams 1944: 29).[1]

*Labor* requires little explication: to produce a profitable crop of sugar a lot of people had to work long and hard. But—why *sugar?* Why was the labor by *slaves* or—at most, according to Williams—by people who were only *nominally free?* And another thing: why should labor in the sugar fields be allocated according to skin-color categories?

These are all important questions, and the literature on them is rightfully large. While I must of necessity begin with a review of these topics for the sake of the reader who is ignorant of the history of the Caribbean and its peoples, this would become a very different work were I to attempt a truly comprehensive review. An adequate account of the history and consequences of slavery and the slave trade should properly occupy many volumes the size of this one. And so it does: the interested but hitherto uninformed reader is urged to turn to the appropriate literature, beginning perhaps with the four volumes of papers devoted to "West Indian Perspectives" edited by David Lowenthal and Lambros Comitas (1973) and the compendious *Peoples and Cultures of the Caribbean* edited by Michael M. Horowitz (1971). The knowledgeable reader will I hope forgive the brevity and over-simplification of my account here, appreciating my eagerness to move on to such contemporary matters as the arrival in Trinidad of the teachings of Sathya Sai Baba.

To begin with, then, let us note that the islands and adjacent territories of the Caribbean Sea vary in almost every way, and so do the peoples who have been drawn to them over the past half-millenium. The history of human interaction in the area is not a pretty one: European nations swiftly wiped out most of the original ("Native American") populations and warred incessantly with one another for local and regional control. Those who managed to achieve control scoured the planet for plentiful sources of labor for their plantations and mines: they needed "plentiful sources" because the conditions of labor were usually literally murderous.

Rarely did Europeans come to the West Indies in search of new homes: the lure was the hope of extracting wealth from the islands, one way or another, to be followed by a triumphant return to one's European homeland and a life of luxury. The mining of gold was an early lure for speculators from the Iberian peninsula, who were the first Europeans to enter the region. Soon, however, they turned to the cultivation of tobacco and other crops, including, eventually, sugar. For the success of all these pursuits they needed labor, and the native inhabitants were not "plentiful" enough, nor were even laborers from Europe, though both sources were drawn upon. Ultimately, the system of enslavement of West African people which came into existence during the sixteenth and seventeenth centuries seemed to provide the speculators with the desired source of a sufficiently inexpensive and seemingly inexhaustible supply of laborers.

Other European nations swiftly became interested in the wealth to be extracted from the Caribbean and laid claims to islands and territories. Among the contending powers, of course, were the British, and in their possessions they too carved out enormous estates. On some islands such estates prospered and inevitably the pressing need for labor led the proprietors to participate in the acquisition of enslaved West Africans. Elsewhere, however, proprietors of less prosperous, or less labor intensive, plantations made do for the most part with laborers from England. These were drawn from the poorest segment of the population, their numbers eked out with shiploads of transported criminals—all known as "indentured servants" (A. E. Smith 1947; Van der Zee 1985).

We might think of these indentured servants, in words reflective of Eric Williams' categories, as "nominally *un*free." They were as "bound" to their masters as any slave, but (in principle, if not always in fact) there was a time-limit on their bondedness, after which they would be free once more. Those among them who managed to survive the conditions of servitude might (in some cases) return home. Many stayed on in the islands in which they found themselves, some as now "free" employees on the estates—overseeing the new "indentured" laborers and the slaves—some attempting to farm on land rejected by the estate owners. On some islands, therefore, a new native but Europe-derived population began to emerge alongside the plantations.

Matters changed radically, however, when the cultivation of sugar spread to the British colonies in the middle of the seventeenth century. In Barbados, Jamaica, and other possessions, all other activities were curtailed or obliterated; enormous estates were carved out wherever sugar could possibly be successfully cultivated, and the use of indentured laborers gave way to the massive importation of West African slaves.

## Slavery

The institution that developed among the Europe-derived societies of the New World and that came to be referred to as "slavery" was an ugly one. Scholars have detailed all the horror, all the viciousness, all the inhumanity of the system (see, for example: Freyre 1964; Patterson 1967). Let us here all too inadequately observe only that "slaves" were humans who had been deprived of their freedom, of control over their own activities, in principle forever, unless freedom was somehow "restored" or "bestowed" by those who had enslaved them. They became "chattels"—equivalent to cattle, to work how and where their "owners" saw fit, with no rights to compensation other than whatever food or necessities their "owners" saw fit to "give" them ("give"—not "pay"—for one does not "pay" laboring chattels). Children of "slaves" were perceived as sharing in their parents' status, or lack of it, and could be bought, sold, put to any work without payment, just like their parents, generation without end.

The impact of living under such conditions was understandably devastating upon individuals, and Orlando Patterson has provided us with a most vivid and penetrating analysis of this in his work, *The Sociology of Slavery* (1967). One dimension of that impact—not necessarily the most painful, but one that has received the attention of anthropologists over the years—has to do with the extent of loss (and retention) of the cultures of origin of the enslaved peoples.

Since the earliest writings of Melville J. Herskovits, both alone (1941, 1966, etc.) and with his wife, Frances S. Herskovits (1934, 1947, etc.), scholars have debated whether the slaves were able to retain important elements of their original languages, beliefs, and systems of social relationship. Those scholars who, like the Herskovitses, believed that such retention had occurred argued that these elements re-emerged after the system of slavery was ended, and became very much part of life in the West Indies. Others, however, claimed that the conditions of slavery had so effectively obliterated the cultural heritage of the Africans that the cultural patterns that ultimately emerged had to be derived either from slavery itself, or from the imposition (or adoption) of European cultural beliefs and practices (cf. Frazier 1948; Greenfield 1966; etc.).

As one who has followed but not participated in this particular debate, I would offer only the minimal, but I think important, observation that the people of West African derivation now living in the West Indies also exhibit patterns that are neither exclusively African nor European—though there are elements present from both cultural systems—but which in many cases may fairly be labeled as distinctively "West Indian."

It is also important for this work, however, to note further that— whatever the cultures, the needs, the deprivations, the successful maintaining of traditions, of the people enslaved—to the people who were enslaving the Africans there was no awareness, during the period of slavery, of anything of value in the cultural heritages of the slaves. To the contrary, rather: religious practices, languages, patterns of leadership and authority, and all such, were viewed as intrinsically worthless, and, even more, usually as potential threats to those in control of the slaves. This attitude continued after slavery ended, as we shall see, and was addressed to those who replaced the slaves in the fields.

In many places in the British Caribbean, the end of slavery, as a formal institution, did not by any means free the descendants of the former slaves from work on the sugar estates—in such places, Williams' "nominally free" laborers of African descent continued to work as had their enslaved parents before them, under much the same conditions, though now for minimal wages and with at least the theoretical right to leave—should an alternative source of employment every present itself. As Eric Williams mordantly noted:

In Antigua, where all the land was appropriated, planters and slaves flocked to the churches when the news of emancipation reached the island, thanked God for the blessing of freedom, and returned to their labors, the slaves now raised to the dignity of landless wage earners paid twenty-five cents a day. The same was true of Barbados, where similar conditions prevailed, except that the Barbadians omitted the thanksgiving (1944: 191).

### Trinidad

Labor problems did emerge for estate-owners—the former slaveown-ers—in some of the Caribbean areas. In Jamaica, in British Guiana, and in Trinidad, among other places, slaves had alternatives and seized them enthusiastically, leaving the sugar plantations gravely depopulated. In Trinidad, this was due in some measure to the comparatively brief period between the establishment of British sovereignty on that island and the arrival of Emancipation.

One of the earliest islands to be visited by Columbus (who gave it its name), Trinidad remained a Spanish possession until the last years of the eighteenth century, and not a particularly prosperous one. Sugar cultivation did not become important until French planters were allowed to settle in the island in 1776, bringing slaves with them from Mar-tinique, Haiti, and other French Caribbean colonies. The population began to increase rapidly, and French, as the language of Europeans, and Patois (a French-African creole) as the language of the slaves, supplanted Spanish throughout the island.

Trinidad, it was discovered, was most suitable for the growing of sugar cane (at least in two substantial flat stretches of land in the island's interior), but the French planters soon found themselves in competition with British counterparts: in 1797, the island came under the British flag, where it remained until independence was achieved in the middle of the twentieth century.

Under the British, sugar cultivation grew in scope and intensity, and the planters imported huge numbers of slaves—from Africa, and also from other parts of the Caribbean, particularly from French-controlled territories where the effects of the French Revolution were precipitating unrest and dislocation. Nevertheless, Trinidad had been late in entering the game. By 1808, the slave trade was formally (if not effectively) ended by England, and in 1833 the Emancipation Act ended the practice of slavery itself in the British Empire (again, in principle, if not entirely in fact). There was still much cultivable but unoccupied land in Trin-idad, and there were sections, particularly in the hilly regions of the north, center and south, which were in any case unsuited to sugar cultivation. Large numbers of the freed slaves moved away from the plantations, leaving the estate owners to seek other sources of plantation labor.

As Eric Williams has pointed out, the ending of slavery did not mean in any way the ending of the system of production of which it had been part. Estate owners, determined to maintain their profits, therefore sought an alternative but equivalent source of labor. They turned, soon, back to "indentured labor"—the mode of labor that had preceded slavery in British New World colonies and had largely been superseded by it, but which had never completely died out: transported criminals, for example, continued to be shipped from England, throughout the period of slavery, as "indentured laborers."

"Indentured laborers," we have observed, were perceived as humans who had relinquished, or been deprived of, their freedom for a period of time. That is, they were not "chattels" but rather "unfree humans," even entitled as such to remuneration: the period of indentureship was for a fixed time, and was understood to be in exchange for *payment*— of one's "debt to society" for convicted criminals, and for passage overseas and for an extended stretch of contracted labor for those who entered into it voluntarily.

Nevertheless, though seemingly something different from slavery, indentureship in practice was sufficiently similar to be able to take the former's place in the world of nineteenth century sugar cultivation. For, whatever the origins and conclusions of indentureship, during the period of actual indenture the "servant" was perceived, and dealt with, as the equivalent of the "slave." Both were put to work in the same way, supervised in the same way by the same kind of overseers, kept in the same kind of quarters on the sugar estates, and given the same kind of food to eat. The monetary payment an indentured laborer received at the end of his service (usually five years, sometimes ten) was not perceived as burdensome by the estate (particularly after deductions for food, lodging, etc.), and even the cost of transportation overseas could be absorbed into the expenses of the estates without cutting significantly into their profits.

A major difficulty, of course, was finding a source of indentured laborers. In the decades following Emancipation, the sugar estate owners cast their nets widely and desperately. Laborers were sought in Portugal, China, even West Africa. The problem, as always, was finding enough of them to fill the barracks of the estates and keep them filled.

Ultimately, the South Asian subcontinent emerged as the primary supplier of plentiful indentured labor, and the production of sugar was able to continue throughout the world pretty much as before well into the twentieth century on estates in such British colonies as Trinidad, British Guiana, Jamaica, Fiji Islands, Natal, etc.—and in such possessions of other European powers as Martinique, Mauritius, Dominica, Dutch Guiana, etc. And, in all of these places, as the years went by, significant segments of the population began to be of South Asian extraction—"Coolies" as they were known to the others, but to themselves they were very much "Indians."

### The East Indians

On May 30, 1845, the *Fatel Razack*—bearing 225 prospective laborers (mostly male) from Calcutta, India—anchored off the coast of Trinidad and began disembarkation proceedings. This date, celebrated for the first time in 1985 as "Indian Arrival Day," is usually cited as the start of the Indian adventure in Trinidad.

By 1920, when the system of the importation of indentured labor finally ceased, approximately 143,900 men and women had been brought from South Asia during the intervening years. They came mostly from northern India (and most of these from what are now the states of Bihar and—eastern—Uttar Pradesh).

The story of their recruitment, shipment, and the conditions they encountered in Trinidad (as in British Guiana, Mauritius, and wherever they were carried to labor on sugar planatations) is not a happy one: indeed, it is more than slightly reminiscent of the accounts of conditions of African slavery (see, for example: Jenkins 1871; Gangulee 1947; Brereton 1974).

The people who managed the estates (Europeans at the top, people of African, or mixed African/European, derivation at the lower levels) tended, as I have noted, to view the indentured laborers as replacements for the previous slaves. The new laborers were housed in the very same slave "barracks" that had been vacated by the freed slaves—with no more concern evinced for South Asian patterns of family life, privacy, rules of association, etc., than had been given to West African practices and needs. Working conditions, again, reflected the perceived needs of the estates, as those conditions had evolved during slavery, and the "drivers" (of the earlier "slaves") continued in office, significantly without even a change in title.

As during the time of slavery, all non-plantation-derived authority and status relationships were perceived as potentially threatening by the estate management, and efforts were made to obliterate them. In practice, this often meant a special degree of hazing of potential leaders and in particular the demeaning of members of Brahman castes among the laborers. Those Brahmans who had been recruited in India (for the terrible famines of the latter half of the nineteenth century—a major impetus to emigration as an indentured laborer—did not distinguish high from low-ranked castes) were often at a disadvantage to begin with. For one thing, most of them were without experience in manual labor. Their caste rules, indeed, often specifically restricted their participation in agricultural work—and required them to eschew meat and alcoholic beverages.

If labor in the sugar fields was onerous for everyone, therefore, Brahmans—along with others without experience in agricultural labor —suffered particularly. Not infrequently, out of respect or simple humanity, Indians more inured to labor in the fields shouldered some of the Brahmans' burdens. "Drivers" who observed this are reported to have often gone out of their way to assign particularly demeaning tasks, such as the cleaning of outhouses, to Brahmans. Some of the other, non-Brahman, Indians acquired the European contempt for the Brahmans, but most defiantly maintained their respect for members of the highest and holiest Hindu *varna* (socio-religious division).

And, though many Brahmans suffered during indenture, members of the group had resources to draw upon. The respect, even adoration, of many non-Brahman Hindus helped to sustain them, and they tended as a body to be better educated, if only in Indian languages, than the rest of the indentured Indians. Not all Brahmans even in India are priests, but almost all consider themselves to be "priestly": holy, set-aside, consecrated. Therefore, despite the opposition of the estate managers, they emerged as the primary religious practitioners among the Hindu Indians. The prohibition to be found among almost all the Brahman castes against drinking alcoholic beverages also helped them materially: the money other laborers drank away in the omnipresent rumshops could be—and often was—hoarded by Brahmans and saved with an eye to the future.

Perhaps significantly, "Marajh" (from *maharajah*—"great ruler") became the preferred term of reference for a Brahman among the Trinidad Indians, and emerged as the most common Brahmanical surname on the island. Though the respectful title "maharajah" for Brahmans was not unknown in India, Brahmans there were rarely actual "kings"; in Trinidad, they became—despite all estate opposition—sources of temporal as well as spiritual authority.

Still, the religions of the newcomers were accorded little or no respect by the rest of the Trinidad population. The indentured Indians—for the most part Hindu, to a lesser extent Muslim—were considered prime candidates for conversion to Christianity, and Roman Catholic and Protestant missionaries were soon moving freely amongst them, with no voice (that carried any weight) raised against their activities. Hindu and Muslim dietary restrictions were of course ignored on the estates, and Hindus were denied permission (until well into the twentieth century) to cremate their dead. Hindu and Muslim religious leaders were even denied permission to perform legal marriages, and those Indians (the overwhelming majority) who insisted on being married according to Hindu or Muslim rites received no recognition: their children were listed as "illegitimate," without the legal right to inherit either name or property from their fathers.

The pressure to slough off Indian practices was enormous. Those Indians who became Christians were given educational and occupational opportunities that were non-existent for those (the majority of the East Indian population) who remained steadfast in their ancestral faiths. Particularly active and successful among the Indians were the missionaries sent by Canadian Presbyterians, who formed what came to be known as the "Canadian Mission," offering schooling, counseling, and other forms of assistance to the Indian population. Many Indians took advantage of the help offered by the Canadian missionaries, though only a small proportion of the Indian population ever formally adopted Christianity.

One reason, of course, was that for many of the Indians the sojourn in Trinidad was seen as a temporary thing: they expected to complete their five, even ten, years of servitude and then return to their homes and families in India with their savings. Some people actually managed to do this, but the majority of the Indians stayed on, sometimes in desperation signing up for additional periods of indenture, and sometimes striking out to find ways of supporting themselves and their families with a measure of independence.

### Settlement

The Indians who stayed on in Trinidad were by no means scattered throughout the island and among its population. Trinidad, in fact, exhibited sharp regional variation in ethnic composition by the end of the nineteenth century. Most of the population in the rural but non-sugar-producing areas was comprised of descendants of slaves derived from West Africa. They also made up a large part of the inhabitants of the urban centers—particularly Port of Spain and its environs—but here were also to be found almost all of the people of either European or mixed European/African descent.

The segment of the Trinidad population of South Asian descent—known derogatorily as "Coolies" and more acceptably as "East Indians"—continued to reside, well on into the first half of the twentieth century, almost exclusively in rural areas, and most particularly, in central Trinidad, in the county of Caroni, and in the south in the counties of Victoria and St. Patrick. These had been, and remained, the main centers of sugar cultivation, and the East Indians continued to constitute the bulk of the sugar estate labor force—even when they were no longer indentured.

They continued to be, in other words, economically "bound" to the estates, the only source of remunerative employment for the overwhelming majority of Indians. Nevertheless, once out of indenture, large numbers of Trinidad Indians (as opposed to those in the colony of British Guiana) managed at least to extricate themselves from the estate "slave barracks." Elsewhere (Klass 1980b), I have suggested that ecology played a part in this—that because there is only one sugar crop a year in Trinidad, as opposed to the two crop seasons in what was then British Guiana, Trinidad plantation managers encouraged their Indian laborers to move away, if not too far away.

In any case, during the last half of the nineteenth century many Trinidad East Indians were able to settle on land adjacent to the sugar estates on which they were employed during crop-time. Some purchased land, others rented plots from wealthier Indians or from the estates. Communities emerged, composed in many cases exclusively of people of Indian descent. Children were born and grew up, in many cases as much at home with Indian languages (particularly *Bhojpuri*, a language of Bihar) as with the dialect of English spoken in Trinidad. The settlers raised rice and other crops, when not working on the estates, and some even became comparatively prosperous. Agriculture, however—whether in the form of estate labor or on one's own fields—remained the primary source of cash income for most Indians.

I have suggested (Klass 1961, 1980b) that the fact that so many of the settlers were themselves emigrants from India—rather than the children or grandchildren of emigrants—contributed significantly to the degree to which they reconstituted Indian culture in Trinidad. On the other hand, of course, it will be understood that life in Trinidad East Indian communities differed from life in Indian communities, back in India. The marriage circles and formal authority structure of "caste" never emerged, nor could most of the traditional caste occupations be resumed. Sources of food and styles of clothing were borrowed, along with other elements of material culture, though many of these were often modified to accord with Indian needs and tastes.

I would argue—particularly given the subject of this study—that the arena of most significant, and yet most subtle, differences between India and Trinidad was that of religion. After all, for half a century or more Indians in Trinidad were largely out of contact with the religious leaders of their homeland and were completely unaware of Indian intellectual ferment, and of the growth of new movements and new ideological concerns. In Trinidad, there were no religious academies and few if any full-time religious leaders: whatever knowledge of religious belief and practice had been brought by the immigrants had to suffice for decades, carried on by men who had to labor in the fields most of the time like their fellows, and who passed on what they could remember to their children. But even more: Hinduism (like Islam) was a religion on the defensive, without prestige anywhere on the island, eliciting contempt, disgust, and derision from all other Trinidadians (see Vertovec 1985: 25).

Nevertheless, Indian cultural practices *were* reconstituted and maintained, and *were* passed along to the new generations. Arranged marriage, joint family, "Hawaiian Cousin" kinship terminology, and even aspects of caste hierarchy continued well into the twentieth century in many, if not all, rural Indian communities. For those who remained true to their ancestral faiths—again, the overwhelming majority—Muslim and Hindu spiritual advisers *did* emerge to provide religious guidance and solace.

### Race, Class, Ethnicity and Religion

What kind of society, then, emerged in Trinidad in the nineteenth and early twentieth centuries? There is no easy, generally accepted, answer to that question. Some scholars perceived accommodation occurring between the different segments, leading to (already achieving, some thought) the formation of a unified "Creole" culture and social system. Others focussed on the differences, the lack of articulation, between the ethnic sections. To still others, and most particularly to M. G. Smith, Trinidad was an example of a "plural society" in which separated ethnic social entities, each with its own distinctive institutions, met and interacted only in the political and economic arenas (M. G. Smith 1955, 1965; Braithwaite 1960; Klass 1960; Crowley 1960; Skinner 1971; Singh 1974; etc.).

The Trinidadian sociologist Lloyd Braithwaite has provided what is universally accepted as the most illuminating analysis of the social stratification system characterizing the greater part of the population—those of African and mixed European/African descent—and, to a certain extent, many of those of European and of Asian descent (Braithwaite 1953). He noted the ways the complex interweaving of "class" and "race" had changed, but had also maintained continuity, as the nineteenth century gave way to the twentieth. And, according to Braithwaite, as the first half of the twentieth century was drawing to a close, Trinidad exhibited an "upper class" that was still largely though no longer exclusively European (usually called "White") in composition; a "middle class" that tended to be comprised of "Coloured" people (of combined European and African descent); and a "lower class" in which was subsumed most of the population considered to be of African (referred to as "Negro") or Indian descent.

"Class" in Braithwaite's usage clearly denotes a population segment exhibiting a common level of economic and social positioning; by "race" he obviously means a biologically distinct community. From the point of view of "ethnicity," however, some of his categories become blurred. Thus, "White" subsumes and obscures the differences between the ethnic communities of British and French descent, while the terms "Coloured" and "Negro" separates sharply people who actually shared an unbroken continuum of values and practices. The "Indian" population—attached by Braithwaite to "Negro" as part of the "lower class"—was itself sharply divided along lines of caste, allegiance to European versus South Asian values and goals . . . and, of course, religion.

Indeed, in his analysis of "race" and "class" Braithwaite barely touched on "religion"—for any of the groups he refers to. Let us observe, therefore, that the overwhelming majority (effectively, "all") the non-Indians of Trinidad in the nineteenth and twentieth centuries were Christians. For a relatively brief period in the middle of this century a small Jewish community existed in Trinidad, and in recent years some non-Indians have converted (or, as many of them claim, reverted) to Islam, some have joined the Rastafarian movement, and a very small number have turned to the religion of Sai Baba.

To label the majority of non-Indians as "Christians," however, is to obscure both important doctrinal differences and differences in position in the social hierarchy. Briefly, Europeans were to be found almost exclusively in the Anglican (for those deriving from Britain) and the Roman Catholic (for the descendants of the French plantation owners) churches. The so-called "middle-class" ("Coloured") was heavily Roman Catholic, too, and the varieties of Baptist and other non-Anglican Protestant churches tended to attract many of the poorest of the "lower-class" (that is, "Negro") population.

The use, in the preceding paragraph, of Braithwaite's categories—"class" and "race"—tends of course to obscure much of the complexity of Trinidad Christian affiliation. There were in fact "Negro" Anglicans and "White" Baptists, and the Roman Catholics encompassed the "racial" spectrum, but the hierarchy of class and color noted by Braithwaite could be observed, if imperfectly, in the membership lists of the various Christian denominations. The East Indian separation-cum-interaction was also reflected: though most Indians were not Christians, some had become Roman Catholics and others made up the bulk of those categorized as Presbyterians.

Despite the problems wrestled with above, there are a number of reasons why this brief inquiry into religious stratification will be useful later in this work. For one thing, most of the schools in Trinidad—up to mid-century, and even beyond—were sponsored by and affiliated with religious denominations. The Catholic church, particularly, supported and ran most of the elementary and secondary schools—and during the nineteenth century Indians were not welcomed by these schools (or at least the Indians felt they were not) unless they willing to convert. Until the comparatively late establishment of the Canadian Mission (Presbyterian) schools, therefore, Indians in Trinidad were isolated from Western education. And, even then, though the Canadian Mission schools did not insist on conversion, the East Indians were always aware that conversion was a primary goal of the Mission—a reason often given for the Indian reluctance to send children, and particularly girls, to such schools in earlier years.

And I would note, too, that "Christianity"—in Trinidad as elsewhere—was the very opposite of a monolithic or unified religion. Christians might be united in their belief that Hindus and Muslims were "pagans" and should be converted to Christianity, but they agreed among themselves on little else. Many Indians were offended by Christian denunciations of non-Christian beliefs, and equally astonished by the conflicts between the various contending Christian denominations. Hindus, particularly, tended to believe, in Trinidad as they had in India, that all religions, however much in error, conveyed spiritual benefit and improvement.

Nevertheless, the Indians who did attend the schools were subjected to intensive proselytizing, and this was not without effect. If some Indians only pretended to convert (in order to gain material benefits) many sincerely accepted the teachings of the Christian missionaries. By the first quarter of the twentieth century, the officials of the Canadian Mission—schools and churches—were Christian Indians. The values and perceptions of Christianity—as these reflected or were distinct from those of European culture in general—clearly penetrated the Trinidad Indian community; even among those who remained steadfast Hindus or Muslims.

Let us note, finally, that Trinidad also exhibited an occupational hierarchy that coincided, in some measure, with the system of social stratification. Wealthier, or more educated, people were to be found in the professions, in government service (police, teaching, etc.), and in commerce. The latter was dominated, in its higher echelons, by people of primarily European (or Chinese) origin, but the lower ranks were drawn from those of mixed African and European descent.

Poor people in the rural areas, perceived as being of primarily African descent, raised garden crops for sale in the markets and to feed their families, fished, sought work in road and sewer maintenance gangs. Many of the rural poor migrated to the cities and worked on the docks or in such other laboring occupations as were available to the city poor and unskilled. Some were able to find employment in the asphalt industry and in the developing oil industry around the southern town of San Fernando. Whatever the shortcomings of these occupations, however, they were considered preferable to work in the sugar fields: that was left to "Coolies."

We may reasonably conclude, therefore, that the South Asian immigrants and their descendants were a minority population on the island—socially, economically, politically, and ideologically imbedded in what was not only a larger and a very different society, but one that was more than uncaring: it was actively hostile to South Asian values and beliefs, practices and relationships.

It should not surprise us, then, to learn that by the time Indian immigrants (first and second generation) were able to escape from the estates to the crown lands, much in their behavior, perceptions and practices had become modified—and more changes could be expected in the following generations.

Still, minority though the Indians were on the island of Trinidad as a whole, they were in fact a majority in the sections of the island in which most of them actually resided. And, in their own communities, not uncommonly they had few or no neighbors who were not of South Asian extraction. Furthermore, while Christianity (particularly the Presbyterian "Canadian Mission" church) did make converts—still, most of the converts did not live in the rural communities, but in towns and cities along with the rest of the Christian, non-Indian, population.

By mid-century, therefore, it was true that East Indians were no longer "Indians"—but they weren't like the rest of the Trinidadians, either. It was this complexity, of course, that attracted scholars (including myself) to the study of such overseas Indian communities.

### Notes

1. For an anthropological exploration of the role of "sugar" in history and society, see Mintz (1985).

# 3

# East Indians at Mid-Century

## Census Reports

A few essential statistics, just to set the stage. According to the Census Report of 1946, the last to be conducted before mid-century (Central Statistical Office [*Annual Statistical Digest*], 1958), the total population of the two islands of Trinidad and Tobago was 557,970, of whom only 27,208 resided in Tobago. Of the total, 46.9% (261,485) were identified as of the "Black race"; 14.1% (78,775) as "Mixed or Coloured"; 2.7% (15,283) as "White"; and 35.1% (195,747) as "East Indian" (Cent. Stat. 1958: 9,12). In other words, the two largest groups—"Black" and "East Indian"—together comprised 82% of the population in 1946. "Black" and "Coloured"—the two groups of full or part African derivation, who also conveyed and maintained the "Creole" cultural patterns of Trinidad—together comprised 61% of the population.

The *Annual Statistical Digest* indicated important differences between the "racial" groups. Among the "Blacks," for example, only 9.4% of those ten years of age and over were considered "illiterate" (self-declared as unable either to read or to write) while a full 50.4% of the "East Indians" were recorded as illiterate (Cent. Stat. 1958: 12).

Again, of the 395,095 people in Trinidad and Tobago who identified themselves as "Christians," 202,702 (51%) resided in either the city of Port of Spain or the surrounding, largely suburban, county of St. George—while of the 126,343 people who identified themselves as "Hindu" only 24,964 (20%) were to be found in those two areas. The three largely rural counties of Caroni, Victoria, and St. Patrick—where most of the island's sugar was produced—accounted for 73% of all Hindus in Trinidad, but only 34% (132,712) of all Christians (some 10% of them "Presbyterian" and therefore presumably mostly East

Indian). Of the 32,615 "Moslems" of Trinidad, 64% (20,879) resided in the above three rural counties (Cent. Stat. 1958: 13).

I pause in this parade of statistics for a personal note. The total numbers of Hindus and Muslims cited above (for all of Trinidad and Tobago, or for each county) were provided in the appropriate table of the *Annual Statistical Digest*: the totals given for numbers of Christians, however, in each case derives from my own computations, since the table provided totals only for *each Christian denomination* (i.e., "Anglican," "Baptist," "Church of God," "Pentecostal," "Roman Catholic," etc.—some twenty-two in all). "Christianity," it seems fair to say, was not perceived by those conducting the Trinidad census to be *one* religion —and clearly not as unified or unitary as they perceived Hinduism to be.

And there is an additional problem: as I noted in the previous chapter, some of these Christian denominations—and most particularly "Presbyterian" and "Roman Catholic"—do include large numbers of Indians: Vertovec (1985) indeed suggests that 95% of Trinidad Presbyterians are of South Asian descent. On the other hand, however, it is reasonable to assume that almost all who were listed in 1946 as "Hindu" and "Moslem" (plus the tiny category "Vedic"—440 people) were East Indians. There are of course Muslims of African descent in contemporary Trinidad, but—at least as far as Crowley could determine—there were none in 1957 (Crowley 1957: 818).

To return to the information provided by the *Annual Statistical Digest*: the sources of income in 1946 were limited—for almost everybody in Trinidad. Of 213,093 people considered to be "gainfully employed," 58,767 were employed in "Agriculture, Fishing and Forestry"— and of these 22,102 were engaged in the cultivation of sugar and another 31,744 in other agricultural activities. In addition, "Sugar Milling" (listed under "Manufacture") employed 3,494 more—all other "Manufacture and Mining" accounting for another 41,166, of which 4,708 were employed in "Petroleum Refining." The total number employed in "Trade and Finance" was only 18,842, and in "Public Service," 17,565. Some 7,693 people provided all the island's "Professional Services" (Cent. Stat. 1958: 46).

Most of the major sources of employment, it should be noted, (including most factories and mines, the oilfields, and particularly the sugar estates and other plantations that employed the rural population) were owned by people of European derivation, quite often non-resident in Trinidad. Further, the upper management of both estate and oilfield were overwhelmingly foreign-born Europeans, most frequently British.

## The Village of "Amity"

Life in Trinidad was undergoing change at mid-century, but much remained as it had always been. As Braithwaite indicated, the rigidities of nineteenth century "racial" hierarchies had softened a little: there were some non-"Whites" in the "Upper Class" and some "Negroes" in the "Middle Class" now—but the hierarchy based on color ascription was essentially intact.

Electricity was in use through much of the island, though people in many rural areas still depended on lanterns or "flambeaux" (rum bottles filled with kerosene and topped off with a cloth wick). There were many good roads—Trinidad certainly compared most favorably in this respect with other West Indian islands—and credit for this and other changes and amenities was given by some to the so-called "American Occupation" (the period, during World War II, when the United States built and maintained military bases received from England in return for desperately-needed over-age destroyers).

In any event, there were good roads now, and automobiles (and therefore taxis and taxi-drivers), along with an international airport, and an important and busy harbor. Things were changing in Trinidad— or at least change was in the wind.

Shortly before the arrival in 1957 of the research group of which I was a member, for example, the Trinidad political scene had undergone a revolution—peaceful, for the most part, but a revolution nonetheless. Titular political power had been wrested the year before from the European ("White," "Upper Class") community and was in the hands of the People's National Movement (PNM)—a party that identified with the non-European (that is, African and Asian derived) majority—under the leadership of Dr. Eric Williams. By the time I departed, one year later, Trinidad was no longer a British colony but part of the new, if short-lived, West Indian Federation.

My own interest was in the so-called "East Indians"—an interest I shared with others, of course. My wife and I settled in a village in County Caroni, and at about the same time Arthur and Juanita Niehoff, who had earlier conducted research in India, settled in a community in south Trinidad (Neihoff and Neihoff 1960). Over in British Guiana, Chandra Jayawardena was completing his study of Indian life in that colony (1963). We, and other students of "Overseas Indians" in the West Indies and elsewhere, amassed a large body of ethnographic data— which served to demonstrate, along with much else, the degree of variation to be observed in Overseas Indian life, from region to region, and from research site to research site.

In Trinidad, for example, the Indians of Caroni were much closer to the major city, Port of Spain, and its suburbs than were the Indians of Victoria and St. Patrick: the latter, however, had more opportunity to seek work outside of sugar cultivation (in the oil fields, for example). Some settlements contained no non-Indian inhabitants; others varied from a few to a predominance of non-Indians. In some communities (as in the village I named "Amity"), the inhabitants were able to raise enough rice to satisfy their needs for this staple of diet, and had excess in addition to sell in the market. In other settlements, East Indians could do no more than plant "garden produce" like their non-Indian neighbors. Again, it was sometimes possible—and sometimes not—to establish internal residential divisions resembling those of the north Indian villages, and based, like the latter, on caste and occupational distinctions.

Amity was (and is) located in the county of Caroni, in the ward of Chaguanas, between the coast and the Chaguanas Ward (and market) center, at the southern edge of the Caroni Swamp. During the period of my stay—1957–58—Amity exhibited four distinct residential (and socioeconomic) subdivisions with a total population of about 4,000 people—almost all of South Asian descent (Klass 1961).

I counted a total of 623 separate households in all of Amity. More than half of these (344) were housed in mud-walled huts known as *ajoupas*—a few of which sported amenities such as wooden floors or galvanized iron roofs. Indoor plumbing was non-existent; electricity was available only to people who lived near the main street; there was only one telephone—in a public box, appropriately near the home of the wealthiest inhabitant. Most of the "good" houses (of brick, cement, and poured concrete) were to be found in "Central Amity"—the dominant subdivision, center of community activities, abode of village wealth and power and prestige.

Not that anyone in the village was *very* wealthy: the richest families—about a dozen—were those owning land on which they could cultivate sugar cane, and only five of these families owned more than five acres each. An annual income of BWI$1,000 to $1,500 was considered "wealth"—though most men enjoying such wealth continued to cultivate rice and sugar and other crops with their own hands; they differed from their neighbors only in that the latter rented pieces of riceland and labored in the estate canefields. For most of the villagers, an annual income of BWI$600 to $800 was considered sufficient to keep a family fed and out of debt.

Of the approximately 900 adult males in Amity, 484 worked as cane-cutters for a nearby large estate, and another 100 for a smaller estate and for the local small-farmers. Some 25 men were employed by the estates in other capacities, from mill to office, and about 100 men of the village, owners of their own bull-carts, were hired by the estates during crop-time. In addition, 207 women from Amity also worked on the estates, performing labor in the fields. In 1957, in short, the East Indians of Amity were almost wholly dependent upon "sugar" for their livelihoods.

Cane-cutters—in 1957, as a century earlier during "indenture"—were paid by the "task": BWI$1.32 (in 1957) for cutting all the cane in a demarcated area, usually 120 feet by 20 feet. Most men averaged two tasks a day; a few of the stronger ones managed to complete three in one day. Private carters received BWI$1.02 for every ton of cane delivered to the crane for shipment to the mill, and many managed to load and deliver six to sixteen tons a day—but the money had to be divided among cart-owners and their hired help.

Crop-time lasted only a few months, however, and there was little hope of employment at other times. Most East Indian families endeavored to raise some of their own food—rice when and if they could, plus garden vegetables. The more access they had to cultivable land—particularly rice land—the more secure (and even prosperous) the family felt itself to be.

There were few other occupations open to them. Some men found work in road gangs—but these and related activities were manned predominantly by men of African descent, and Indian men considered themselves unwelcome. In any case, few men found such jobs. Some men became shopkeepers (groceries, rumshops, soft-drink "parlors"), but in rural settlements such as Amity they were inevitably few in number, and profits were small. Besides, in most villages, they had to compete with already-established Chinese shopkeepers. Many young men, seeking an avenue out of the canefields, dreamed of becoming taxi drivers, but here again (Klass 1961: 79–81) the opportunities were limited and the rewards were not high (though, in general, a distinct cut above those of the cane-cutter).

Educational opportunities were also limited, and as we have seen half the East Indian population (including almost all the women) were illiterate. Amity had a "Canadian Mission" school, and in the early 1950s another school had been started under the aegis of the Sanatan Dharma Maha Sabha, the largest Hindu religious organization in Trinidad, and a body to which more attention will be given later in this chapter.

In any event, in 1957 there were barely half a dozen "bookkeepers" in Amity and about the same number of elementary-school teachers—the only men who could claim any but the most minimal of educations.

### The East Indian "Way of Life"

It is difficult, of course, to say what was "true" of "all" East Indians in Trinidad in the middle of this century—to assume, for example, that what one observed in one settlement was characteristic of the entire East Indian population. With care, however, one may offer certain generalizations.[1]

After all, if East Indian communities differed markedly in composition, in accessibility to the city, in economic opportunity, and much else—and they did—the rural East Indians of Trinidad were also very much in contact with one another. Women in Amity who had never been to Port of Spain traveled regularly throughout *rural* Trinidad to visit family members. Indians in settlements that contained no non-Indians usually had relatives who lived in the midst of people of African and European descent. Hindus even had relatives who were Christian, and they too visited back and forth.

This continual East Indian movement and interaction reflected the maintenance of one particular practice of north Indian derivation—that of village-exogamous marriages. The fact that so many marriages took place between young people of widely separated communities also pointed to the widespread observance of another practice deriving from India—that of "arranged marriage." In Amity, at mid-century, as in many other Trinidad East Indian communities, the overwhelming majority of marriages were arranged by parents. Most commonly, the father of a teen-aged girl would set out to find a husband for his daughter, and he would approach the father of an eligible young man, rather than the young man himself.

Things were changing: marriages by Hindu and Muslim religious leaders were now legal, though most East Indians were still living in legally unrecognized "under the bamboo" unions. Again, many young people tended to chafe at the notion of marriage "arrangement," claiming they had acquired (or planned to acquire) their spouses by "free choice." For most of them, however, in practice the term meant only that—after the initial contact between fathers—the two young people were accorded the right to meet, and to accept or reject, the prospective spouses chosen by their parents. There were cases—a small minority in the community I studied, but more common in other places—where a marriage was initiated by the young couple themselves, although once they had chosen each other it was still customary for them to turn the rest of the proceedings over to their parents.

Even apart from matters of propriety and the observance of traditional rules, it is hardly surprising that the young people left so much in the hands of their parents. After all, at mid-century, in Amity, most

brides were in their teens—usually between fourteen and eighteen—
and the grooms were only a little older. There was no "dating," and
adolescents had very little experience with unrelated members of the
opposite sex. Joint-family households—in which married brothers lived
together with their wives and children, all under the authority of the
oldest man and woman—represented the ideal and very often the
practice. New brides shouldered many of the household burdens, and
younger women—married or unmarried—were not allowed to go far
from the house without male chaperons.

Thus, the older, and more experienced, family members did most of
the work of arranging marriages for the younger ones. And, when they
did so, most parents—if perhaps not all—gave attention to the "caste"
membership of the prospective spouse. In Amity, in 1957–58, I identified some thirty-nine "nations"—the English term used in Trinidad
as a translation of *jati,* more customarily translated as "caste." Overwhelmingly, I found, the marital unions of Amity had been made
between boys and girls of the same—or very closely ranked—castes.
Men of the "high" castes—of the Brahman and Chuttri (*kshatriya*)
*varnas,* the two highest caste groupings—were particularly rigid in their
observation of the rule of endogamy (Klass 1961: 62, *et passim*).

What was especially striking about this was that there was no sign
whatever, in Amity or elsewhere in Trinidad, of the ubiquitous "caste
*panchayat*" of South Asia—the regulatory body of a given caste which
holds and can exercise the power to expel a member who violates a
rule as important as that of endogamy. Community ostracism had
sometimes occurred in the past, as a punishment for marriage across
too-wide a caste gulf, but by 1957 it was no longer possible to achieve
this in Amity. The worst thing likely to happen to young people who
married out of caste was parental disapproval and rejection, and even
this was by no means inevitable. Nevertheless, despite the absence of
any sanctioning body, marriage in Amity was far more likely to take
place within the caste than outside it.

It was obvious, of course, to me as to other observers, that the
"caste system" of India had not been reconstituted in Trinidad. Not
only were there no signs of caste *panchayats* and assemblies, but other
important elements and attributes of the classic "system" were missing
or present in only the most attenuated form.

I observed, for example, almost no signs of the traditional socioeconomic relationships of "caste." "Redistribution"—for some of us a basic
feature of that system (see Klass 1980a; Neale 1957)—simply did not
take place. Though obligation relationships reminiscent of *jajmani* (Kolenda 1963; Wiser 1936) were very much in evidence, they were not
in any way expressions of traditional intercaste relations, and redistri-

bution of food occurred regularly only at the feasts at weddings and other social and religious events. In other words, apart from those of Brahman priests and an occasional barber or musician, services were not offered by "representatives" of groups having monopolies over them—in fact, only Brahman priests could be said actually to monopolize any service. While by no means an insignificant exception, the Brahman case (even if we add that of the barbers) is hardly enough to produce or reflect a "caste system."

There was a statistically demonstrable *tendency*—but by no means a *rule*—for people to congregate in districts made up of similarly ranked castes: the highest to be found in the greatest proportions in "Central Amity"—but a few households of the lowest-ranked castes could also be found here. Members of the higher-ranked castes tended not to eat in the homes of those they considered particularly "low"; for one thing, traditional dietary restrictions (specifically the avoidance of beef and pork) were observed by many. On the other hand, such rules were often ignored by other members of the same caste, and again there were no institutionalized sanctions to be imposed on those who ignored the restrictions.

But there were indeed signs of change: more young people than older ones expressed a lack of interest in caste membership, or in observing the rules—marital, dietary, or whatever. It could be argued, of course, that the preponderance of close-caste and village-exogamous marriages was due solely to the fact that marriages were arranged by parents while their children were still quite young, so what I was observing were the rules of the *parents,* not of the coming generation.[2]

Still, there were distinct differences to be observed between even young people of different castes on such matters as use of obscenity in public, occupational aspirations (including attitudes toward crab-catching and other traditionally "low" occupations), degree of responsibility expressed toward children by parents, and toward parents by children. And it must be remembered that the parents in Amity who were arranging marriages at mid-century were themselves the third generation (or more) since the original immigrants.

If the "caste system" had not been reconstituted in Trinidad by people of Indian descent, *something* of "caste"—call it "values," "perceptions," "eidos," or what you will—had survived and was clearly still affecting the lives of Trinidad East Indians at mid-century.

Not all the values of the East Indians, of course, could be attributed simply to the manifestation of "caste" principles and attitudes. The avoidance of beef and pork, or even of flesh itself, reflects the tenets of Hinduism and of South Asian religion in general. The observed kinship terminology and relationships, family structure (including husband-wife, parent-child, sibling-sibling, interactions) and so on, are not even restricted solely to South Asian societies, though in many ways the patterns of that region differ markedly from those deriving from Europe and Africa.

My conclusion, simply put, was that—in Amity, and by extension throughout East Indian Trinidad—despite all "loss" and change and Westernization, the way of life was more "North Indian" than it was "West Indian." And, further, this Indian "way of life" presented problems for those who followed it: it was not in accord with the non-Indian "way of life" of Trinidad.

### The Politics of Religion

The problem of accommodation for those caught in the pull between these two very different cultural systems was particularly apparent in two aspects of East Indian life: "religion" and "politics." To some scholars, it may be, these two might seem odd bedfellows, but for any examination of Trinidad East Indian life it is difficult, and I believe ultimately disadvantageous, to isolate them from each other.

We have observed, for example, that a Brahman priest was often called "Marajh" by his fellow indentured laborers, and was perceived, not without reason, as a source of alternative and antagonistic authority by many who ran the estates. This joint role of the Brahman in Trinidad—religious and political leader—was maintained well into mid-century, and had by no means totally disappeared even by 1985.

One source of this joint role was surely the contribution made by Brahmans to the survival of Hinduism in a hostile environment. Even after indenture had come to an end, the religions deriving from South Asia—both Hinduism and Islam—were accorded little recognition or respect. Hindu holidays, rules of diet and dress, religious practices and ritual needs, were variously ignored, mocked, or forbidden. Christian missionaries were given free rein to attempt conversion, and converts were welcomed and applauded as people who had emerged from darkness into light.

By mid-century, changes were beginning to take place, but it was very much only a beginning. When I arrived in Amity, marriages performed by both Hindu and Muslim "Religious Officers" had become legal. Nevertheless, in 1957 the majority of Amity marital unions were still non-legal. Many, of course, reflected ceremonies performed before the enactment of the Hindu Marriage Act only a decade earlier, but some were unions of more recent vintage, performed by Brahman priests who were not yet legally registered "Marriage Officers." This meant, among other things, that almost everyone in the community, with the exception of a few very young children, was officially illegitimate.

Interestingly, and perhaps significantly, they didn't *have* to be, no matter how legally unacceptable the original marriage ceremony had been: a brief visit by parents—at any time in their lives—to the Ward Center Registrar for a civil ceremony could make their children "legitimate." The fact that almost everyone refused to do so therefore apparently reflected, first, a widespread belief that there was little to be gained by the act, for either parent or child—and secondly, and even more, a feeling of resentment toward a government that appeared to hold their religion in contempt. They *were* married, men and women would tell me, and they rejected the law's contention that they were not and that their children were illegitimate.

Again, at the first East Indian funeral I attended in Amity, I heard men expressing their bitterness at having to bury the deceased: why, they wished to know, was cremation—so important to Hindus—forbidden by law? Hindu dead were buried in a nearby cemetery because the living had no choice . . . but in most cases no stone was erected, and no grave care given: effectively, the remains were treated as if they had been cremated and had dissipated into flowing water and blowing wind.

There were other things that made it seem, to the villagers at least, that Hinduism was accorded little of the respect given in Trinidad to Christianity. Thousands of Hindus gathered every year in a field in north-central Trinidad to observe the festivities and colorful pageantry of the holiday of "Ram Lila"—but the event was invariably given short shrift or none at all in the newspapers. Similarly, the island-wide annual excursion of great numbers of East Indians to the beaches of the coast to observe "Kartik Nahan" received no notice—but a ceremony in a rural church attended by a few dozen Christians was likely to get newspaper coverage.

In earlier years of this century, the differential treatment in the newspapers might have gone largely unnoticed, but by mid-century radios were making their appearance in the East Indian communities and literacy in English was on the increase. There were still older people whose horizons ended at village and kin-network boundaries, but more and more of the younger generation were becoming aware of the world—particularly the Trinidadian world—around them.

Young East Indian men had taken up the sport of cricket, and a few of their number had received national and even international renown. Taxi drivers traveled throughout the island, and particularly into urban areas, and were acquiring a familiarity with non-Indian patterns of behavior, speech and activities. Many young men of Amity and the surrounding area now traveled to Port of Spain to observe the Carnival festivities—and some expressed irritation at the way "Coolies" were ridiculed in Carnival costumes or the songs of the calypso tents.

The term "Coolie" itself—long current throughout the island and used by all the non-Indian strata—was challenged now, and was avoided in press and radio, and in conversations with (though not always about) East Indians.

### Contact with South Asia

Unquestionably, the emergence of an independent India and Pakistan on the subcontinent constituted an important source of pride and confidence for the descendents of immigrants from the former British colony of India. In addition, movies from India had become extremely popular in the areas of East Indian concentration. Trinidad East Indians derived much more than entertainment from these movies: princely robes were copied for bridegroom's garments, movie stars were idolized and their mannerisms copied, and pronunciation and grammar were much affected by movie standards—though the villagers (unbeknownst to themselves) actually spoke dialects or even languages originally quite distinct from the one that was to become standard Hindi in independent India.

It was certainly the case that India-derived language, education, and religion had begun to undergo, at mid-century, significant change and reorganization. Indeed, one scholar, Richard Huntington Forbes, suggests that Trinidad Hinduism began to be influenced by modern India at an even earlier period—1917 to 1939—with the arrival of missionaries from India heralding the teachings of Dayananda, founder of the *Arya Samaj* movement:

he criticized the Brahmans for encouraging superstition and keeping the people in ignorance . . . and he argued that Hindu ideas and practices regarding caste were gross distortions of the original Vedic concept of four *Varnas,* a system in which a person's status and occupation in society were determined, not by birth but by *Guna, Karma* and *Swabhav,* or temperament, actions and individual merit. Furthermore, Dayananda emphasized the idea . . . that all men should not only be allowed but should be encouraged to read and preach the Vedas (Forbes 1979: 4).

Such teachings apparently precipitated a great deal of furor in Trinidad. Brahman priests inveighed against the newcomers, while many people—particularly among the educated and wealthy segment of the East Indian population—flocked to the lectures and began to adopt the practices the missionaries recommended. *Arya Samaj* meetings, it was said, always began punctually (unlike the ceremonies presided over by village Brahman priests), and followed rules of order and democratic process, including the keeping of minutes.

A particularly influential "Vedic Missionary," Pandit Mehta Jaimini, was said to have introduced the use of the sacred term *om* to the non-Brahman East Indians in Trinidad: "Like the Gayatri Mantra, which is the essence of [Arya] Samaj teachings, the word *OM* appears to be part of that 'secret' knowledge, jealously guarded by the priest caste, or *Brahmans*" (Forbes 1979: 15).

Brahmanical opposition and internal squabbles ultimately brought about the collapse of the *Arya Samaj* movement in Trinidad, and by 1957 it was hardly more than a memory—but it was a stubborn memory, and many elements (and probably even participants) seem to have re-emerged in the days of the Sai Baba movement.

Orthodox opposition, led by hereditary Brahman priests, was centered in two organizations at first. Both claimed to represent the *Sanatan Dharma*—the ancient and ageless faith known to the world as "Hinduism"—and in 1949, triumphant over *Arya Samaj* and other perceived heterodoxies, they merged into one body, the Sanatan Dharma Maha Sabha of Trinidad and Tobago, under the leadership of Bhadase Sagan Marajh, one of the wealthiest men of the East Indian community. Though not himself a practicing priest, he was, as his name indicates, a member of the Trinidad "Marajh" or Brahman caste—and Brahmans have, throughout the life of this organization, predominated in its leadership.

Under Bhadase Marajh's dynamic leadership, the Sanatan Dharma Maha Sabha embarked in the 1950s upon an ambitious program of building schools throughout rural Trinidad. Quite intentionally, a Sanatan Dharma School was constructed, as challenge or supplement, in almost every locality where there was a Canadian Mission School. In addition, Hindu day schools were also built in isolated areas where no schooling of any kind had hitherto been available.

In a number of cases, teachers and even headmasters came to the Hindu schools from the Christian ones, declaring they had always remained, in their hearts, devout Hindus, but had been forced by economic circumstances to pretend to be Christians. In the Hindu schools, Hindi was taught (standard Hindi of India) and time was devoted to Hinduism; its philosophy, rituals, and music. The primary medium of instruction was English, however—and for the most part the curriculum duplicated that of the other schools of Trinidad, for children were being prepared for island-wide competitions for entry to favored secondary schools. The traditional Indian reluctance to send girls to school diminished swiftly, and in many areas seemed to disappear completely: East Indians, at mid-century, had become convinced that education was important for all children—that it could provide an avenue for them and for their families out of the cane fields.

Credited with the building of schools and the maintenance of temples and shrines, and. despite charges of corruption and favoritism, the Sanatan Dharma Maha Sabha increased in prestige and influence among the Indian population. There were, however, other—non-Maha Sabha—religious voices and organizations. East Indian Muslims, for example, had their own religious organizations and leaders, and were at work constructing their own schools and temples. They shared some concerns and problems with the Hindus—but for them the enormous Hindu majority constituted an additional and important problem in its own right.

As Muslims they looked for inspiration to Pakistan and to the Muslim world in general, and Arabic and Urdu were as important in their schools as Hindi was in the Maha Sabha schools. Muslim abhorrence of Hindu religious practices (most particularly of the adoration, through paintings and statuary, of a pantheon of human and human/animal deities) certainly rivaled that of Christians, though the Christians seemed hardly aware of the beliefs, or even the existence, of Muslims—except, as some Muslims complained in 1958, to turn one Muslim holy day ("Hosein"—known in Trinidad as "Hosay") into a variety of "Carnival."

It should be noted, too, that the Hindus themselves were by no means uniform in their beliefs and practices. There were many sects, many distinct practices, and most of these could be traced back to the original immigrants who came from diverse regions of the subcontinent. The small segment of the East Indian population of south Indian ("Madrassi") descent, for example, continued to observe particularly distinctive customs and rituals. Again, among people deriving from such Indian castes as *Bauri* and *Chamar,* there were regular goat and pig sacrifices to divinities such as the goddess *Kali,* intended to protect the devotees from illness and other calamities.

In Amity, however, as in most East Indian villages, Brahman pandits were the dominant religious authorities. They performed weddings and presided at religious events at peoples' homes and in village temples and shrines. They functioned as "gurus" or teachers, instructing children and young people in "proper" behavior. Though many in the village objected that the pandits themselves tended to be both "immoral" and "ignorant" ("instruction," it was said, consisted usually of no more than the giving of a "mantra," a sacred secret word or phrase to be repeated by the student in his or her prayers) still, for a long time they were pretty much the only game in town (Klass 1961: 147–149; 216–218).

### The Swamis

In the early 1950s three men came to the West Indies from India, stopping first in Trinidad. They were emissaries of a worldwide Vedantic mission, and they became known as "the Swamis." They traveled around the island, each living for a while in various different settlements, preaching and teaching. While they did not attack the Maha Sabha, or disdain the village pandits (and thus avoided head-on clashes with either) they were perceived, particularly by many young men hungry for spiritual sustenance, as an inspiring alternative.

After a few years, two of them went on to British Guiana (now Guyana), leaving the third in Amity. Many young men—some from Amity and some from distant communities—gathered around him and attended his lessons. Soon, he too left for British Guiana, but by then a nucleus had formed that was to have a great impact on Hinduism in Amity and among the East Indians of Trinidad.

One of his disciples (referred to in my study of Amity as the "Brahmcari"—the young ascetic who lived in and administered the "Siwala," then the main temple of Amity) formed a "Divine Life Society"—"dedicated to the improvement of the religious and moral life of the village" (Klass 1961: 150) during the time of my study. He left Amity a few years later to study in India and then to preside over his "Divine Life Society" as it acquired members throughout the island. Within a few more years it had come to encompass many temples in many communities, with large numbers of devotees who were attracted to this new movement deriving from India, thoroughly orthodox, but unconnected to the Sanatan Dharma Maha Sabha.

Another disciple in Amity became the founder of an orthodox but anti-Brahman "every man his own priest" movement—in the village, but again with followers outside it. He offered to teach men and women—of any caste—to perform the ceremonies that had been considered the province of Brahmans alone. Under his direction, groups were forming at the time of my visit, in Amity and elsewhere, to study Hindi and even Sanskrit, and to learn the "bhajans" (hymns) and "hawans" (fire rituals) that they now understood to reflect the Hinduism of contemporary India (Klass 1961: 149–152).

The two village "pandits" (priests) were of course Brahmans, but they were not accepted by the villagers as being part of the community leadership, largely because both were widely believed to be guilty of sexual peccadillos (Klass 1961: 216). For the most part, however, high-caste membership and political authority went hand in hand in Amity, with certain qualifications. Political leaders were invariably male, for one thing—women were expected to be passive politically; to vote, for example, as the men of their family instructed them.

Education gave a man prestige, and the resident Headmaster (of the Sanatan Dharma School) was part of the Amity power structure. Wealth was even more important—most of the leaders were among the wealthiest residents of "Central Amity." But not all: two wealthy men, resident in the "best" district, were never included in any roster of leaders. Both "happened" (as people said) to derive from "low" castes, but I was assured by many that no one refused to accord them respect just because their relatives raised pigs in the back alleys of Amity—it was simply, so it was said, that they utterly lacked leadership qualities.

My own conclusion was that most Amity East Indians sincerely and consciously subscribed to Western notions of equality—but in practice (and even unconsciously) still responded in political contexts in terms of India-derived values, motivations, and criteria. Nor was this true only of the East Indians of Amity: Clarke reports much the same political attitudes and responses for the East Indians of south Trinidad (1986: 139–141). Even more: the Hindu East Indian members of the Legislative Council (the colony's elected parliamentary body) during the period of my stay were all of the two highest *varnas*—Brahman and Chuttri.

### National Politics

As in the case of religion, however, the customary East Indian political relationships were in flux at mid-century. The participation of East Indians in the larger political scene had been almost nonexistent before 1955—although, to be fair, the participation of people of African descent in the governing of Trinidad was until then hardly greater than that of Indians.

True, there had been elections for many years to the "LegCo" (Legislative Council) and there had been political parties reflecting many positions—but control of the island was effectively in the hands of the British Colonial Office, and of the European minority in Trinidad. True, there had been non-European members of the "LegCo" for years— but, again, such power as that body had was invariably in the hands of men of primarily European descent.

Then, in 1956, a new party emerged and came to power—the PNM, or People's National Movement—under the leadership of a distinguished scholar, Dr. Eric Williams, a Trinidadian of "mixed" ancestry: European, African—and Indian! The "Doctor" became "Chief Minister" in 1956, and when Trinidad and Tobago would achieve independence at the end of the sixth decade, he would become "Prime Minister." And, from the very beginning, the highest echelons of his party included men of the East Indian community as well as those of others, for he preached equality for all and a joining of hands to build a better Trinidad.

The PNM leaders of East Indian derivation, however, were predominantly Muslim or Christian, and the same pattern appeared to characterize PNM supporters among the East Indians nationwide. The party rose to power upon the votes of large numbers of people of African and mixed African/European descent, but attracted far less support among Hindu East Indians. In fact, active opposition formed against what many East Indians perceived, despite the speeches of Eric Williams, to be "a Negro party" (see Malik 1971, Gosine 1986, for extensive analyses of these and related issues).

Supporters of the PNM were puzzled: why was Eric Williams' program for social and economic reform so attractive to the poor of African descent in the urban areas, and not to the equally poor East Indians in the rural areas?

In Amity, in fact, I observed that many of the poorest among the cane laborers were indeed attracted to the PNM during the elections of 1958. The leadership of the community, however, like that of East Indian population at large, swung behind Bhadase Sagan Marajh, head of the Sanatan Dharma Maha Sabha and leader of a new political coalition, the Democratic Labour Party (DLP), that had arisen to challenge Dr. Williams and the PNM.

Many non-Indian Trinidadian supporters of the PNM were confused and embittered by the political behavior of Hindu East Indians. An explanation that had wide currency in Port of Spain was that, at the orders of the Maha Sabha, Brahman pandits forced their congregants to swear with their hands on receptacles filled with "Ganges water" that they would vote for the DLP.

In Amity, however, I observed no such thing. The pandits there played no part whatever in the 1958 contest. Rather, the community leaders agreed with Bhadase Sagan Marajh that the PNM was the party of "Negroes"; that it was both necessary and good that Indians have their own separate political structure to protect their interests and particularly their identity. When Eric Williams indicated (as he did when he spoke in Amity) that he was opposed to all discrimination and separation, that he refused to see differences between poor "Negroes" and poor "Indians"—because to him both were simply poor *people*—East Indian leaders interpreted his remarks to mean that he wanted the ethnic groups to intermarry and become one "Creole" population. The village leadership did not have to impose such views on their followers; most Indians in Amity shared them and, given the history of relations with the non-Indian population, were deeply suspicious of the PNM.

And, it must be observed, there was another reason East Indians supported the DLP in large numbers. It was not because of oaths on "Ganges water": the leaders of Amity believed that they had a debt to Bhadase Sagan Marajh that they were in honor bound to repay. Under his leadership, and (they believed) with the infusion of some of his own money, the Maha Sabha had built the Amity Hindu School, along with all the others. East Indian village leaders were patrons who provided for their clients, and expected respect and obedience in return. They were clients of "Bhadase" and therefore had a similar obligation to support him, and to line up their own clients in turn—and they did (Klass 1961: 221–229).

Those men of influence and education in Amity who were either attracted by Williams' program, or who had doubts or suspicions about the DLP leadership and program—and there were such—faced a dilemma. Some simply stayed away from the hustings, and others buried their misgivings for all the above reasons and joined with their fellows: in their view there was nowhere else to go.

Bhadase Sagan Marajh was elected to the LegCo, but neither the DLP nor its (and his) various successors ever succeeded in toppling either PNM or Eric Williams. On the one hand, therefore, the PNM, to the day of Eric Williams' death, never drew the votes and support of the majority of the nation's East Indian voters or political parties (see Malik 1971). On the other hand, East Indians continued to feel threatened, unrepresented, and politically powerless. The Trinidad East Indian scholar, Kelvin Singh, observed in a paper published in 1974: "The Indian population . . . has remained in a general situation of powerlessness, and this largely accounts for the fact that economically and socially their position in the society has not changed significantly from what it was in the period before 1946" (Singh 1974: 65; and see Dookeran 1974 for a similar view).

1974, however—the year of publication of the volume containing Singh's paper (*Calcutta to Caroni: The East Indians of Trinidad* edited by John La Guerre)—saw the beginning of what were to be far-reaching changes for all the people of Trinidad, including the East Indians.

### Notes

1. My own knowledge and understanding of island-wide patterns of marriage, settlement, and much more has been immeasurably enhanced by Colin G. Clarke's extensive study of ethnic relations over time in the town of San Fernando (1986); the interested reader is urged to consult it.

2. See also Mahin Gosine (1986); particularly Chapter 2; "East Indians: Culture and Group Structure" (pp. 40–62).

# 4

## Persistence and Change

### The Problem of "Caste"

Times change, politics change, life styles change, individuals come and go, and even "culture," that most tenacious of human artifacts, changes all the time it remains the same. Or, from the opposite perspective, it remains the same all the time it seems to be changing.

Thus, Kelvin Singh, as we have observed, saw little change taking place in East Indian life. In his paper, *East Indians in the Larger Society,* published in 1974 but using data compiled in earlier years, Singh described the Trinidad East Indians as a remarkably static, impoverished population:

> The most significant fact of the Indians, today, is that after more than a hundred and twenty years of economic struggle, attended by a good deal of privation . . . the Indian community in Trinidad, by and large, is still the lowest income earning section of the society. The data of the 1960 census revealed that Indians had the lowest median income, with a fairly large gap between itself and the second lowest group, the Negro population, Europeans being at the top, as hitherto (Singh 1974: 61).

Other observers, however, were convinced that significant changes were in fact taking place. In papers delivered at a symposium in 1975 at the University of the West Indies (Faculty of Social Sciences [etc.], 1975) two scholars, J. M. Alleyne and Courtney Boxill, concluded that the processes of "Creolization" were well under way, and that the future would see a change (as Boxill's title had it) "From East Indian to Indo Trinidadian" (Alleyne, Boxill 1975).

Clearly, the issue is a complex one, exhibiting different facets in different contexts, and inviting different—but equally valid—conclusions given different kinds of questions.

For example, in 1967, in a volume that for the first time assembled together the research of some of the scholars who had worked in different "Overseas Indian" communities (*Caste in Overseas Indian Communities* edited by Barton M. Schwartz), Colin Clarke reported on his 1964 study of East Indians in San Fernando, the largest town, or second city, of Trinidad. As might be imagined, the milieu was markedly different from that of Amity in the Caroni cane fields. San Fernando, Clarke observed, claimed to be "the industrial capital of Trinidad"—among other reasons, because "a large proportion of the 7,000 men who work at the [adjacent] Texaco oil refinery live in San Fernando" (Clarke 1967: 165; for a more thoroughgoing analysis see Clarke 1986).

East Indians comprised only 25.8% of the population of the town, and they differed significantly in certain ways from the island-wide East Indian patterns ("Proportionally, Presbyterians are more than twice as numerous locally as they are nationally, and Hindus are three times as numerous nationally as they are locally" [Clarke 1967: 167]). Nevertheless, the rules, practices, and values of San Fernando East Indians were not markedly different from those of the inhabitants of Amity I had observed almost a decade earlier: most marriages were arranged by parents, and—despite a survey indicating that a majority of Hindu East Indians personally disapproved of caste endogamy—Clarke observed that 73% of marriages were in fact "varna endogamous" (Clarke 1967: 186–191). He noted, further, that while occupational and "pollution" dimensions of caste had largely disappeared, "caste is equated with prestige," particularly for Brahmans who dominated in religious and often in political affairs. "Caste," he concluded, "does not seem to have been especially eroded in the industrial, multiracial, and multireligious environment of San Fernando" (Clarke 1967: 191–197).

A somewhat different view was advanced by Arthur Niehoff in another paper in the same volume (reflecting research conducted at about the same time I was in Amity). Niehoff contrasts the social organization of the East Indians of the Oropouche Lagoon region of south Trinidad with that of communities in India he had studied earlier. Though the small towns in which he conducted research were, respectively, 90% and 75–80% "Indian" (Niehoff 1967: 150), he concluded that "caste is functionally a matter of little concern in this [Trinidad] Hindu community" (Niehoff 1967: 162). He found little evidence of "residence clustering by caste," and intracaste marriage probably just as common as intercaste marriage—even though most marriages were arranged by parents, and though the India-derived extended family system was, he observed, still flourishing.

Again, Barton M. Schwartz, who—in 1961 and again in 1964—also studied a south Trinidadian East Indian community, came to much the same conclusions as had Niehoff. In "Boodram," he wrote, "caste does not exist" (Schwartz 1967: 141). By this he meant, first, that the key elements of caste as he understood that institution (such things as corporate caste units, economic and social functions, etc.) were missing in Trinidad. Secondly, Schwartz—like Crowley, Alleyne, and Boxill—was convinced that "Creolization" was occurring at a rapid rate. Thus, though he noted that "the overwhelming tendency is for East Indians to marry other East Indians"—he argued, nevertheless: "Forces at work in Trinidad are moving in the direction of cultural and racial integration. It may not be too long before this tendency is significantly altered" (Schwartz 1967: 124).

Whatever the future might or might not hold, however, it would seem that despite local variations and the different perspectives and experiences of the observers, East Indian life in Trinidad during the 1960s was not significantly different from that of the previous decade—or even half century, or more.

### Return to Amity

In 1972–73 a re-study of Amity was conducted by Joseph Nevadomsky—apparently, as he himself records, because his "well-intentioned but perhaps naive original project did not survive actual field conditions" (Nevadomsky 1983a: 180). Whatever his initial reasons, his decision has provided us with an opportunity to see Amity as it was some fourteen years after my first visit, and some thirteen years before my second visit (in 1985). Of possibly greater significance, Nevadomsky's study took place *just before* the "oil boom" of 1974, an event which, as we shall see, transformed all of Trinidad and Tobago—including the East Indian population.

Nevadomsky's doctoral dissertation—*The Changing Family Structure of the East Indians in Rural Trinidad* (1977)—has not as yet been published, but he has drawn upon his findings for scholarly articles, and the observations in the succeeding pages about Amity in the 1970s derive from two of these (1983a, 1983b).

As the title of his dissertation indicates, Nevadomsky was particularly interested in indications of change. In one of the articles he observes: "The focus of the present paper is on the processes of economic change and changing patterns of social mobility. . . ." (Nevadomsky 1983b: 63). How different, then, was Amity from the community I had observed fourteen years earlier—and how different was it to become in an equivalent period of time after 1973? In the preceding chapter I offered a brief description of the community as I had seen it in the late 1950s; now I propose to compare the community as Nevadomsky found it in the early 1970s with the community I revisited in mid-1980s.

In 1958, I saw Amity as a village of some 4,000 people. In 1973, Nevadomsky found a population of about 6,500 (Nevadomsky 1983b: 65), an increase of over fifty percent. By 1985, however, the population had seemingly mushroomed by almost one hundred percent over that of 1973—to more than 12,000! This was not due solely to natural increase (though that has played a part) but also to considerable immigration, reflecting significant changes in occupation, and also important changes in Trinidadian (and particularly Indian) residential patterns.

Again, Nevadomsky observed:

By 1972 the village had undergone a considerable physical transformation. In contrast to 1958, some 70 per cent of the houses are now made of concrete blocks . . . most of the homes have electricity and pipeborne water. Telephone lines were installed in 1973. About half the households have a refrigerator, a third have an automobile, a quarter have a modern gas cooker, and nearly a fifth have a television set (Nevadomsky 1983b: 66).

By 1985, I can report, almost one hundred percent of the houses were of concrete construction (which means, specifically, according to the usual modern middle or even upper-class specifications to be found anywhere in Trinidad). Similarly, almost every family had at least one television set, a refrigerator, a modern gas stove, and an automobile—according to the estimates of Headmaster Ramsingh, who had worked earlier with both myself and Nevadomsky:

I would say about 80% of the households have automobiles—but you have quite a percentage of those 80% having more than one vehicle—about 10% of these. Between 90 and 100% have [gas burners]. . . . I would estimate that in ["Amity"] about 10% of the people own videos. Refrigerators, it will be nearer 90%. Washing machines will be about 40%. . . . Now almost every household has water . . . and water tanks—about 50%. . . . And a pump—if you don't have a pump, it is useless (*Personal Communication*).

In other words, in 1985 Amity was not *approaching* the island-wide middle-class norm in appearance and possessions—by 1985 it had reached and very possibly surpassed that norm: one can no longer treat it as an isolate, and certainly not as a "little community"—in twenty-seven years, it has become a residential ("suburban"? "bedroom"?) community very much part of the island life, and even more a part of urban Trinidadian life.

Similarly, Nevadomsky recounts differences, between 1958 and 1972, in agriculture: changes in amount of land devoted to rice and cane cultivation, changes in income of sugar workers, changes in agricultural work-patterns and land inheritance, etc. By 1985, however, a term such as "change" has become completely inappropriate: there has been a thoroughgoing economic transformation. At the time of my second visit, for example, not one household in Amity was raising its own rice.

Again, it was noted earlier that in 1958 out of some 900 male adults (about one-fourth of the total population) some 700 were engaged in sugar cultivation, the majority as estate cane-cutters earning an average of BWI$2.89 per day, when they worked. In addition, between a hundred and two hundred women from the village were employed by the estates, again primarily as cane-cutters.

In 1972, according to Nevadomsky, the nearby estate had reduced its labor force by twenty-two percent, to 625 men and women, "many, if not most" of whom came from Amity (Nevadomsky 1983b: 69). Even if all did, and assuming that adult men still comprised approximately twenty-five percent of the population (approximately 1,100), the 425 men of the total cane force would constitute less than forty percent of the adult males of Amity, admittedly a significant decrease in the economic importance of the activity.

But in 1985 estate records indicated that only 318 persons from Amity—221 of them men—were employed as cane laborers, full, part-time, or whatever. Thus, if there were approximately 3,000 adult males in Amity, then less than eight percent of the men were cane laborers, making the occupation one of the very minor ones of the community! But perhaps even more to the point, the estate records indicate that (a) almost all the cane laborers were over forty years of age—from which we may conclude that an insignificant number of young men (and, as it happens, no young women at all) are attracted to the occupation—and (b) that while the income of cane-cutters, according to Nevadomsky, had more than doubled by 1972 (to TT$6.88 for a day's work), in the next thirteen years it was to increase to TT$57.92 for a day's work!

Cane-cutters, in other words, were earning at least as much for a day's work as anyone in Trinidad outside of the skilled and professional occupations. Therefore, if few could now complain that the remuneration was unreasonably low, why were not more people seeking jobs in the cane fields? The objections to it that I heard were: the work was particularly onerous; it was tainted with memories of indenture and slavery; employment in the cane fields was still a seasonal occupation— and there was little new hiring going on.

On the basis of all the information gathered over the years about this village, I would therefore argue (a) Amity's economic and occupational structure in 1958 was not far different from that at its founding in the late 1870s; (b) by 1972, it is true that this structure was undergoing change, but it was still recognizable; but (c) by 1985, it had changed into something totally different: rice cultivation had simply disappeared and sugar-related activities played an exceedingly minor role. The economic pattern was no longer the traditional "rural East Indian" one but now reflected the new nationwide economic and occupational circumstances.

### Marriage, Family—and "Caste"

Amity social organization, by 1985, had undergone a similar transformation, though perhaps not—at least in all respects—as complete a one. Again, there is always the problem, when one is attempting a comparative analysis of data, of establishing an appropriate standard for evaluation. Thus, we have seen that Schwartz and Niehoff, while coming to conclusions somewhat different from mine about the nature and significance of "caste" among Trinidad East Indians, nevertheless join with me in the conclusion that Indian family patterns and relationships had survived and continue strong. Nevadomsky, however, challenges that conclusion most emphatically—he compares what was observed in Trinidad with descriptions of family structure in contemporary India, and writes:

> The traditional Indian family is supported and sanctified by a caste and religious system of a particular kind. As soon as one of these constraints is removed or transformed the system either collapses or undergoes change and a new pattern of integration develops. In short, Trinidad's East Indians are a long way from India in space, time and social structure (Nevadomsky 1983a: 209).

Few would care to challenge that ringing last sentence: the difficulty, of course, is that at the very same time Trinidad East Indians seemed also to be far from *Trinidad* in social structure, though not in time and space! I suggest we recognize that what we have is that sometimes disconcerting mix of extensive change and remarkable continuity, and if we ignore one because the other is more in accord with our views, we run the risk of distorting the data.

In any case, from Nevadomsky's account we have learned that the rules of marriage and of family life had changed from 1958 to 1972. And, as I observed in 1985, they had continued to change for the next dozen years—though not in all respects. Thus, by 1985 the rule of village exogamy simply no longer existed, and marriages between boys and girls of the same village were not only frequent but excited no more comment than did exogamic unions.

I was tempted at first to relate the loss of this rule to the sheer size of contemporary Amity, and to the number of recent "squatters" who have moved into abandoned sugar estate land adjoining the village, but I heard of no cases of such a rule in any Indian community, anywhere on the island. The closest thing to it was the account given to me by an educated, urban Indian of a recent conflict in his ancestral village when a boy and a girl of two neighboring families wished to marry: though not related by blood or marriage, the two families were descended from founding ancestors and had lived side by side for generations. There was a strong feeling, in this one case, that the boy and girl were "village kin."

Furthermore, in Amity and indeed throughout the Indian community of Trinidad, the practice of initiation of marriages by parents rarely occurs any more: as far as I could determine, the young Indian man and woman initiate their own marriages in what can only be considered typical Trinidadian/Western "free-choice" patterns. That is, young people meet at school or at work, or wherever, go on unsupervised dates without asking parental permission, and do not ordinarily discuss with either parent what happens during a date. When a dating couple decide to marry, they so inform their respective parents (who are expected to pay for the expenses of the wedding), but they rarely seek permission or parental approval.

Age at marriage, too, is within the Trinidadian/Western parameters. In Amity, in 1985, two teen-aged girls became convulsed with amusement and disbelief when their mother reminisced about how she had been married, thirty years before, at the age of sixteen: both of her daughters said they expected to be in their twenties (like their older sisters) before they would consider getting married.

Still further: young Indo-Trinidadians see the same movies, watch the same television programs, and idolize the same movie and rock music stars as do their counterparts in non-Indian Trinidad—and, indeed, in the United States or Canada. Whether or not they all perceive and react to these stimuli in exactly the same way, it is surely reasonable to assume there is considerable overlap or similarity of interest and expectation.

Nevertheless, there still seem to be a few areas of significant divergence from the non-Indian norm. Most particularly, and despite Barton Schwartz's prediction, Trinidad Indian opposition to intermarriage has not disappeared (see Gosine 1986: 23–24); Indians throughout Trinidad still tended to marry Indians, and marriages between Indians (particularly Indian women) and Afro-Trinidadians still encounter considerable difficulty. In 1985, an Amity father, as he proudly invited me to attend the marriage of his daughter to a European, made a point of telling me that he never interfered in his children's marital choices. It was now their business, not his, he said: "Unless it is a Negro—then I kill!"

There are other, and perhaps more significant, ways in which the Indians of Trinidad have resisted, and continue to resist, becoming unhyphenated "Trinbagonians." For one thing, the Indian community as a body is—from evidence soon to be reviewed here—as reluctant as it ever was to merge *politically* with those of African descent. Nevertheless, and on the other hand, if at mid-century the East Indians were clearly different from their ancestors and cousins in South Asia, by 1985 those differences had become even more pronounced. At the same time, as we shall see, the Trinidad Indians had become much more aware of those differences than their parents had been thirty years before.

Nevadomsky believes, we have seen, that the changes in East Indian practices reflects the "collapse" of India-derived institutions such as caste and religion. There can be no argument, of course, that most political and economic dimensions of Indian "caste" were never, and could never have been, reconstituted in Trinidad. On such questions, however, as the reconstitution, the continued presence, and the significance, of social and religious dimensions of caste at mid-century and immediately thereafter, there was considerable disagreement among observers. At any event, if such dimensions were present then, they have clearly undergone substantial change in the succeeding decades.

One would seem to be justified, in such a situation, in concluding that that by 1985 the Trinidad "Indians" were no longer meaningfully representative of South Asian culture—and equally justified in concluding that they were somehow still set apart from Afro-Trinidadians, at least from their own point of view. Surely, there was no clear consensus about what they wanted their community to become: more South Asian, more Western, or more Trinidadian/West Indian?

Given that, what was the attraction to the Trinidad Indian community of Sathya Sai Baba—a holy man no one in Trinidad had heard of before 1970, and one who lived in a part of India which no Indo-Trinidadian ever claimed as an ancestral homeland?

It will help us to evaluate the ramifications of Trinidad Indian ethnicity, I suggest, if we raise our eyes from the issue of structural conflicts attendant upon the simple impossibility of reconstituting "India" in Trinidad. We must take into account not only that the Indians were in Trinidad, but that Trinidad was in the world. Why, for example, was change among the Indians so rapid after 1974—what has the "Oil Boom" to do with caste and religion and rules of marriage?

### While Oil Boomed

In 1974 life in Trinidad and Tobago began to change for everyone —more, and in more ways, than ever before. This change was of course related to, in fact clearly derived from, the effects of the world-wide leap in oil prices. The consequences of that economic event, however, must be seen within a specific political context: the former colony was now a nation—with a government capable of nationalizing industries.

Trinidad, like other islands in the Caribbean, had throughout its history served as a source of wealth for people overseas; the inhabitants themselves shared only meagerly in that wealth. Absentee landowners had long garnered the profits of the sugar estates, and the first half of the twentieth century saw only a shift in the pattern of ownership (with absentee shareholders replacing the landowners) but none at all in the flow of wealth. Similarly, during this period the profits from oil also in the main went overseas, with Trinidadians benefitting only from opportunities for employment in the oil fields.

All that was to change sharply by the mid-70s. Legislation restricting foreign ownership of Trinidad enterprises was first enacted in 1973, and in August 1974 the oil industry of Trinidad was completely nationalized, so that the profits (and they were huge as both the price and the demand for oil spiraled upward) went into government coffers: "By early 1975 oil production had hit 200,000 barrels a day and the economy was growing at an enviable 5% per annum. In 1976 the World Bank estimated that Trinidad had achieved a per capita income of £775 to put it third in Latin America and eighth in the developing world" (Cross 1980: 16).

Further, by 1977 the sugar industry was also nationalized, and so by the end of the decade the government of Trinidad had control over all levels of employment in both industries, in addition to the profits and their disbursement. Oil, however, was the sole source of the new prosperity, for the profits from sugar had been declining before the industry was nationalized, and the decline continued unabated. To complicate matters, the newly nationalized sugar industry discovered it was not eligible for the favored treatment the former British company had enjoyed, and heavy world competition, along with rising costs in Trinidad, curtailed profits even more.

The cultivation of sugar therefore dropped off sharply in the ensuing years. In 1973, 40,065 hectares of land were devoted to sugarcane—by 1982, only 25,235 hectares were so utilized (Central Statistical Office

[*Annual Statistical Digest*] 1984: 121). In 1973, Trinidad and Tobago had exported 148,516 tons of sugar—by 1982 the export figure had dropped to 50,582 tons (Cent. Stat. 1984: 119).

But what did the price of sugar matter when the revenues were pouring in from oil? In 1973 (the year before nationalization) the export of crude petroleum produced a total revenue, for those who shared in it, of TT$265,226,300. In 1982, the total revenue—destined solely for Trinidad and Tobago, now—from the exporting of this *one* petroleum product alone was TT$2,679,250,500 (Cent. Stat. 1984: 164–165)!

Most of the revenue from oil was channeled back into the nation's economy so as to benefit as many people as possible. Government loans, for housing and for starting businesses, were easily obtainable at low interest. By 1985, the ubiquitous ajoupa, or "trash house" (with mud walls and floor, and a thatched "trash" roof), had completely disappeared—it was said that two or three were maintained near the main airport as a tourist attraction! Even wooden houses, once the characteristic homes of somewhat wealthier Indian and non-Indian laborers, became rarer as even the poorest people, when they build at all, erected new homes of cinder block, concrete and steel.

Small (and not so small) businesses mushroomed and prospered, particularly those that participated in the construction boom: building supplies, hardware, material transport, etc. Jobs in sales as well as in construction trades paid well and were easy to obtain. The value of real estate rose and continued to rise.

The oil revenues were also channeled into enormous joint government/private enterprise ventures: factories producing canned food, bottled drinks, etc. The profitability of these enterprises—their viability without government subsidy—was apparently of less importance than their ability to provide jobs. In 1981, of the 221,617 people employed in what the *Annual Statistical Digest* categorizes as "Large Establishments," 64,110 were in "Manufacturing" (including sugar and petroleum production), and another 15,047 in "Construction." But perhaps the most striking figure in the table is that of "Central and Local Government" employees: 94,500 (Cent. Stat. 1984: 87)! The government directly and without intermediary provided almost 43 percent of all employment outside of farming and small establishments.

There was little reason, now, to stay down on the farm; everyone sought ways to draw upon this new wealth. Indians, particularly, turned away from agriculture—and not only from labor in the canefields, but even from rice cultivation for home consumption.

### The New Indian Occupations

Young people could now dream of professional—or at least white-collar—careers, for government money was also being channeled into education. The educational system was transformed: religious groups (such as the Catholic Church, the Canadian Mission, and the Sanatan Dharma Maha Sabha) maintained titular control over their respective schools, and unquestionably controlled religious instruction, but the funding for teachers' salaries and most other educational expenses soon came to be derived from government revenues. Along with that, nationwide curriculum standards were imposed. More schools, and most particularly secondary schools, were constructed and staffed, and the University of the West Indies grew and prospered. By 1985, a graduate of the university with a good academic record could expect to get a starting teaching job paying a salary in the neighborhood of TT$3,200 per month—a salary surpassed only by those of his or her fellow graduates entering fields such as engineering.

I said "his or her" in the preceding paragraph advisedly: women were now well-represented in the UWI student body and in the profession of teaching. And East Indians, both male and female, appeared to be represented in that profession even beyond their proportional share: one knowledgeable official estimated that perhaps sixty percent of Trinidad teachers, in 1985, were of East Indian derivation. If true, that is a particularly startling figure given the fifty percent illiteracy rate among East Indians reported in the 1946 census!

Indians entered government service in capacities other than those of the teaching profession, but apparently not in similar proportions: while there are Indian policemen, soldiers and sanitation employees, these occupations are still perceived (by all) as manned overwhelmingly by people of African descent.

Young Indian women, however, were attracted in large numbers, upon graduation from secondary school, to government clerical employment. In 1985, as far as I could determine, seclusion and familial guarding of young unmarried women occurred no more frequently among the Trinidad Indians than it did among any other segment of the population. Rather, young Indian women moved freely out into the world of business and government service, traveling alone and without supervision on public transportion to their places of employment.

I heard no parental expression of concern—in Amity, at any rate—about whether their daughters might be sexually active while away from home. In south Trinidad, Aisha Khan reports (*personal communica-*

*tion*), such freedom of movement for unmarried young women was indeed sometimes accompanied by parental anxiety, and daughters were expected to be mindful of their reputations. What I heard in Amity, however, was for the most part concern over whether their daughters might become attracted to men of African descent. On a number of separate occasions Indian men—some old but some young ones, too— told me earnestly that they believed a plot existed to hasten the assimilation of Indians into the Afro-Trinidadian ethnic community— by premeditated assignment of Indian young women entering government service to jobs alongside attractive Afro-Trinidadian men!

As I have already noted, agricultural production diminished, and the role of agriculture in Indian life diminished even more. The wages of cane laborers rose dramatically, but nevertheless laborers were hard to find. Rice cultivation was increasingly abandoned throughout the island, and in 1985 I was unable to find a single resident of Amity who was still producing a crop of rice.

Men in Amity say that the oil boom was perceived by rural Indians, by and large, as providing an opportunity for entering private, rather than government, employment—an opportunity, particularly, to move toward owning one's own business. Young Indians sought sales jobs in the rapidly proliferating shops and markets, many with the hope of eventually opening their own stores. Hardware businesses, along with building suppliers and transport companies, appeared in 1985 to be largely owned and staffed by Indians. Taxi driving—long a favored occupation of Indian men—became even more popular. Vehicles became more easily obtainable and the demand for public transportation all over the island burgeoned because more and more people were traveling long distances to their places of employment.

One particularly startling development (at least for me) was the sudden movement of Indians into skilled trades—carpentry, welding, construction trades, electrical trades, automotive repair, etc.—in all of which they had had comparatively small representation even as late as the beginning of the 70s. Men in Amity, who had been able to penetrate those trades in the wake of the oil boom, claimed their opportunities had come about because the increased demand for people with such skills had coincided with a substantial departure of those who had long monopolized them (primarily men of African descent) into government employment, particularly in the oil fields, and into the new industries.

The influx of what was for most Trinidadians, whatever their ethnic identification, considerable and novel "wealth" appears to have precipitated an island-wide spending spree. New houses, we have noted, went up everywhere. In 1985, it was estimated that there were approximately 250,000 television sets in Trinidad, or approximately one per family, and almost as many automobiles. Approximately 35,000 families were believed to own video cassette players. On the other hand, with the diminution of agricultural activity, less and less of the food in the shops and emerging supermarkets was home grown; increasingly, shelves were stocked with items imported from all over the Caribbean, from the United States and Canada, Europe and the British Commonwealth. In 1958, I observed (Klass 1961: 244) that rural East Indians spent comparatively little on clothing. In 1985, an average family in Amity expected to pay three to five thousand (TT) dollars for their daughter's wedding sari—the trousseau itself (often entirely Western in composition) might cost thousands more!

### *Travel*

For the purposes of this study particular attention must be drawn to one area or type of expenditure: that for travel. Within the island, automobiles (both private and in the form of taxis) came to provide the major source of transportation for the entire population—and rush hour traffic jams on major roads near the urban centers now rivaled those anywhere in the world. This increase in private automobiles, and in public taxis and minibuses, has served to bring the people of all parts of the island into closer contact, and to diminish regional isolation. In 1958, Amity was, in important ways, an isolated community: by 1972 it might fairly have been described as a suburb of the nearby town of Chaguanas. By 1985, however, for many of its inhabitants Amity had become simply a bedroom suburb of Port of Spain.

That change merely reflected what was happening throughout Trinidad. There were people residing in the attractive and expensive community of Diego Martin north of Port of Spain who commuted each day to their jobs in the oilfields of San Fernando. In short, regional differences are disappearing throughout Trinidad, and the isolated community is becoming a rarer phenomenon.

And, in addition, for many Trinidadians travel abroad by airplane had become almost a routine event. People of all ethnic groups had relatives living and working in Canada, England and the United States (it was estimated, for example, that about four hundred residents of Amity had migrated to North America, and that about twenty percent of the current residents had relatives abroad) and there is continual visiting back and forth. The pattern of visitation was intriguingly similar to (and possibly even as frequent as) that of familial intervillage visiting back in 1958.

Trinidadians, however, went abroad for reasons other than to visit relatives or even to seek overseas employment. Study at the universities of Great Britain, Canada, and the United States is highly valued, and is not limited by any means to the children of the urban and wealthy. Furthermore, so many Trinidadians, and among them Indians most particularly, traveled in 1985 to Florida in order to shop that there were organized shopping excursions for them to join at the Miami airport (and, indeed, at Caracas and New York and other cities) taking busloads of Trinidad visitors from one shopping mall to another!

In 1958, as I noted in an earlier chapter, I knew elderly women in Amity who had never been to Port of Spain once in their lives; in 1985, some of their daughters flew regularly, two or three times a year, to Panama City where they could buy dry goods the sale of which in Trinidad would more than cover the cost of the flight.

And, for Trinidad Hindus particularly, the emergence of almost-casual overseas travel has meant the real possibility of a visit to India. For some, this has meant an opportunity to search out "roots"—to try to find one's ancestral village, and perhaps even contemporary relatives. Many, however, who had little information about their ancestors' origins, perceived a trip to India simply as a religious pilgrimage. Package tours abounded, advertising visits to all (or many) of the holy sites of India. The more educated (and wealthier) could make up their own religious itineraries, and such trips could be combined with stops in Bombay and Delhi (and then in London and perhaps New York) for shopping.

To sum up, a substantial portion of the Indian population of Trinidad has became remarkably cosmopolitan (so unquestionably have the non-Indians, but in this study I am focussing on Indians). Many have traveled abroad, and more than once; many more have relatives abroad; and almost everyone knows someone who has been abroad. From movies, and particularly from television, the Indians are as aware of world events—of things happening in politics, in economics, in fashion, in entertainment—as people in any community in any country on the planet . . . and more, I truly suspect, than most.

And yet, I would argue, in certain ways they remain Indo-Trinidadians—a community of people of South Asian derivation resident in Trinidad and Tobago. They are tied to the nation's economy and political system, among much else, and the majority still identify themselves primarily as Hindus, though they have become, at least in my view, "Trinidad Hindus"—something not quite the same as their seeming co-religionists in India.

### Creolization or Westernization?

In view of all the foregoing one might easily demand of me whether there really is much point to this micro-analysis. Should we not, in other words, say that for all practical purposes Indian culture is gone or moribund, and that "Creolization" is pretty much complete? We could—but there are still problems for which the "Creolization" conclusion provides little illumination.

On the one hand, as we have seen, by the summer of 1985 most of the former "East Indians" of Trinidad and Tobago had adopted the "Trinbagonian" way of life—in language, in social and economic patterns, in material goods, and in aspirations. Even more, they shared with the rest of the island's population a commitment to Western education and egalitarian values, and were well aware of their economic and other ties to North America (Canada and the United States) and the British Commonwealth.

And yet, for all of that, when we peer closely at certain important dimensions of Indian life we observe what some might consider remarkable evidence of continuity—in culture content and in structure. For example, all the change in the direction of "Westernization" or "Creolization" that has taken place in social relations has of course had its impact on "religion"—but there has been no turning away from Hinduism or Islam to Christianity, nor even significant decrease in public or private observance of "Indian" religions. If anything, it could well be argued that such observance has intensified, increasing the differences between Indo- and Afro-Trinidadians.

Similarly, we saw that at mid-century East Indians rejected social and political amalgamation with West Indians, despite all overtures from the latter group. In 1985, in the face of all the "changes"—and despite the shrinking of the island of Trinidad into one seemingly tightly-knit "village"—that rejection, as we shall now see, continued fully in effect, and apparently characterized the majority of the Indian community.

The issue is further complicated, I would argue, by the interplay of change and persistence *within* the Indian community. That is, on the one hand Indo-Trinidadians have resisted becoming unhyphenated "Trinbagonians" and have continued to find themselves in conflict with their Afro-Trinidadian neighbors.

On the other hand, the Indo-Trinidadians are often very much in conflict with one another—and sometimes such a conflict takes place within the person himself or herself: in either case, however, this might be viewed as a conflict, both social and ideological, between "Homo hierarchicus" and "Homo aequalis."

For these Indo-Trinidadians, let us note still one more time, are people who have lived for generations in the West, and have adopted and incorporated much of Western (read "European") values and practices. Indeed, much of that which is rejected turns out, upon examination, to be of what is perceived as *Afro*-Trinidadian in origin—and not of what is assumed to be of European derivation.

Thus, as we have seen, sequestration of women has come to an end, along with arranged marriage and marriage at an early age. In this, however, the Indians clearly see themselves as adhering to European rather than Trinidadian standards (despite the fact that other Trinidadians adhere to the same practices). And, further, marriage of daughters to men of European descent—particularly to American and English men—is often a source of pride to the Indian family. Nor does there appear to be much objection to the marriage of sons to foreign women, except in that the couple are likely to take up residence somewhere far from the Indian parents. Daughters who marry foreigners go away too, of course, but while this saddens parents (who tearfully play and replay the videotapes of the weddings) the departure of daughters from the parental neighborhood is in any case still quite frequent. Apart from those constrained by economic circumstance, sons rarely continued to reside in the parents' house (neolocality appeared to be pretty much the rule in 1985), but in the normal course of events they are not too far away.

Still, as we have seen, marriage with members of the Afro-Trinidadian community is still frowned on by Hindu and Muslim Trinidad Indians—and to a great extent even by Christian Indians. Young men in 1985 whispered the same kind of accusations I had heard a quarter of a century before from their fathers: there was a conspiracy among Afro-Trinidadian men to foster marriages with Indo-Trinidadian young women.

It would be tempting to offer, as explanation for this unwillingness to intermarry, the classic spectre of "caste pollution"—but I agree with most observers that even by the 1950s there was little concern among Trinidad Indians about ritual pollution, and what little there was is long gone: pork and beef are sold in the butcher shops of Amity, and for those who do not wish to cook there is even a Chinese "take-out" restaurant.

Whatever the percentages of intracaste/intercaste marriages once observed by myself, Clarke, Schwartz, Niehoff and others—things are unquestionably different today: both young Indians and their parents agree that caste membership—with one possible exception—plays no role whatever in the choice of marriage partners. Members of Amity families that, in 1958, had been ripped apart by controversies over intercaste marriages, reminded me of those disputes—and went on to enumerate the number and scope of recent intercaste marriages in their families. Indeed, it was often the case that literally no one knew the original caste of some of the inmarrying spouses.

The one exception,however, is an interesting one. Many non-Brahmans, in discussions about marriage, noted that they believed that many—perhaps most—*Brahmans* still preferred to have their children marry other Brahmans, or at least Chuttris, members of the next highest *varna*. An examination, therefore, of the role the Brahman plays in the contemporary Indo-Trinidadian community will help to illuminate the nature of the clash of Western and South Asian values.

### Brahmans and Trinidad Hinduism

Young Brahman men whom I consulted reported to me that, while there was no parental effort to *arrange* a marriage, they had indeed been urged to look for Brahman girls, and I was told that a young Brahman man who chose a non-Brahman as a prospective wife could expect disapproval from his parents—though rarely to the point of disinheritance if he persisted in his choice.

But, again, even Brahmanical opposition to intermarriage need not be interpreted in terms of fear of "ritual pollution," though the objections are probably strongest among Brahmans who serve as village priests, or "pandits." It seemed to me, in my discussions with Brahmans about this issue, that the source of the objection was in a pride of ancestry rather than a fear of pollution: a feeling that Brahmans were a distinguished group in Trinidad, as they had been in India, and that what they were endeavoring to preserve was something akin to being of Norman blood in England, or a Mayflower descendant in the United States.

There can be no doubt, of course, of the predominance of Brahmans in all aspects of Indian life in Trinidad, from politics to commerce to the professions. But it is in religion particularly that many Brahmans claim more than importance: they claim total, and sole, authority. Not all Brahmans make such a claim, of course, and not all non-Brahmans bow to it—but despite all objections and even the formation of dissident religious groups, Brahmanical control of Trinidad Hinduism was as much the rule in 1985 as it was in 1957.

The people of Amity, like most of those in Trinidad who identify themselves as Indians, continue to consider themselves Hindus. Most marriages in the community continue to be performed by Brahman pandits: two were resident in Amity in 1958, and one of them was still following his profession in 1985. The other pandit (now deceased) has been succeeded by his son.

For many of the contemporary residents of Amity, "religion" consists, as it did during my first visit, essentially of sponsoring weddings and other occasional or periodic rituals—as on one's birthday—conducted by those pandits. Important Hindu holidays are celebrated as before in Amity—with only minor changes ("Holi" is now more commonly referred to as "Phagwa," and the Amity celebration is now really part of a nationwide observance, at least among Indians). Though beef and pork are sold in some of the shops of Amity, it is only fair to note that many people claim they do not eat such foods. Vegetarianism in fact is perceived by Indians throughout Trinidad as an inevitable, perhaps necessary, first step for one seeking spiritual enlightenment or improvement.

Amity now boasts a number of temples in addition to the old "Siwala" (now "Siva Mandir"). Two or three of the new ones were constructed as essentially private chapels by wealthy men as acts of piety, and two public temples were erected to serve specifically as alternative places of worship by those who felt alienated from the Siva Mandir. One of these is part of the chain of Divine Life temples that dot rural Trinidad, and the man who was once Amity's Brahmcari is now the Swami who directs this movement: it is orthodox Hindu, and an affiliate of a larger organization in India, but it rejects the authority of the Sanatan Dharma Maha Sabha in Trinidad. In Amity, services at the Divine Life temple are conducted by another of the disciples of the original Swami who came in the early 1950s.

A third disciple, named Basraj Bridglal (referred to in my earlier study as "Basdeo"), who had broken away from the Siwala in the early 1950s because he challenged the exclusive right of Brahmans to serve as religious officiants, died in 1982. Before his death, however, he had gathered about him many people in Amity (and outside it) who shared his views. With their help, and with the support of another India-based religious group (the *Bharat Sevashram Sangha*), he constructed a "Vishnu Mandir" and it continues to prosper: after his death, the world organization dispatched a Brahmcari from Guyana to take up residence in the temple. Though the new Brahmcari now served as spiritual adviser to the congregation, Mr. Bridglal's friends and followers, non-Brahmans all, continued to administer the temple in the spirit, they earnestly believed, of his teachings and principles.

One of Mr. Bridglal projects, however, has been totally abandoned, though it was one that was particularly important to him. He had trained some nine young non-Brahman men in the rituals normally performed by pandits, and made their services available to the community. None, I was told, was able to make a go of it, and eventually all returned to their former occupations.

Informants said that even the most faithful of Basraj's supporters preferred—in time of crisis or of celebration—to engage the services of a "real" Brahman pandit. Some—who sincerely respected Basraj

Bridglal and his teachings, but who had nevertheless turned to "real" Brahmans—tried to explain their mixed feelings to me: in principle, they said, they believed Basraj was right and that Brahmans should have no monopoly on divine attention. Further, they (like many others in Amity, in 1985, as in 1958) professed little respect for the learning, manners, or piety of Brahman pandits. Nevertheless, they admitted, they found they were simply not as satisfied by a ritual performed by a non-Brahman: in their hearts they were not convinced that a religious event had truly taken place.

The issue is by no means confined to Amity and to the disciples of Basraj Bridglal. The question of the right of Brahmans exclusively to preside over religion was raised in my presence by many educated Indians living elsewhere in Trinidad. Well-to-do, frequently, and long away from their ancestral villages, many of them seemed to find rural Brahman pandits embarrassing reminders of their rude origins. Even more, many of these urban Indians have been to India, and have read (if in English translation) contemporary Hindu philosophical and theological works. They have studied philosophy, sociology and Western science at a university, and find the Brahman pandits largely ignorant of such matters. And yet, when such Indians have a wedding to celebrate—or wish to sponsor one of the week-long "yagnas" (reading from the *Ramayana* or *Bhagavad Gita*) which have become popular throughout Hindu Trinidad—they must turn to a Brahman pandit. They prefer, they say, one whose speech will not embarrass them—one well-educated in both Eastern and Western traditions—but such are hard to come by.

To some extent, the Sanatan Dharma Maha Sabha appears to be aware of the problem. The Secretary-General (Mr. Satnarine Marajh, son-in-law to the late Bhadase Sagan Marajh) reported that the organization plannned in the near future to set up a training school for pandits, staffed with teachers imported from India. As of 1989, however, no such "training school" had materialized.

Of course, only young Brahman men would be eligible for admission to such a seminary, and this may add to the irritation already expressed by many Hindus about the continued Brahmanical control of the Maha Sabha. At a gathering I attended at Maha Sabha headquarters, for example, a fellow guest—an observant Hindu, though not himself a Brahman—indicated to me his resentment of the overwhelming representation of Brahmans on the governing council of the Maha Sabha: he said he could accept the principle that only Brahmans could be pandits, but by what right should all governing and administrative positions continue to be controlled by them?

## Black Power

The members of the Trinidad Indian community continue to be enmeshed in two political arenas, and we cannot talk long about one without returning to the other. They are simultaneously Indians and Indo-Trinidadians. As the latter, they are citizens of the larger nation, and are very much involved in nationwide politics. At mid-century, I reported in my earlier study, the majority of East Indians rejected the overtures of Eric Williams to join with West Indians in what he hoped would be a racially-blind People's National Movement. The reasons for their rejection are of course open to debate: the fact that they did so reject his overtures is not (see Malik 1971, etc.).

Though Eric Williams and the PNM remained in power without a break in the decades following Independence, the majority of the East Indian voters continued to support opposition leaders, of other parties. Trinidad and Tobago remained a parliamentary democracy, however, with free elections and a general absence of racial or political violence.

A change occurred in the late 1960s, however, with the emergence of a "Black Power" movement. Many of the leaders were students at the University of the West Indies, and were fully aware of the experiences and theoretical positions of similar movements in other parts of the world. The "Black Power" movement grew in size and strength, and in 1970 there seemed a serious possibility that it would topple not only the government but the democratic parliamentary structure (see Gosine 1984, 1986, for a comprehensive analysis of the Indian response to the "Black Power" movement).

The proponents of "Black Power" challenged the leadership of Eric Williams and the PNM on ideological grounds—claiming that all social, political, and economic difficulties in the island could be attributed to "White" mistreatment of "Black" people, and that Williams, the PNM, and the parliamentary system were all captives or symbols of "White" domination over "Blacks." From the perspective of the "Black Power" movement, therefore, "Indians" were not to be distinguished from other "Blacks": the movement opposed all political and social forms of separation or distancing between people of African and Indian descent, and made serious efforts to bring Indians, particularly Indian students and workers, into the movement. Young men and women traveled throughout the rural districts of Trinidad, pleading with their Indian counterparts to join them (see Gosine 1986: 107, 113–115, *et passim*).

Many Indians—particularly university students—were indeed attracted to the movement, and participated in its activities, particularly as it made a thrust for real political power. It does not appear, however, that a majority of even Indian students, let alone workers, ever joined the "Black Power" movement. Mahin Gosine, after reviewing the details of Indian rejection of "Black Power" overtures, sees "ethnicity" in all its aspects as the source of the rejection:

> In a society like Trinidad the polarization of ethnic interests within the political arena makes it difficult for one group to accept any degree of control by the other. This is because politicians tend to use their own ethnic group as a power base to achieve and maintain their political positions (Gosine 1986: 214).
>
> In ethnically heterogeneous and developing societies, competition for scarce socio-economic resources is structured along ethnic lines. Historically, the ethnic group that held political power in Trinidad allocated itself a larger share of the resources of the society (Gosine 1986: 215).
>
> The group structure of the East Indians was another force that affected their level of participation. The East Indian community is not a homogeneous one; it is divided into a number of religious and caste groups (Gosine 1986: 217).

A number of young Indians, who were at the University during the rise of the "Black Power" movement, and who say they shared some the ideals of that movement, appear to agree with Gosine's conclusions. Many told me they could not in the end stand with their Afro-Trinidadian colleagues because the movement resolutely ignored all Indian concerns and interests. The reaction to this, according to Gosine, was that:

> Being East Indian became more important than religious differences, general orientation towards life, or political party affiliation. The preservation of their ethnic identity as a people in the face of a movement considered hostile to them gave them a unity they had not had before (Gosine 1986: 220–221).

Kusha R. Haraksingh, another Trinidadian scholar who studied the "Black Power" movement and its reverberations, refers to: "a marked resurgence of Indian cultural activity, including of course a religious dimension, especially following the disturbances of 1970. The latter trend is distinguished by the prominent role of young persons" (Haraksingh 1984: 16).

Surujrattan Rambachan—by 1985 a figure of growing significance in both national politics and the affairs of the Indian community—was one of the "young persons." He and his associates founded the Society for the Preservation of Indian Culture (SPIC) on the UWI campus during those tumultuous days, and they were instrumental in bringing about the first observance on that campus of the Hindu holiday of Diwali (*personal communication*).

In a major 1985 ethnic confrontation, Mr Rambachan and other young Indian leaders insisted that Indian holidays be treated with more respect, that "Indian Arrival Day" be a national holiday, and that more time be given to "Indian culture" on radio and television.

From the Indian perspective, it would appear, to be "Black" meant more than simply to be dark-skinned, or to have a history of persecution by "Whites," as the advocates of "Black Power" insisted—it also meant, in practice, to extoll one's *African* ancestry and heritage. This difference between Indian and African perspective appears to have been the root of the conflict that erupted in 1979 over a popular calypso (one of the characteristic topical songs of Trinidad, associated particularly with the observance of Carnival).

First prize at the 1979 Calypso Monarch Competition went to a singer named "Black Stalin" for his song originally entitled "Caribbean Unity" and known popularly thereafter as "Caribbean Man." According to Ramesh Deosaran (1979), the song was hailed by Afro-Trinidadians as "important and moving." Indeed: "At the 1979 . . . graduation ceremony of the . . . University of the West Indies, the song was sung by the university choir as a symbol of 'Caribbean togetherness' " (Deosaran 1979: 9).

Indian students (and teachers), however, protested the singing of the calypso at graduation ceremonies, because they felt that lines such as:

Dem is one race—De Caribbean Man
From de same place—De Caribbean Man
That make the same trip—De Caribbean Man
On the same ship—De Caribbean Man


". . . applied only to people of African descent and . . . implied that people of other . . . races were left out in this 'message' for Caribbean unity" (Deosaran 1979: 9).


The controversy spilled into the editorials and "Letters to the Editor" columns of the Trinidad papers, and became quite vitriolic at times. Some writers, including Mr Deosaran, saw the calypso as "racist," and indeed as "sexist," while others found the objections totally baffling. Deosaran concluded—quite reasonably, it seemed to me—that, "It is clear from the data in the controversy that the two different groups . . . [Africans and Indians] were responding to the situation on the basis of different perceptions of national identity" (Deosaran 1979: 19).

### Recession

Perhaps as a result of the "Caribbean Man" controversy, perhaps for other reasons as well, there certainly seemed to be little consensus in Trinidad and Tobago, in 1985, about ethnic or racial terminology, and particularly about who is or is not "Black." Most Indians, of all social and educational strata, tended to avoid the term almost entirely, referring on the one hand to "Indians" or "East Indians" and on the other to "Africans" and "Negroes" (educated, urban, Indians tend to use the former and rural Indians the latter).

The term "Caribbean" as used in the calypso precipitated particular concern in the minds of many upper-class Indians: in the nation of Trinidad and Tobago people of Indian derivation are approaching numerical parity with those of primarily African derivation, and their position in the economic, political, and social scheme is roughly equivalent. Use of the term "Caribbean" as an ethnic derivation, however, immediately makes the Indian a member of a small minority in the larger *Caribbean* (African-derived) population of the total West Indies. Of course, the short-lived "Federation of the West Indies" (1958–60) has long since been buried, but does the recent interest in "Caribbean" identity, some Indians worried, presage some "Afro-Trinidadian" push for its reincarnation?

And there were other sources of anxiety for the Indians of Trinidad. With the death of Eric Williams in 1983, new politcal alignments came into being, and PNM control of the government began to face serious challenge. In the elections of 1986, the PNM went down to defeat for the first time, and the defeat was a crushing one. Indians constituted an important component of the triumphant new party, but the leader was a distinguished Afro-Trinidadian.

The new party—the National Alliance for Reconstruction—was careful to define itself as reflecting multi-ethnic interests, and as representing all the diverse people of Trinidad. Nevertheless, there were Indians—even supporters of the new coalition—who still questioned (some angrily, some fearfully) whether the Afro-Trinidadians would ever accept an *Indian* as Prime Minister. According to Kevin Yelvington, Indian support of the NAR dwindled from a high of 86 percent in 1986 to a low of 16 percent in 1988 (Yelvington 1991).

It must be noted, however, that changes and pressures in the political scene were not solely due to the death of Eric Williams, or to ethnic conflict. Recession, if not quite depression, began to succeed prosperity by 1984. An international oil glut, and the sharp reduction in oil revenues for the producing nations, had its impact on Trinidad and Tobago as it did other oil-producing nations.

As oil revenues decreased, jobs became more difficult to come by in the government sector as well as in private enterprise. The government began to evaluate the viability of some of the enterprises it had subsidized, and some of them were closed and others more stringently operated. Construction fell off sharply, and so did business for the firms and activities associated with it. Unemployment increased sharply for both young and old, and by the summer of 1985 breadlines began to be seen on the streets of Port of Spain.

In the rural areas, where most of the Indians still live, there were also signs of economic depression. Young men, claiming there are no jobs to be had anywhere, congregated on the roads and in rumshops and "parlors." During a visit to a village in south Trinidad, near Fyzabad, I was told that two or three Indian farmers were seriously considering growing rice in the coming year for the first time in more than half a decade.

It is too early (and for someone like myself, too difficult) to predict the economic, political and social consequences of all this, but many Indian Trinidadians glance fearfully in the direction of Guyana, and hope that the ethnic violence and political instability that has plagued that sister nation (with a similar history of African and Indian interaction) will not have their counterparts in Trinidad and Tobago if bad economic times have come to stay.

Some Indians speak of joining their relatives and friends now settled in Canada and the United States—and indeed in recent years emigration from the island nation has increased, and not just for Indians—but for most of the population, Indian or otherwise, Trinidad and Tobago is both home and hope for their future. In any case, of course, Indians do not speak of returning to the ancestral homeland—India—from whence their ancestors departed . . . except, of course, for spiritual sustenance and inspiration. Of that, as we shall now see, there is plenty.

# 5

## The New Avatar

### *The First Sai Baba*

On May 23, 1940, a fourteen-year-old boy named Satyanarayana Raju, a resident of the small south Indian village of Puttaparthi (not far from Bangalore, in what was then the state of Mysore), announced to his family and friends that he was in fact the reincarnation of a famous holy man known as Sai Baba of Shrdi (or Shirdi), a village far to the north in the pre-Independence state of Gujarat.[1] The so-called "Saint of Shrdi" had in fact died in 1918, some eight years before the birth of the boy—who now called himself "Sathya Sai Baba" to distinguish himself from his claimed previous incarnation as "Shrdi Sai Baba."

Observers reported that the boy was able to materialize objects with a wave of his hand, and to perform other "miracles." Many people— among them former devotees of Shrdi Sai Baba—became convinced that the boy was indeed the holy man reborn. More and more people began to come to Puttaparthi as pilgrims, hoping to see the reincarnated holy man and acquire his blessing. Then, on July 6, 1963, Sathya Sai Baba announced that he (like Shrdi Sai Baba before him, he said) was in fact an avatar of *Shiva*. Ultimately, he was to claim that he was also *Shiva's* consort, *Shakti,* and that he was *Vishnu,* and the divine essence known to Hindus as *Bhagavan*—and more.

He was, in other words, claiming to be the transcendant Godhood of the universe (whoever or whatever humans anywhere have worshipped under a name that translates as "God") now made manifest in a human body. Those who follow him accept his claim.

In addition, then, to accepting him as an new avatar of God, his followers believe that he has lived, and will live, a number of human lives. Specifically, it is believed that he *was* Shrdi Sai Baba, he *is* Sathya Sai Baba, and he *will be* reborn again as Prema Sai Baba. These three persons—human men—are not thought to be related in any social or biological sense; they are quite different in appearance (there are a few photographs surviving of Shrdi Sai Baba, and Sathya Sai Baba has distributed to some devotees tiny representations of what he identifies as his next and final incarnation). Prema Sai Baba, it is believed, will be born sometime after the death of Sathya Sai Baba, and will complete the mission of the first two Sai Babas—by spreading the reign of love (*prema*) throughout the world.

Since, to the devotees of Sathya Sai, his is a successive three-lifetime divine incarnation, it would seem reasonable to begin with an account of the life and teachings of the first Sai Baba. Let us observe as we begin, therefore, that in terms of teachings, as well as in appearance and lifestyle, he who was known as the "Saint of Shrdi" differed markedly from the man of Puttaparthi who calls himself Shrdi reincarnate—and yet there are certain interesting similarities.

The literature on Shrdi Sai Baba is limited, and—indeed like much of the information on Sathya Sai Baba—derives largely from the writings of devotees. Further, a large part of the contemporary discussion of the life and works of Shrdi Sai Baba tends to derive from or relate to accounts of Sathya Sai Baba. The following account of the "Shrdi saint" therefore draws heavily upon those few works—among them particularly, Arthur Osborne's *The Incredible Sai Baba: The Life and Miracles of a Modern-Day Saint* (1957)—that focus primarily on the life and teachings of Sai Baba of Shrdi.

Whatever the source we turn to, nothing is known about Shrdi Sai Baba's childhood. Even his name is an appellation taken or acquired later in life. *Sai,* Osborne claims, is derived from the Persian word for "saint" and *Baba* from the Hindi familiar form for "father" (Osborne 1957: 3). The followers of Sathya Sai Baba, as Swallow observes (1982: 125, fn. 4), prefer to seek Hindi or Sanskrit derivations for *Sai* such as "the supreme Mother of all." In any case, all that Osborne can offer on Shrdi Sai Baba's origins is: "It is fairly certain that he was born of a middle-class Brahmin family in a small town in Hyderabad State" (Osborne 1957: 3). It is by no means "certain" to all, however. Another biographer, Mani Sahukar, a devout follower of Shrdi Sai Baba, rejects all efforts to penetrate the mystery of the saint's origin, arguing: "Shri Sai Baba's appearance was an affirmation of the Immaculate Conception" (Sahukar 1971: 15).

As a matter of fact, it is clear that Shrdi Sai Baba intentionally resisted and foiled efforts to learn about his past. Osborne gives the following account (though without citing his sources) of an attempt by a magistrate to interrogate Shrdi Sai Baba:

"What is your name?" he began.
"They call me Sai Baba."

"Your father's name?"
"Also Sai Baba."
"Your Guru's name?"
"Venkusa."
"Creed or religion?"
"Kabir."
"Caste or community?"
"Parvirdigar."
"Age?"
"Lakhs of years" (Osborne 1957: 20).

Shrdi Sai Baba had apparently also related the name of his guru (Venkusa) to some of his followers—one of the few bits of information about his past he had ever vouchsafed—and had identified Venkusa as a Hindu teacher. In addition, those early followers also believed that Shrdi Sai Baba spent some years during his childhood absorbing the teachings of a Muslim fakir.

These speculations to one side, however, all that seems to be known for certain was that in 1872 a boy of about sixteen years of age— coming from parts unknown—appeared one day in the village (or small town) of Shrdi, in what was then the Bombay "Presidency," perhaps arriving as part of the entourage of a wedding party (Sahukar 1971: 17). He settled in Shrdi, ultimately taking up residence in a mosque (after first requesting accommodations, and being denied them, in a Hindu temple) where he lived until his death in 1918—leading some Hindus to insist that he had really been born a Muslim.

It is clear that Shrdi Sai Baba fostered the ambiguity about his origins for reasons deriving from and reflective of his ideological concerns. His answer, for example, to the question about his caste— "Parvardigar"—was, according to Osborne, intended to imply that he had progressed above and beyond caste distinctions (" 'Parvadigar' is a Divine Name; it is recognized that one who has attained self-realization is above the four castes" [Osborne 1957: 20]). And his reply to the request for his "creed" identification—"Kabir"—was similarly accounted particularly significant by his followers.

Kabir was a teacher (poet, saint) who lived in India in the late fifteenth and early sixteenth centuries. Charles White (1972) describes him as a theist and ascetic "who made major contributions in creating links between Muslims and Hindus" (White 1972: 867), and whose teachings foreshadowed those of Shrdi Sai Baba. It is interesting to note, in fact, that a similar uncertainty exists about whether Kabir was born a Hindu or a Muslim (White 1972: 867).

Shrdi Sai Baba, who identified his creed as that of Kabir, and whom some of his followers considered a reincarnation of Kabir, clearly was of the opinion that Hinduism and Islam taught the same basic truths. Though most of his followers were Hindu, and most of his teachings derived from Hindu scriptures, he habitually referred to God as Allah, or even as "the Fakir" (Osborne 1957: 40).

### The Miracles in Shrdi

Shrdi Sai Baba is said to have performed miracles regularly, almost from the time of his arrival in Shrdi. He changed water into lamp oil; he stopped storms; he healed the sick; he predicted future events. The ash collected from his hearth began to be famous for its miraculous qualities, and devotees begged for small quantities of this *udhi* (sacred ash) so they might drink it or rub it on their bodies: White terms it "a sacramental substance" (White 1972: 869).

Osborne argues that the miracles were intended only to gain the attention of people so that they would then listen to what was more important (i.e., his teachings) and he quotes a reputed saying of Shrdi Sai Baba: "I give my devotees what they want so that they will begin to want what I want to give them" (Osborne 1957: 15, 100).

Actually, Osborne—though he places the saying between quotation marks—phrases the remark slightly differently the second time he cites it. I mention this because it points up the fact that what we know today of Shrdi Sai Baba's teachings is by hearsay alone: the holy man wrote no books and dictated no lectures for posterity. All that remains are the tales told by his devotees.

Indeed, there was apparently some doubt about whether Shrdi Sai Baba had even *read* any books; a doubt only laid to rest when he discoursed learnedly and casually one day on a passage from the Bhagavad Gita. According to Osborne, the holy man claimed that acquiring knowledge would not contribute to the attainment of self-realization (and thus the end of the cycle of rebirth). Rather (in a quotation attributed to Shrdi Sai Baba):

". . . there is no need to give [the disciple] Knowledge but to remove the veil of ignorance that hides the existent Knowledge. . . . The universe is the efflorescence of the indescribable Maya, which is ignorance; yet ignorance is needed to illuminate and dissolve this ignorance. . ." (Osborne 1957: 12–13).

Again, the devotee Mani Sahukar reports that Shrdi Sai Baba taught that:

it was not by reading pages and pages from the *shastras* that a man could assimilate wisdom. True wisdom lay concealed in one's own *atma*. Even in order to understand what meditation is, one must first and foremost understand the meditator (Sahukar 1971: 50).

But without instruction, how was this to occur? Shrdi Sai Baba would do it all, simply through his presence: "The Guru does not teach, he radiates influence" (Osborne 1957: 88). And Osborne quotes another habitual saying of the holy man: "Stay with me and keep quiet. I will do the rest" (Osborne 1957: 89). Sahukar lists, as one of Shrdi Sai Baba's "assurances": "If one meditates on me, repeats my name and sings about my deeds—he is transformed and his *karma* is destroyed. I stay by his side always" (Sahukar 1971:59).

It will be clear to those familiar[2] with the various approaches advocated within Hinduism for the achievement of *moksha* (the release from continuing rebirth), that Shrdi Sai Baba was an advocate of *bhakti*—the path of prayer and devotion, as set against *jnana* (knowledge), or any of the other paths advocated by other teachers. On the other hand, however, it would seem that Shrdi Sai Baba did not dismiss *jnana* or *seva* (selfless service)—it was simply that, in Sahukar's words, "the Sage of Shirdi did favour the path of *bhakti* for attaining salvation" (Sahukar 1971: 52). To put it another way, seek *moksha* any way you wish—but the path of "devotion" is the one recommended by Shrdi Sai Baba—and you need only direct that devotion toward him, and he would do the rest: "If you make me the sole object of your thoughts and aims you will gain *Paramathma*" (Sahukar 1971: 59).

But, after all, could an ordinary mortal accomplish such things? Increasing numbers of his devotees concluded that he was more than mortal. Some considered him a reincarnation of Kabir, others of *Shiva* (and thus a manifestation of God), and from 1908 onward many Hindu followers adored and even decorated the living person called Shrdi Sai Baba as they would a picture or statue or other representation of actual divinity.

Muslim followers, apparently, were made uncomfortable by this devotion: they revered him as a holy man, living in a mosque, who referred to God as Allah, and who taught that while both Islam and Hinduism were true paths to God, one need not—indeed one *should* not—convert from one's ancestral faith. Some were even willing to carry his slippers on a pillow in a religious procession; but to call him "divine" and to worship his physical body was a step that many Muslims could not take (Osborne 1957: 54–56). More recently, as we shall see, many of those who are drawn to Sathya Sai Baba from Christianity and Judaism report similar conflicts. In any event, in the

case of Shrdi Sai Baba, ultimately his Hindu followers began to out-
number those who came to him from Islam.

Wealth was offered to him by devotees, but he accepted little, and
even that apparently with reluctance. He did make a practice of asking
for a few rupees from those who came to him with requests—but his
followers claim .that this reflected only his use of money as symbols
for other things (e.g., a demand for six rupees meant that the supplicant
was being asked, really, to relinquish "the six vices" [Osborne 1957:
79–80]).

In fact, Shrdi Sai Baba required of his devotees neither surrender
of property, nor "renunciation" (of material goods and pleasures), but
only that, in their minds, they surrender totally not only possessions
but body, mind and soul—to him (Osborne 1957: 11, 82). Then, as
has been noted, he would do the rest: no rituals were required of his
devotees, no incantations—"striving is largely through devotion to the
Guru" (Osborne 1957: 93).

In fact, unlike most (though not all) gurus, Shrdi Sai Baba even
refused to give his disciples *upadesa,* or formal initiation, and he
discouraged them from going elsewhere (to gurus or to Brahman priests)
for it. Osborne concludes: "If such a one as Sai Baba . . . took this
responsibility it means then an invisible type of *upadesa* was in use
whether the disciples were aware of it or not" (Osborne 1957: 83–84).

Charles White sums up the career of Shrdi Sai Baba with the
following observations:

> Sai Baba established himself as a saint through the performance of
> miracles; and it is chiefly because of his renowned *Siddhis,* preternatural
> powers, that his reputation has continued to grow long after his death.
> One can read volumes of collected experiences of his followers who have
> believed that it was the direct intervention of Sai Baba that brought them
> health, wealth, or remedy in some pressing life situation (White 1972:
> 869).

His life and miracles—his "visitations" to people and places far
away—are indeed still remembered vividly throughout India, despite
the years that have passed since his death, and some of the *udhi*—the
sacramental ash—which he gave to people and which is said to have
effected miraculous cures, is still in use. Many people, in fact, do not
consider him dead, though they believe that he did achieve union with
the universal Godhood in 1918, but feel that he is "still alive and
active" and close to them (Osborne 1957: 48–49).

Some might argue that there is a curious inconsistency or contradiction in this account of Shrdi Sai Baba and his teachings. Was he

not, on the one hand, primarily concerned with the attainment of *moksha*—with the ending of one's interest in material pursuits and the things of this world by total immersion in prayer and devotion? But, on the other hand, as White has observed, is he not remembered particularly for his miracles—for the "wealth" and "health" he is believed to have brought his devotees? The answer to both questions is "yes." It would appear, therefore, that the lay Hindu man or woman (or, for that matter, Christian or Muslim or Jew, as the career of the later Sathya Sai Baba demonstrates) can be attracted to a teacher who preaches the way to *moksha*—and also to someone with miraculous powers to ease the burdens of this life—but is particularly attracted to someone, like the two Sai Babas, who can offer both.

After his death, Shrdi Sai Baba's place—for some—was taken by Upasani Baba, a disciple of the Saint of Shrdi, and then in turn by a female disciple of Upasani Baba, known as Mata Godavari. At the ashram founded and presided over by these two, however, miracles are rarely performed, according to White, and the emphasis is on Hinduism without any linkage to Islam (White 1972: 870–872).

For many of his devotees, however, and for many other people in India and in the rest of the world, Shrdi Sai Baba—*himself*—was in fact born again less than a decade after his death, and grew up to be Sathya Sai Baba.

### Sai Baba of Puttaparthi

The life of the second Sai Baba has been very different from that of the first. For one thing, the stories of his birth and childhood—if somewhat mythologized and romanticized—are known to all his devotees: he was born in the village of Puttaparthi, not far from the city of Bangalore, and has formally resided in or near his birthplace throughout his life.

It is true that most of the accounts of his life, miracles, and teachings have been written—as in the case of his predecessor—by devotees. In addition, however, there are taped recordings of his sermons and hymns (the latter frequently sung or led by Sathya Sai Baba himself). These are widely distributed, as are movies and videotapings of both special occasions and his regular daily *darshan* (in both religious and secular South Asian literature, a public appearance of divine or royal personages)—the term used by devotees for the times Sathya Sai Baba walks out of his ashram and greets and strolls among those who have come to set eyes on him. And, still further, there are numerous collections of his talks and sermons in many different languages, prepared by his closest associates under his direct supervision.

To take just one example of the reverence with which the story of his life is treated:

As the morning sun gently kissed the fading night away, in a remote and tiny village hidden from the glitter and gaze of modernity, and as temple flowers sanctified the sacred home of the Raju family in Puttaparthi, India, Divinity manifested itself on earth fifty-eight years ago proclaiming to one and all that a new and golden era was being ushered into the hearts of men.

So begins the editorial in the issue of *Satya*—the official publication of The Co-ordinating Committee of Sri Satya Sai Baba Centres of Trinidad and Tobago—commemorating the fifty-eighth birthday of their leader (Ramadhar 1983: 5).

Indeed, the story of the birth, in 1926, of the baby—then named Satyanarayana Raju—to Easwaramma (now often referred to as "The Chosen Mother"), wife of Pedda Raju, is even the subject of children's playlets, and the miraculous nature of the birth—including the appearance of a cobra (a symbol of *Shiva*) in the bedclothes—is related in almost all accounts of his life. Writers among his devotees, such as N. Kasturi (1969) and Howard Murphet (1971), have portrayed his childhood as one of "sweetness" and "devotion" and have related that he became, at an early age, a leader among the children of his natal village, many of whom are said to have called him their "guru."

According to Murphet:

Satya began his formal education at the village school where he showed himself bright and quick in learning. His special talents were . . . for drama, music, poetry and acting. He was even writing songs for the village opera at the age of eight (Murphet 1971: 53).

While he was still in school, it is reported, he began to materialize candy and other items for his friends, with a simple wave of his hand. Word of this spread, and he began to acquire a reputation as a performer of *siddhis* (miracles). Then, on May 23, 1940, he announced to friends and family in Puttaparthi that he was in fact the famous Sai Baba of Shrdi—reincarnate (Murphet 1971: 56–57).

There was apparently little stress or conflict associated with the emergence of Sathya Sai Baba first as a reincarnation of Shrdi Sai Baba and then, ultimately, as both *Vishnu* and *Shiva*—and thus as God Incarnate. His followers in India see nothing in the announcements of the divine nature of Sathya Sai Baba that is in any way in conflict with orthodox Hinduism. A devotee of Sai Baba, born in India but now temporarily resident in Trinidad, insisted that the issue of whether or not Sai Baba was actually God—actually capable of performing miracles—was not of interest to her or her husband:

> *[My husband] never asked him any questions, because basically we believe in the* teachings *of the person. We don't sit in judgment over the man as such. See, any religious teaching should bring about a change in us. I have to have good attitudes . . . I have to be truthful. If his teachings have brought about a change in me [then] I think I could follow him. . . .*
>
> *You require some "symbols"—so that you can identify yourself with the "symbol" and it is easier to comprehend. That is why they say that every family has its own "god"—the idea behind it is that you familiarize yourself with that "god" so that the moment you close your eyes you think of* God— *of that one image. . . . So, since Sai Baba is a living idea, it makes it easier for you to imagine him than a picture of a "god." So you try to have faith in some one (*Interview Reference # 01).

Undoubtedly, some who heard of him rejected his claims (as many in India still do) but others began to flock to Puttaparthi from the earliest years. The accounts of his miracles spread, and more people came—many of them already devotees of Shrdi Sai Baba. By the late 1960s, the name of Sathya Sai Baba was known all over India, and was beginning to attract attention overseas. Tal Brooke, a lapsed American devotee, has provided a vivid if antagonistic description of the Americans and Europeans who flocked to Puttaparthi during this period to sit at the feet of Sathya Sai Baba (Brooke 1979).

### What Sai Baba Gives

Though Sathya Sai Baba claims to be the reincarnation of the "Saint of Shrdi" he has made no effort to look like the latter, or to behave in ways attributed to the older holy man. Shrdi Sai Baba was bearded, carried a staff (at least in the pictures of him as an old man, the only ones of him that exist), and wore a kerchief-like head covering. Sathya Sai Baba is clean-shaven (though it is clear from the dark shadow to be seen in many photographs that he could have a heavy beard if he wished to), and bare-headed.

His hair, in fact, constitutes—as many people seeing his picture for the first time will comment—his most unusual physical feature: it is black (touched with gray in recent years), and gives the appearance of a mass of tightly curled wires—though it is said by many actually to be soft to the touch. Puffed up as it is around the sides and top of his head, it is often described, in the United States and in Trinidad and

Tobago, as an "Afro"—an observation of some significance in places
where hair form is considered a marker of "racial" membership. One
Indo-Trinidadian devotee, reporting on a visit to Puttaparthi, commented:

> *I always tell them nobody can say what kind of hair is that on his head.*
> *Because the slightest breeze blow, all the hair will part up and you can*
> *see his scalp. The hair will drop and you will see all inside . . . a real*
> *Afro wouldn't shake. . . . What I saw, over there, Baba was walking,*
> *coming across over to us, and on this Afro hair I saw something big, in*
> *a circle, like with stars around it, over his head, while he was coming*
> *(*Int. Ref. # 02).

Many of the *siddhis* said to be performed by Sathya Sai Baba
resemble those attributed to his predecessor: both are famous for cures
of the very ill, for manifesting themselves to devotees in distant places,
for materializing objects. I have not seen any assertion, however, that
this similarity in itself constitutes any kind of proof of the relationship
between the two holy men. In any event, Sathya Sai Baba is famous
for one particular kind of materialization—the regurgitation on certain
holidays of a large stone *lingam* (considered to be a representation in
phallic form of *Shiva*)—that was never attributed to his forerunner.
One of the most frequently performed of Sathya Sai Baba's mater-
ializations, however, is interestingly both similar to and different from
an activity associated with Shrdi Sai Baba. The latter, it will be
remembered, frequently gave gifts of ash—called *udhi*—to visitors. This
ash was considered by devotees to have miraculous powers, but was
not in itself miraculously produced; it was in fact known to come from
the ash of Shrdi Sai Baba's hearth. Sathya Sai Baba also distributes
quantities of ash—known to his devotees as *vibhuti*—but he produces
this ash himself: with his sleeve hiked up to expose his bare arm (and
thus the absence of any hidden cache), he moves a hand in a circular
motion and quantities of gray sandalwood-perfumed ash are said to
flow from his fingers into the cupped hands of his devotees.
We have seen that Shrdi Sai Baba lived in a mud-walled and decrepit
mosque through most of his life; in fact, only in his last years, and
apparently most reluctantly (Osborne 1957: 57–58), did he permit the
mosque to be repaired and made slightly more comfortable.
Sathya Sai Baba is also reported to ask for no contributions from
his devotees—indeed, not even the "symbolic" rupees requested by
Shrdi Sai Baba—and those who represent the "Sathya Sai Organization"
announce proudly and constantly to all visitors that he has forbidden
the collection of any "dues" whatever, or even the establishment of

membership rolls. He is quoted by his devotees as saying laughingly, when offered gifts of money: "What need has *God* of money? Here— let Me give *you* something!" And, it is said, with a wave of his hand he materializes a gold or silver locket or ring and bestows it on the visitor. The Trinidad informant previously quoted gives this account of the visit of an *Afro*-Trinidadian member of his group:

> *she dressed up in a nice yellow sari, with flowers in her hair and everything. And she went outside and bought a big* big *mala [necklace] with big yellow flowers, to carry to Baba. And when we went into the interview room again we sit at Baba's feet, and she took the mala and give it to Baba. And Baba say, "No no no! That flowers—it looking nice now, but by tomorrow it fade—no use!" He said, "Give me the flowers from your heart." And he never take the flowers from her. Then he materialize, with a wave of his hand, some sweets and he give it to her, and he ask her, "What form of mine do you want?" And she said, "Baba, I want* you.*" Baba said, "No, you don't want me—you want Christ! You don't want me." And Baba raise up a ring with Christ (Int. Ref. # 03)*

### What Sai Baba Receives

Nevertheless, though Sai Baba refuses gifts, wealth has certainly come to Puttaparthi. Visitors from all over India and from other parts of the world come by the thousands to see the "Godman"—and on special occasions, such as his birthday, it is said the crowds number in the hundreds of thousands. The villagers of Puttaparthi offer accommodations and food, and sell souvenirs. Sathya Sai Baba is believed to disapprove of much of this: his entourage provides food and shelter for visitors at much lower cost, and on occasion he warns devotees not to be taken in by some of the more unscrupulous vendors and apartment renters. Still, he seems unable—or for some reason unwilling—to put an end to the milking of pilgrims.

He himself no longer resides in the village itself, but at "Prasanti Nilayam"—a large and imposing ashram with well-cared-for grounds, a short distance from Puttaparthi. He also has a summer residence, called "Brindavanam," (after the legendary home of *Krishna*) in White-field, a formerly-British suburban community a few miles outside of Bangalore. He has a fleet of expensive cars at his disposal, and many other amenities--all provided for him, it is said, by wealthy devotees.

His personal needs are said to be small; though he makes no pretence of living like an ascetic, he eats simply and resides in a comparatively small apartment in the ashram. Nevertheless, he and his devotees appear to feel that he requires the large buildings and surrounding grounds, as well as the other amenities, in order to cope with the crowds and otherwise effectively carry out his mission. Without fuss or formality, it is said, all expenses are taken care of by wealthy devotees—all arrangements made and all needs provided for—so that Sathya Sai Baba himself will have no distractions.

But those devotees who feel a need to contribute actual money to him are not in fact completely dismissed. Though he will not accept gifts of money personally, people are advised to contribute instead to charitable enterprises; such acts fall under the heading of "right action" or *seva*—the giving to the needy without expectation of return—and lead to the accumulation of favorable *karma*.

Any contribution to any charity, it is said, would be equally meritorious, but those who wish may contribute specifically to charities set up by Sathya Sai Baba himself. These "funds"—over which he is believed to exercise no personal financial control—are administered as acts of devotion by wealthy and experienced businessmen. He does, however, guide and advise about the charitable disbursement, and these funds have provided for the construction of schools and colleges, and for the care of the poor and ill. Among other projects, Sathya Sai Baba undertook to "adopt" (support completely) six thousand poor villages in India by his sixtieth birthday in November 1985, through these funds.

It has never been charged, as far as I have been able to learn, that Sathya Sai Baba has ever impoverished anyone by demanding (or accepting) that person's wealth and possessions.

His followers in India come from all classes and castes, but it seems fair to say that there is a weighting among them toward the upper classes—businessmen, professionals, government officials, etc.—and toward the wealthy, and even the very wealthy. While it is true that Sathya Sai Baba neither directs his teachings solely toward the wealthy, nor in any way excludes the lowly and impoverished—it is equally true that the wealthy and important are particularly attracted to him, and that he makes no effort to turn them away, or to insist that they relinquish or distribute their wealth.

We will return to what Sathya Sai Baba teaches about himself and what he asks of his followers in a succeeding chapter, after a necessary glance at the larger context: similarities and differences between Hinduism and religions of the West. I would note, however, that few would argue that those teachings deviate significantly from traditional Hinduism. There are a few distinctive elements, and as we shall see a few modern emphases (ones that he shares with other contemporary or recent Hindu teachers) but nevertheless there is little that could be considered either revolutionary or unacceptable to mainstream Hinduism. In other words, people who considered themselves Hindus before they became devotees to Sathya Sai Baba, have no reason to feel they have gone outside their original faith. Devotees drawn from other faiths make the same assertion, but it can be, and often is, challenged.

The most controversial element for Hindus in his pronouncements, probably, is the claim that he is an avatar of *Vishnu,* a manifestation of *Shiva,* and the representation on earth of *Divinity* of all faiths and in all names and forms. Still, given the nature of the Hindu perception of "divinity," as we shall see, this does not put him outside the fold: indeed, it is exceedingly difficult to get "outside" of Hinduism!

In any case, Sathya Sai Baba responds to questions about his divine nature by saying: "Everyone of you is an Avatar. You are the Divine, encarsed [sic] like Me in human flesh and bone! Only you are unaware of it!" (Mc Martin 1982: 10).

Few Hindus are likely to find that formulation intrinsically objectionable—but still, for some, it is difficult to believe that this diminutive man with the shock of bushy black hair is not only, as he claims, one with the avatars *Krishna* and *Rama,* who came to inspire and uplift, but is also *Shiva,* the dimension of divinity concerned with endings and death.

The true devotees—whatever their natal faiths—have no difficulty with any of these matters. To them, Sathya Sai Baba is God in all the forms known to humans anywhere. He can take on any shape, speak any language, perform any miracle he wishes to—including the bringing of the dead back to life.

As Sathya Sai Baba says, and as his devotees firmly believe:

You have come into this prison of incarnation through the errors of many lives. But I have put on this mortal body, of My own free will. You are bound to this body with the ropes of the three Attributes. I am free, untouched by them, for the Attributes are but My playthings. I am not bound by them . . . I use them to bind you. You are moved this way and that by desire. I have no desire except the one to make you desireless (Mc Martin 1982: 10).

In that last sentence, there can be no doubt, he wishes it to be understood that he is speaking as the voice of the incarnate Godhood.

But what exactly does he *mean* by that? The words he uses must inevitably be translated into other languages: do they then convey the same message to people not only of different speech but of different religious traditions? Sathya Sai Baba, we have observed, claims to be "God"—but does he mean by that exactly what a monotheist understands that term to encompass? When he speaks, are his words to be received as what in another faith might be called "Divine Revelation"?

In short, it is not enough, for the purposes of this study, simply to observe that an Indian religious movement has acquired followers elsewhere in the world, and specifically in Trinidad. As we have seen, Trinidadians of Hindu extraction—particularly the educated and westernized ones—are often more at home in English than in Hindi (and none know Telegu, the language of Sathya Sai Baba). To understand the attraction of Sathya Sai Baba's teachings for people outside of India, and particularly for Trinidadians, we must address ourselves to a clarification of theological terminology and an exploration of underlying similarities and differences between the religions in contact.

### Notes

1. Indian state or provincial names and boundaries have undergone change over the years. Puttaparthi, I noted earlier, is in the contemporary Indian state of Andhra Pradesh, and Shrdi was in Gujarat when Satya Sai Baba was a boy, in the "Bombay Presidency" when the young Shrdi Sai Baba first arrived in it, and is now in the contemporary Indian state of Maharasthra.

2. For those who are not familiar, this issue and similar ones relating to the differences between Hinduism and the religions of the West will be explored (and I hope clarified) in the following chapter.

# 6

## Eastern Thought and Western Religion

### The Concerns of Religion

True belief in God and knowledge of the existence of a higher reality represent a leap in consciousness for most of us modern rationalists. Sai Baba can help many of us make this great leap, and after it is accomplished the quest for self-realization can begin in earnest (Sandweiss 1975: 155).

If we were asked to list the attributes in our concept of God, the spiritual parent, most of us would name these: compassionate concern for our welfare, knowledge of what that welfare truly is, the stern strength to make us take the nasty medicine when necessary, the power to help and guide us along the narrow way to our spiritual home, the forgiveness and mercy of the father who welcomes with joy the returning prodigal. . . . These are surely the salient qualities in man's mental image of God. And these qualities—all of them—those who have the eyes to see have seen in Sai Baba (Murphet 1971: 207).

Devotees turn to Sathya Sai Baba for many reasons. In the previous chapter, an India-born devotee of Sathya Sai Baba was quoted as observing that the teachings of the holy man were of more importance to her than the question of whether he really was or was not "God." For overseas devotees, however (including, as we shall see, those in Trinidad) the issue of Sai Baba's *divinity* appears to be of all-consuming interest. Writers such as Murphet and Sandweiss give it central importance, and Tal Brooke entitled his book *Lord of the Air* (1979) because he wished to communicate his belief that Sai Baba is not God—but the Devil.

Well, the reader may ask, is that not the central issue: what else *is* religion but a search for God?

The problem is indeed a profound one, and requires attention in this work, because it illuminates the ambiguous nature of the interface between what Sathya Sai Baba says—and what is heard by his devotees. Furthermore, I would argue, that very ambiguity is a crucial component of the acceptance of his teachings by people deriving from extremely different religious traditions.

To begin with, then, let us observe that the assumption that all religions are concerned with superhuman power may well be an example of ethnocentrism. Émile Durkheim rejected the assumption, though for other reasons, early in this century.[1] It remains, nevertheless, a widely accepted view, and even in anthropology there are scholars who continue to define religion in terms of belief in a superhuman power (cf. Spiro 1968), and who therefore might insist that all ideological systems entitled to be called "religions" are by definition "theistic." This does raise problems, of course. Are the so-called "ancestor-worship" belief systems to be considered "religions"? If it could be demonstrated that Theravada Buddhism or Jainism deny (or at least ignore) the existence of gods, must we then consider the followers of those systems to be "atheists"?

It seems to me, in any event, that a particularly troublesome aspect of this attribution of concern about "divinity" to *all* religions is the potential distortion of the fundamental beliefs of the religions of South Asia, and not just of Buddhism. As Sarvapalli Radhakrishnan, in his seminal work, *Eastern Religions and Western Thought*, observes: "Both Judaism and Christianity take their stand on revelation . . . for the Jews and the Christians, God is a supreme person who reveals His will to His lawgivers and prophets" (Radhakrishnan 1939: 8).

And, on the other hand, he points out: "For . . . [Hinduism and Buddhism] religion is salvation. It is more a transforming experience than a notion of God. In theistic systems the essential thing is not the existence of the deity, but its power to transform man" (Radhakrishnan 1939: 21).

This distinction may surprise or even irritate those who are particularly aware of the great theological complexity and subtlety to be observed in both the "Western" and the "Eastern" belief systems. Is Radhakrishnan perhaps oversimplifying the differences? Is not "salvation" of crucial importance in Christianity and Judaism? Are there not Hindu and Buddhist texts that wrestle with the nature of "divinity"?

All true, of course, but the question at issue here is: *With which concern does the belief system begin?* The "theistic" religions, Radhakrishnan argues, begin with "God"—while the others (the "Eastern" or "South Asian" or—perhaps more definitively, at least in my view—the "karmic") begin with "salvation" . . . though both go on to other things, and ultimately seem even to intersect.

Thus, for example, it may certainly be observed that Hinduism gives much attention to the universality of *Brahman* (another term defined traditionally as "Godhood" or "all-pervading divinity")—while the fate of the human soul is unquestionably of great moment to the followers of the "theistic" religions. It becomes important, however, given the difference in essential concern noted by Radhakrishnan, to question whether we are on safe ground when we accept without reservation such translations as *Brahman* into "Godhood" or for that matter "soul" into *atman*.

Let us note, however, that what may seem "important" to the scholar attempting to classify, distinguish, and clarify, may be thoroughly unimportant to a devotee—and particularly to a devotee in Trinidad who is burdened, in Wallace's words, by "too many elements," and who is seeking to "simplify the repertoire."

For Sathya Sai Baba, as we have seen, claims to represent "God" or "Godhood" as that term/terms is understood in all faiths: his followers, of course, accept that claim, and in so doing indicate that they share his belief that the fundamental concept of divinity is the same everywhere, whatever the word for "God" may be in a given language.

Whatever his claims, whatever the eagerness of his devotees to believe them, I would nevertheless ask: is his "universal" message in fact universally received in an identical way?

Following the lead given by Radhakrishnan, I would argue that the words do not mean the same thing to all who hear it, and that therefore before we can turn to the specifics of Sai Baba's teachings we must attend at least briefly to the significance of differences in theological terminology, concepts, and assumptions.

I am of course aware that theologians and other scholars of religion have long debated the similarities and differences among and between all these varieties of faiths, and I join the debate with trepidation. My comments will be seen to be limited and even superficial: they are intended to be. I hope to provide illumination in only two respects— the minimal introduction needed by those with little familiarity with South Asian religion (who may perhaps be more conversant with or interested in some of the other anthropological issues I am pursuing in this work), and the delineation of those particular aspects of South Asian religion which, in my view, relate to the attraction of people in and out of India to Sathya Sai Baba and his teachings. I hope, therefore, that students of the pertinent scholarly disciplines will forgive me if I

severely limit, in this discussion, my review of their findings and
positions.

My concern for the moment is with the fundamental differences in
religious perception and concern noted by Sarvapalli Radhakrishnan.
For him, as we have seen, the major religions of the West—specifically
Judaism, Christianity, Islam along with their various offshoots and
derivatives—constitute "theistic" belief systems. That is, they begin
with a concern with an overarching, distinctive, and unitary divinity.
All other concerns of these belief systems stem from that initial one.
Following his lead, therefore, when I refer to "the theistic religions" I
mean primarily this set—though I do not necessarily mean to exclude
other theistic religions to which my comments may also apply.

I propose, further, to refer to the set of South Asian religions
(Hinduism, Jainism, Buddhism) as the "karmic" belief systems—by
which I mean to indicate my sense that in these religions the primary
concern is with a law of the universe that is believed to govern the
affairs of human beings and to determine the vicissitudes of every
human "soul."

Is that all I mean to say about *karma*? By no means, but there is
another term we must consider first. The underlying issue, when one
speaks of *karma*, is the fate of the deathless component of the human
being, and so before we can approach the issues of "Godhood" or
"salvation" in the karmic religions (and we must, because Sathya Sai
Baba claims to be one and to convey the other) I suggest we must first
understand something of what is meant by *atman* or *atma*: usually
defined as "soul" or "innermost self."

### *"Atman" and "Soul"*

Is not the "usual definition" sufficient for all reasonable purposes?
Do not *both* terms—"atman" and "soul"—convey a sense of the im-
material but intrinsic dimension of humans; the part that is of divine
origin, innately pure and undefilable, that with which all humans are
endowed, something that is immortal and perhaps eternal but still
capable of experiencing joy or anguish as a response to the activities
and thoughts of the human within which it is housed?

It is my impression that those who use either term do in fact mean
to imply all of the above, and I further agree that both terms enable
the user to encompass issues such as: materiality versus spirituality (or
at least "non-materiality"), capacity for moral (and immoral) behavior,
mortality versus immortality, and the relationship of humans to divinity
on the one hand and to animal life on the other.

And yet I would argue that, if we probe deeper, there are important differences between the two terms. This difference between "soul" and "atman" looms particularly large when one attempts to examine what Sathya Sai Baba teaches, and what his devotees—East and West— understand him to be saying.

Whatever the view of the nature and source of the "soul," for example, it cannot be said the "soul" carries the burdens of, or rewards for, behavior in previous human lifetimes. Further, the fate of the "soul" after the death of the human is decided in some way by the overarching and distinctive "divinity"; there is, in other words, a "divine judgment." To be more specific, there is general agreement that the divine presence ordering the universe includes in that ordering a set of rules of behavior for humans—the details of which may vary from religious group to religious group.

Thus, as Radhakrishnan has observed, "the essential thing" for the theistic faiths is the power of the deity "to transform man." To depart from the divinely inspired rules is, variously, to "sin" or to "transgress"—to turn away from God or to cause God to turn away—and the result of such behavior is to cause suffering to one's "soul" (whether by torment after death, by the negativity resulting from the absence of God's grace or pleasure, by total extinction, or whatever).

What I am arguing, then, is that despite all the very significant differences that keep the theistic religions apart, there are nevertheless fundamental assumptions that they hold in common—and that these are different from the fundamental assumptions held in common by the South Asian karmic religions.

In this latter group, there is a belief common to all the faiths that the "atman" (by whatever term it is actually called) exhibits an immortality extending into the past—that is, far (perhaps eternally) back into the period preceding the birth of the human it presently inhabits. This past immortality is coupled with a future immortality, and so— since humans are manifestly mortal and ephemeral—it is believed that the "atman" continually transfers after the death of each mortal human to a newly born one, and so on and on, perhaps forever.

Again, there are of course major and minor differences between the contending component religious groups about the nature or composition of the "atman." Some question whether there actually *is* an "atman" (or "divinity," or "universe," or—as in Theravada Buddhism—anything but the consequences of "desire"). There is dispute about why it exists, if indeed it does, about whether it can be found in the non-human or even non-organic parts of the universe, and so on. Many Hindus, and Sathya Sai Baba's followers among them, believe that the "atman" is actually a particle of the universal Godhood that permeates, or constitutes, the universe; one that is temporarily separated from it and seeks reunion. Many followers of the theistic faiths, on the other hand, would insist on a distinction between "God" and the "universe" (the latter encompassing "human" and "soul"); others would disagree.

There are nevertheless certain clear and essential differences to be observed between "atman" and "soul": "soul" implies identity with *one* human being, whereas "atman" implies serially multiple identities with many humans.

Thus, from this perspective it does not matter if proponents of a particular theistic sect suggest that the "soul" does not come into being at the moment of birth of a human, but persists eternally, say, in some heavenly vault: this is still "soul" and not "atman" because, whether newly minted or lifted from some divine shelf, the "soul" brings no experiential baggage with it—its adventures begin with that of the living human with which it merges, its first and only one. And, after the death of that human, it may be believed that the "soul" is extinguished, or it may be assumed to continue to exist in some form or realm or other: it is still different from the "atman" in that the "soul" does not go on to another human existence carrying with it the consequences of former experiences.

There is still another important difference between "atman" and "soul": the faiths deriving from South Asia concur almost universally in the belief that the primary religious or spiritual concern of every human should be to so live as to prevent the further transference of that person's "atman" to another body, after death. But, in the theistic religions, as Radhakrishnan has pointed out, the primary concern is with "revelation."

To put it another way so as to emphasize this particular fundamental distinction between the two contrasting sets of belief-systems, the karmic religions see as the over-riding issue "stopping the wheel of endless rebirth" (if not this time around, at least in some reasonably proximate rebirth)—while the theistic religions have as their over-riding issue "getting right with God": learning what it is that the divine presence that orders the universe has decreed as the proper behavior for humans.

In theistic religions, therefore, we must introduce "God" (or the concept of divinity) at the beginning of any discussion: "Our Father, who art in Heaven," "There is no god but God and Mohammed is his prophet," "Hear O Israel, the Lord our God, the Lord is One."

In karmic religions, I am arguing—following on the heels of Radhakrishnan—the immortal but transferrable "atman" is the primary concern, given whatever is the prevailing view of the nature of *karma*— of the law of the universe that governs the conditions of that transference.

There are of course other issues of importance in the religions deriving from South Asia, as there are in all faiths, and, as in all, the issues are interrelated. What behavior is required of those who would interrupt the cycle of rebirth? Do any personified "Gods" actually exist? If so, do they have anything to do with the rebirth of the "atman," or with the interruption of the rebirth cycle?

The nature of "divinity" is indeed a most important issue for many of the karmic faiths—but I join with Radhakrishnan in arguing that it is not the primary issue for them; and further that we (both Eastern and Western scholars) have introduced a distortion into the study of the South Asian religions because we have assumed they have the same intrinsic priorities and concerns as do the theistic religions. Before we can contemplate "divinity" in a religion such as Hinduism, I would therefore argue, we must attend to the issue that takes precedence— that of *karma*.

## The Law of Karma

It should hardly be necessary to point out that a concept as basic and important as karma undergoes much local and sectarian variation in South and Southeast Asia—and is also the subject of much Western scholarly analysis and disputation. The interested reader is urged to consult the literature, and two excellent starting points are the collections of papers on the subject edited by Ronald W. Neufeldt (1986) and by Charles F. Keyes and E. Valentine Daniel (1983).

Here, however, we must confine ourselves to the minimal review of the topic necessary for those, not familiar with the subject, who wish nevertheless to appreciate the assumptions and traditions underlying Sathya Sai Baba's assertedly "universal" message.

Thus, Charles F. Keyes, in the "Introduction" to the book he co-edited with E. Valentine Daniel, notes the varieties of approaches to karma presented in their collection, but concludes nevertheless:

> It is when faced with the ultimate conditions of existence that peoples of South and Southeast Asia are most likely to find karmic ideas meaningful. As Babb has noted for Hindus below: "Whatever else the doctrine of karma might be, it is a theory of causation that supplies reasons for human fortune, good or bad, and that at least in theory it can provide convincing explanations for human misfortune" (Keyes 1983: 3).

Keyes is citing Lawrence Babb's paper, "Destiny and Responsibility: Karma in Popular Hinduism" (Babb 1983: 163–181), in which the point is in fact made that in "popular Hinduism" other explanations may be offered, in specific circumstances, for good and bad fortune: wicked people may be working evil magic, the gods may be interfering in human affairs, and so on (see also Klass 1978: 182–189). Even then, however, the final explanation—the ultimate fall-back—continues to be the notion of karma: a universal regulation to which human fate is somehow subject.

But, as many scholars have observed, karma is inextricably related to and involved with other concepts: the law has relevance for humans because, so it is believed, the human essence—the atman or its equivalent—is an immortal something that existed long before the birth of the living person, and that will continue to exist long after that human being is dust. It is further assumed that the atman must and will transfer upon the death of a person to a newborn human, and that it will continue to do so unless and until its cycle of endless rebirths is somehow interrupted. Finally (for our purposes), it is understood that this immortality of one's atman—or at least this transference—is profoundly unfortunate and undesirable: the ending of the cycle of rebirths, all believe, should be the goal of every living human. One, if one is lucky, achieves *moksha*—sometimes translated as "salvation" but more meaningfully as "release."

The "Law of Karma," then, governs the continuing transfer of the atman as well as the conditions under which that endless progression may be halted. In other words, such issues as continuing "rebirth," ultimate cessation of "rebirth," and the fate awaiting the particular newborn human, are all fundamentally not matters of chance or of divine judgment: they are reflections of the way the universe is constructed, much as are the consequences, say, of the Laws of Thermodynamics. Indeed, Terence Penelhum, in his "Critical Response" (a review of the papers about the "doctrine of karma" in Neufeldt's book) specifically concludes: "By saying it is a fact of nature, I mean that it is thought of as more akin to such general principles as the Laws of Thermo-dynamics or Gravitation, than to such intrinsically religious principles as that of Providence or Original Sin" (Penelhum 1986: 339).

How then may one achieve the goal desired by all—the ending of the cycle of atman rebirths? At this point the different faiths diverge. The founders and later theologians of the contending faiths have offered different views about the nature of the atman, about the reasons why the "Law of Karma" operates as it does, about the specific conditions of "rebirth"—and most of all about what "cessation of rebirth" means in theory and in practice.

In the case of Hinduism—the *Sanatan Dharma* to its adherents; the ancient and everlasting doctrine—the atman of a living human is generally (well, reasonably "generally") understood to be a separated

particle of the universal divine substance that permeates the cosmos—
that *is* in fact the cosmos. We may refer to this universal divine
substance as *Brahman* or "Godhood," but not as "God"—if by the
latter term we mean to imply sentience, or will, or separation from the
rest of the universe. For, in this case, the belief is that the physical
universe, and the Godhood, and the atman—are all in the end one
and inseparable; even the seeming separate identity of the atman is in
a deeper sense only an illusion.

This issue of division in divisionlessness, of particle and substance
and individuality and the absence of individuality could take us into
deep and churning theological waters and even into anthropological
shoals that for this work we had better skirt. The oceanic metaphor is
a useful one (cf. Babb 1983: 180), however, for it is invoked in most
of the religions of this complex (specifically including Hinduism, Jainism, and many sects of Buddhism). That is, the atman may be compared
to a bubble of froth: it is ocean water just like all other ocean water
(read "Godhood") that has become momentarily and seemingly separated and distinct from the rest of the ocean. This seeming distinction
is, as we know, illusory—sooner or later the froth will merge back into
the ocean and again be indistinguishable from it, and so too will the
atman ultimately merge back into "Godhood."

Let us now pause and consider how very different these beliefs are
from the equally fundamental beliefs of the theistic complex of religions—most particularly that a unitary divine power (creator of the
universe, but still to be distinguished from that universe) imposes order
and meaning upon the universe in all spheres, including the moral
sphere; that which encompasses human behavior. In this set of belief
systems, therefore, the nature and experiences of the soul become
subsidiary or derivative issues. In a karmic religion, and particularly
in Hinduism, the nature and experiences of the atman constitutes the
fundamental issue, and "divinity" is—as we have just seen—subsidiary
or derivative.

### Achieving Moksha

One thing, according to Hindu teachings, that will diminish karmic
"separation" and thus bring a given atman closer to ultimate reunion
with "Godhood" is behavior that is understood to be the antithesis of
a *material* activity or interest. The amassing of possessions and the
enjoyment of the pleasures of the senses, for example, are *material*
concerns; the abandonment of sensual pleasures and the distribution of
one's wealth to the needy are therefore *non-material* (or, some might
say, *spiritual*) actions.

And, in addition, one draws closer to "Godhood" by turning one's
very mind away from material matters to a contemplation of "divinity"
in almost any way or form. The universal "Godhood," we have noted,
is seen to be implicit in—in some measure to be represented by—any
deity worshipped by any group of humans. Another way of putting it
is that it is the act of worship itself that is important, for whatever
form it takes and to whomever it is addressed, it constitutes an effort
by a human being to reach out to *divinity,* to draw close to *divinity*—
which in the end is *Brahman.*

Thus, implicit in the Hindu perspective, and very often explicit in
the teachings, is the belief that all creeds, all objects worshipped
anywhere on earth by anyone, all rituals intended to be expressive of
religious feeling—do indeed serve to draw one's atman closer to ultimate
reunion. It therefore follows for many Hindus that all human religious
teaching—however distorted, confused, or feeble—is of some value in
that all religion derives from the urge of *Brahman* and atman to reunite.

However, while all religions—and indeed "religion" itself—are seen
by Hindus as having "merit" (to be understood here as meaning that
which contributes in some way to the eventual reunion of an individual
human atman and the universal "Godhood"), nevertheless, the beliefs
and practices of religions other than Hinduism are considered less
effective than the latter because they contain more error. Most Hindus
would of course concede that all teachings contain *some* error—since
they cannot escape the contamination, the inherent confusion and illusion of the material universe in which they are embedded—but the
least amount of error, it is felt, is to be found in the teachings and
sacred writings of Hinduism. These, Hindus believe, provide the surest
avenues to *moksha*—in this case the attainment of complete and permanent merger with the universal "Godhood."

It will be understood by now, I hope, that the foregoing definition
of *moksha* is inevitably simplistic: it does not reflect the wealth of
literature on the subject, nor the different perceptions of the differing
karmic religions. Still, however defined, it is clearly very different from
the theistic concept of "salvation" with which it is often confused.

Indeed, even within Hinduism there is difference of opinion about
the best way or ways to achieve *moksha*: some advocate the path of
knowledge and discipline; others advocate fervent prayer; still others
favor good works, and there are those who advise combinations of all
three. Some teachers, as well as teachings, are considered by different
segments of the population to be inherently more meritorious. Given
the coupled assumptions, however, that, while no human teaching can
ever be wholly free of error, yet nevertheless *all* spiritual teaching
conveys some "merit"—theological debate in Hinduism rarely if ever

rises to the level of acrimony often to be observed in the religions—
each claiming exclusive divine revelation—of the theistic aggregation.

There may in fact be another reason: the messages offered by Hindu
teachers are remarkably similar in content. There have been innovators,
of course—Shankara, Ramanujan, etc.—and as I have indicated there
are often points of difference between teachers. Still, teachers and
followers alike have wide areas of fundamental agreement. For example,
I am not aware of any Hindu religious leader who has challenged the
belief that "bad karma" (a future for an individual's atman in which
the probability of merger with "Godhood" is appreciably diminished)
derives from increasing involvement in the material universe, including
pleasures of the senses and other attachments to life.

And, again, all Hindus are apparently in agreement that by slipping
the attachments to materiality, individuality and life itself—the relinquishment and avoidance of sensual and material pleasures, along with
truly selfless service to others—one achieves "good karma" leading
eventually to the attainment of *moksha.*

The disagreements are, as I have indicated, more questions of strategy
(i.e., does "relinquishment of sensual pleasures" count for more than
"selfless service to others" or vice versa? Are *both* necessary?) or they
relate to what are, within this belief system, essentially peripheral
matters: e.g., how much attention need be given to the traditional
personified divinities of Hinduism, such as *Shiva, Vishnu, Ganesha,
Saraswati,* etc.?

Some Hindu teachers (and Buddhist, and Jain) appear to hold that
such "gods"—named and personified deities, whether of the Hindu or
non-Hindu religious traditions—are really only reflections of human
error and of imperfection in the attempt to reach out for and compre-
hend the ineffable indescribability that is true transcendent "Godhood."
Proponents of this view advocate (at least for those who attain the
proper degree of enlightenment) the turning away from the propitiation
of personified deities to the contemplation of the non-personified "Godhood." Others, however, teach that if it helps the seeker after *moksha*
to focus on *Shiva* (or *Allah,* or any other personification of divinity)
the practice need not be discontinued.

This view of divinity—as variously unitary or multiple, important
or peripheral, and so on—can be confusing to the theist for whom the
centrality and uniqueness of divinity are fundamental. Ninian Smart
has noted the *kathenotheistic* tendencies in Hinduism ("one-god-at-a-
time-ism"): "Although the composers of the hymns may on various
occasions address themselves to various gods, within the context of a
given hymn the god addressed is supreme" (Smart 1984: 81–82).

From the Hindu perspective, Smart's observation might seem both obvious and irrelevant: all gods are reflections of the one "Godhood" and are therefore "supreme." Indeed, so even are humans who can lead others closer to the *Brahman* that longs to be reunited with their atmans. Sathya Sai Baba—who claims to be a manifestation in human form of that "Godhood"—tells his followers that if they will only take one step toward him, he will take many more toward them.

### The Godmen

There are important differences of opinion among those who stand forth as teachers or practitioners of Hinduism. Some, for example, emphasize learning, and some emphasize prayer, and others urge both, and so on. I have argued, however, that the underlying message—that the way to escape the wheel of continuing rebirth is by relinquishing the ties to "materiality"—is substantially the same for all.

Why, then, does the religion need so many "teachers"? To put the question slightly differently, if their messages are inherently so similar, what is their attraction? One is tempted to observe that if you hear one "guru" you have heard them all. If such an observation is overly simplistic, and it is, it is also obvious that the Hindu teachers convey much more than the content of their teachings.

Peter Brent begins his account of *Godmen of India* with a quotation he attributes to the great fifteenth century Indian teacher known as Kabir: " 'In the midst of the highest heaven there is a shining light; he who has no Guru cannot reach the palace; he only will reach it who is under the guidance of a true Guru' " (Brent 1972: 1).

Some scholars—D. A. Swallow, for example (1982: 123)—would have us remember that Brent's work is "unashamedly popular." But the term "Godman" is, as Swallow herself finds, a useful one for encompassing and summarizing the myriad terms actually used by Hindus, and Brent's book is particularly helpful in focussing our attention on the ways the Hindu "Godman" is like—and very unlike—the "teacher" or "religious leader" of the theistic religions.

In the case of the latter, I would suggest, distinctions have to be made among those who are vessels for divine revelation—those through whom God speaks—and those who have been chosen by God to expound and clarify that revelation, and those who are simply more learned or more pious than their neighbors, and so on.

Similar distinctions exist in Hinduism, as we shall see, but the principle implicit in the observation cited above, attributed by Brent to Kabir, serves to blur those distinctions and to a certain extent even render them irrelevant. Brent concludes:

The function that the Master, the Guru, performs is complex and perhaps essential. He is, first, the focus of the disciple's attention and emotion. . . . Second, the Guru, a human being demonstrably similar to the disciple, sets the experience within a human scale. . . . Third, it is clear that the Guru can help the disciple directly, either by explaining difficulties, helping to solve problems . . . even by violence. Fourth, he is the repository of . . . doctrine. . . . Fifth, he is the example, the proof that the way leads somewhere. . . . And possibly, sixth, he may be a source of a developed mental power which, transferred to the disciple, can transform the latter's inner life (Brent 1972: 339).

It may even be argued that "Godmen" convey "merit" by their very existence, at least for those who listen to their words and do them homage: that merit accrues from the simple adoration of one's guru (as it does, for many Hindus traditionally, from the adoration of any Brahman). And why should it not—if one believes, as many Hindus do —that there is even "merit" to be acquired in the worship of the most distorted and erroneous deity of the most benighted religion? Sathya Sai Baba is quoted as saying: "We have heard the Guru being praised as equal to God. The Guru sows the seeds of virtue, of wisdom, and of faith in the heart of the pupil" (Mc Martin 1982: 223). Again, he is elsewhere reported to have said in a talk entitled, "The Guru is the Guide":

Once you have secured a Guru leave everything to Him, even the desire to achieve liberation. He knows you more than you yourself ever can. He will direct you as much as is good for you. Your duty is only to obey and to smother the tendency to drift away from Him. You may ask, how are we to earn our food, if we attach ourselves to a Guru like this? Be convinced that the Lord will not let you starve; He will give you not only anna [money] but Amrita, not only food but the nectar of immortality (Kasturi 1981a: 50).

Note, in the foregoing, the equation of "guru"—in principle, *any* teacher—and "God." Note, too, the injunction to obey the guru in all things and to relinquish any tendency to question or challenge the guru. Is the Hindu "guru," then, not identical to the Western "cult-leader"? Swallow, in the paper cited above, does in fact refer to the movement that has grown up around Sathya Sai Baba as a "God-Man's Cult" (Swallow 1982: 123), but it is difficult to see how his teachings on the nature of the guru and on the relationship between leader and disciple differs significantly from those of traditional Hinduism.

N. H. Maring, in the entry under CULT in the *Encyclopedic Dictionary of Religion,* cites scholars who have attempted to distinguish "cults" from other religious bodies by: ". . . their small size, localization, dependence upon a leader with magnetic personality, and beliefs and rites that deviate widely from the norms of society" (Maring 1979: 958).

Milton Yinger—one of the scholars from whom Maring derives— struggles with the term, noting many of the objections that have been raised, but in the end decides to continue to use it: ". . . to refer to a group at the farthest extreme from the universal church. . . . It is usually small, short-lived, local, and built around a charismatic leader" (Yinger 1970: 279–280).

D. A. Swallow, who has written about Sathya Sai Baba's followers in India, decided—after wrestling with the implications of the term "cult"—that with all of its problems the term remains a useful one, and that it can be applied equally to such movements as the one that has grown up around Sathya Sai Baba and the one that follows the teachings of Sri Aurobindo (Swallow 1976). A diagnostic feature for her is the centrality of what Yinger calls the "charismatic leader."

I indicated earlier my discomfort with the pejorative connotations of "cult"—but now I want to question the very applicability of the term to any subdivision of Hinduism, in terms of the accepted definition of "cult." I turn resolutely from issues such as "smallness" (what number shall constitute the boundary of "cult" and "sect"?) and "short-lived" (how are we to know, except in retrospect, whether a set of religious teachings is destined to survive the test of time? Is the term only to be applied in the cemeteries of ideology?). There is a much greater problem when the term is applied to any variety of Hinduism: every guru is almost by definition a "charismatic leader"—shall Hinduism then be defined as an amorphous mass of "cults"? Swallow seems to perceive this problem, for she observes that, despite the differences between the teachings of Sri Aurobindo and Sathya Sai Baba: "Both . . . are recognisably in the tradition of Indian holy men. Both are ascetics and both are credited with godlike powers" (Swallow 1976: 237).

Where then shall the line between "cult" and "non-cult" ("sect"? "religion"?) be drawn? There are differences between and among all the "Godmen," and those differences are important to objective scholars and devotees alike, but they must be discerned as within the context of Hinduism—where the differences may both exist and at the same time be meaningless to the devotee, for whom the "guru" is in the end a pathway to *God*.

## The Avatar

The variety of "Godmen" to be found in South Asia is great indeed. There are holy men who do not necessarily preach or teach—who simply wander, begging bowl in hand. The term *sannyasi* is usually applied to them. They are living exemplars of the possibility of complete relinquishment of material and sensual interests and concerns: they have abandoned family and possessions, they accept no comfort and only the barest of necessities (and to give such a one a handful of rice is to acquire much "merit"), they are manifestly intent on eradicating any sense of individuality or personhood, and they are obviously much further along the path to "moksha" than the people they move among.

Similar to the *sannyasi,* but nevertheless distinguishable, is the *sadhu*—the "itinerant or *asram*-bound full-time specialist" (Bharati 1970: 277) who will expound on Hinduism to those who gather at his feet. And for some observers, the *swami*—the teacher who will even sometimes travel to instruct the non-Hindus of Europe and the United States—is simply a variety of *sadhu* (Bharati 1970: 270).

All of these, however, are to be distinguished from the *pandits*—Brahmans, almost invariably, trained in the performance of their hereditary rituals, residing with their wives and children in the countryside. In Trinidad, until the coming of "the Swamis" in mid-century, such pandits were pretty much the only kind of Hindu religious leader known—or at least observed.

The differences between all these become important when one wishes, say, to analyze the different strains and patterns of Hinduism. Agehananda Bharati, for example, argues that the pandit is the conservator of traditional ritual, and the sadhu (often) of traditional teachings—but that among the swamis (or "scientific" sadhus) we find the proponents of the "Hindu Renaissance"—the de-emphasis of ritual, caste, and "superstition," and the concurrent emphasis on the humanistic and universalistic dimensions of Hinduism (Bharati 1970).

In our evaluation of Sathya Sai Baba and his teachings we will have to return to these theological issues, and indeed to Bharati. The point I am making now, however, is that—whatever their roles and practices, whatever their teachings—to their devotees all the foregoing are "gurus." All, in other words, are likely to be treated by their respective followers as "Godmen"—and this was equally true of the village pandits of Trinidad. Contributions to their support constitute a source of "merit," as would any contribution to the construction or maintenance of a temple—or for that matter any succor to the needy given without expectation of reward or return.

Consider, then, the implications of the presence on earth of an actual *avatar*—the physical appearance among us of *God* (personified) or of *Godhood* (transcendant and normally unpersonified) itself. One adores one's guru "as if" he were a "God"—but occasionally in the history of Hinduism, though very very rarely, it turns out that he actually *is* God! It follows that any attention to, or connection with, a true avatar is indeed a source of much "merit." The very act of gazing upon him brings one immeasurably closer to *moksha*—but imagine if he speaks to you . . . touches you . . . allows you to touch him! Might he even be prevailed upon to assume some of your "bad karma" burdens?

Sathya Sai Baba of Puttaparthi claims to be such an avatar; he is thus guru and more than guru. He is *Shiva*; he is *Vishnu*—he is Jesus Christ or Allah or any personification of "divinity" worshipped anywhere on earth, for he is ultimately and essentially the transcendant "Godhood" of the universe now somehow crystalized in a human body.

But how can this be? Is not the universal "Godhood"—the all-permeating everything—the very antithesis of materiality, of individual personhood? How can "Godhood" incorporate?

I have neither the knowledge nor the need (for the purposes of this study) to address this last problem. The interested reader is urged to pursue the matter in the appropriate literature. What is pertinent here is the observation that Hinduism admits of the possibility of *avatar*—divinity in a human form. True, the literature refers to avatars in the *past* (*Rama* and *Krishna,* among others) and in the *future* (e.g., *Kalki*). An avatar in the *present* can of course raise problems—is he a true avatar or merely a charlatan (or even a madman) claiming to be one? What proofs would be sufficient? What if some authorities accept his claim, and other authorities—equally authoritative—reject it?

For some, the solution to the problem lies in the assumption that an avatar is not bound by the laws that encompass mere humans. That is, if a personified God can perform miracles from on high, the same miracles can be performed by the deity who is now an avatar on earth. *Rama* could perform miracles, *Krishna* could, too—and so therefore must anyone who claims to be an avatar. Those who take this view claim, literally, that "God can do anything!"

But this, inevitably, raises more questions. If an avatar—say, Sathya Sai Baba—can, with the wave of his hand, materialize gold and silver, heal the deathly ill, bring the dead back to life . . . then why stop with only a few demonstrations? Why not shower the needy of the world with wealth? Why not put an end to all sickness and suffering? At the very least, why help my neighbor with a miracle—and not help *me*?

Sathya Sai Baba of Puttaparthi is besieged, like others who are believed to be capable of miracles, by those beseeching such divine interventions, and, while he has responded, he has only responded occasionally and selectively.

For those, of course, who are not convinced he is an avatar there are still further questions: When is a "miracle" truly a *miracle*? Is curing someone dying of cancer a miracle—or merely the power of suggestion?

Truly, the way of the avatar is not as easy at it might seem at first glance. With that in mind, let us turn to the specific teachings of Sathya Sai Baba.

### Notes

1. He concludes a lengthy inquiry with the words: "Religion is more than the idea of gods and spirits, and consequently cannot be defined exclusively in relation to these latter" (Durkheim 1965: 50).

# 7

# The Power of Sai

## Baba Says

Baba Says
If you take one step
towards me
I take ten steps
towards you (Mc Martin 1982: 373).

Sri Sathya Sai Baba has not, so far, written or dictated a book constituting his "teachings" or "theology." What are available, however, are collections of his sermons, lessons, speeches, and remarks, put together by various of his devotees and distributed by the Sathya Sai Organization—apparently with his knowledge and approval.

Still, the foregoing statement that a collection of his lessons is published with "his knowledge and approval" does need a bit of explication. On the one hand, material to be published (in any and every language) is indeed submitted to him, for he and his followers believe that Sathya Sai Baba alone speaks for Sathya Sai Baba—and that no one else is empowered to "explain" his message:

*"The most frequent error made by Sai devotees and Sai organizations in overseas countries is to give credence and power to people who may have had interviews—had things materialized—had vibhuti coming from their pictures, or whatever. Your relationship to the Lord is between your heart and the Lord: no individual or organization can interpose in that relationship. . . . As far as your own spiritual life—that is between you and the Lord. . . . Do not ask other people to lead you—that is not possible. . . . Only Bhagawan Shri Sathya Sai Baba is leader"* (from an address by Dr. Michael Goldstein, Chairman, North American Sai Organization, to members of the Trinidad and Tobago Sathya Sai Centres, July 27, 1985 [see also Kasturi 1981a: 352]).

But, on the other hand, it could also be argued that there is no real necessity to submit written materials to him (except perhaps as a matter of form or courtesy) since, as God, he already knows what each of his devotees is writing, or doing—or will do. Thus, Dr. Samuel Sandweiss, an American psychiatrist and devotee, reports—in the last pages of a book he wrote about his own experiences—that he brought the manuscript to Sathya Sai Baba for evaluation, and that the Godman then summoned him to a group meeting:

> For fifteen minutes he enveloped me in his marvelous aura of energy— answering all my prayers, assuring me that the circuit had been completed and he was receiving my offering in a way I could never have imagined. He spoke about the purpose and meaning of the book as I had visualized it and in a way which convinced me that he understood and accepted it. Finally, regarding me with love and gentleness, he said, *I am satisfied.* [Note: Sandweiss invariably places Sathya Sai Baba's spoken words in italics, without quotation marks.] Then he looked into each of our eyes with an almost mischievous smile and added, *And I haven't even read this book yet* (Sandweiss 1975: 225).

The Sai Baba movement, therefore, as we see—despite the number and worldwide distribution of its membership—lacks any interpreters or leaders other than Sathya Sai Baba himself. The movement's organization has at its tasks the propagation (never the interpretation) of his message, the carrying out of his programs (for education, for service, etc.), the provision of sites for satsangs (group prayer meetings), and so on. All of these tasks are essentially "lay"—there is no spiritual voice other than that of Sathya Sai Baba, with whom every devotee is encouraged to commune directly. Nor, as Swallow has observed, is any change in this structure planned for the future:

> His sect, despite the lay organisation, simply consists of an accumulation of followers, each of whom feels he has a direct line to the guru. It is unlikely that the Sathya Sai Baba cult will, in the future, become a formalised sect, with an elaborate doctrine or set of rules, or a body of teaching ascetics carrying on a particular tradition. He has prognosticated that he will once again take human form, and so has no need to groom a successor (Swallow 1976: 311).

Some observers might conclude that this particular set of elements— an absence of a formal doctrine or set of rules, one voice of authority speaking primarily in a language known only to the inhabitants of one south Indian state, a worldwide and very diverse network of followers— exhibits great potential for conflict. It is only fair to observe, therefore, that there are few signs, thus far, of any disagreement or division within the organization or among the followers. The problems that have surfaced, and they are on the whole modest, were alluded to in the citation above from Dr. Goldstein's address: the occasional officious devotee or local leader who claims a special knowledge of what Sathya Sai Baba "means" or "wants"—and the persons who proclaim that the godman actually speaks through them, or performs special miracles in their homes or shrines.

Nevertheless, there is clearly room for possible misinterpretation—given the universal problem of translation from one language to another, and particularly from one religio-cultural context to another. In a talk entitled, "The Message I Bring," Sathya Sai Baba proclaimed:

> I have come to light the Lamp of Love in your hearts, so that it shines day by day with added lustre. I have not come to speak on behalf of any particular Righteousness like the Hindu Righteousness. . . .
>
> All religions teach one basic discipline; the removal from the mind of the blemish of egoism, of running after little joys. Every religion teaches man to fill his being with the Glory of God and evict the pettiness of conceit. It trains him in the methods of detachment and discrimination, so that he may aim high and attain liberation (Mc Martin 1982: 25).

Would the leaders of "all religions" indeed agree with this summation of their teachings and goals? Did all those listening to this address—as it happened, in Nairobi, Kenya—agree with one another, and with him, on the meaning of the "liberation" to be obtained through religion?

Clearly, of course, those who become his devotees perceive no problem. For them, though his teachings must be derived from an assemblage of unconnected talks and lessons, the message they convey is nevertheless coherent and consistent. He teaches, for example, that he is God—one with all forms of divinity known to humans anywhere—that (as we have just seen) his message is the one that all religions teach—that distinctions of language (or race or nationality or ethnicity) are irrelevant.

Such a message may indeed be attractive to foreign devotees everywhere, but it is unquestionably particularly attractive to devotees of Indian descent in Trinidad, struggling, as we have seen, between the claims of both "Homo hierarchicus" and "Homo aequalis," aware at all times of conflicting calls of religious allegiance and ethnic identity.

For those who accept Sathya Sai Baba, such conflicts cease to have meaning, because, as God, he both supersedes and encompasses everything:

There are many who observe my actions and start declaring that my nature is such and such. They are unable to gauge the sanctity, the majesty and the eternal reality that is Me. The power of Sai is limitless; It manifests forever [from a sermon given at Brindavan in 1974] (Mc Martin 1982: 16).

Believe that all hearts are motivated by the One and Only God; that all faiths glorify the One and only God, that all Names in all languages and all Forms man can conceive, denote the One and Only God [from the talk delivered in Nairobi, Kenya, in 1968] (Mc Martin 1982: 25–26).

And, God is and can be only One, not more! "There is only One God and He is Omnipresent! There is only One Religion, the Religion of Love! There is only One caste, the caste of Humanity! There is only one language, the Language of the Heart" [from a talk at a temple in Madras in 1967—but a constantly quoted saying, almost the Credo of the movement] (Mc Martin 1982: 53).

So God is "one"—and Sathya Sai Baba is that "one"—and God is "omnipotent": "God is all-powerful, God is everywhere, God is all-knowing" (Mc Martin 1982: 56). And yet, in the same address, he also observes: "God has no will or wont. He does not confer or withhold. He is the eternal Witness" (Mc Martin 1982: 56). And, in effect, this last observation explains why he cannot cure all the sick and ailing who come to him. Even God cannot interfere with the "Law of Karma"—though he can alleviate the pain and even, at times, absorb the misfortunes of some humans:

You might say that the karma of the previous birth has to be consumed in this birth and that no amount of grace can save a man from that. Evidently someone has taught you to believe so. But I assure you, you need not suffer from karma like that. When a severe pain torments you, the doctor gives you a morphine injection and you do not feel the pain, though it is there in the body. Grace is like the morphine, the pain is not felt, though you go through it! Grace takes away the malignity of the karma which you have to undergo. You know there are dated drugs, which are declared ineffective after a certain date; well, the effects of karma is rendered null, though the account is there and has to be rendered! Or, the Lord can save a man completely from the consequences, as was done by Me to the bhaktha whose paralysis stroke and heart attacks I took over some months ago, in the Gurupournami week! [from a talk at Prasanthi Nilayam in 1964] (Kasturi 1981a: 165).

### Sai Baba and Hinduism

Sathya Sai Baba's dismissal of caste—or, at least, proposed revision of the meaning of caste—takes on great importance for many of his

Overseas Indian devotees, as we shall see. Nevertheless, his statements about caste, like those on the unimportance of ethnic distinction (as when he proclaims the universality of his message) should not be interpreted as rejections of Hinduism. His teachings clearly reflect Hindu theological concerns and his own personal identification with Hinduism. Indeed, Sathya Sai Baba continually acknowledges that, while he is indeed transcendant "Godhood," he is at the same time an Indian and a Hindu and even, in appearance, a human male:

> For example, you must have noticed that I never call a woman alone for the "interview." I call women only in groups of ten or fifteen. I want that you should note this and infer that one has to be extremely cautious in dealing with the other sex, for, though I am above and beyond the Human Attributes [, since] this body is obviously masculine, I want to teach both men and women how they have to regulate their social behaviour and be above the slightest tinge of suspicion, or of small talk (Mc Martin 1982: 18).

Indeed, despite his efforts, rumors about his purported sexual proclivities are spread in India by some of those who reject his claims to divinity (see Brooke 1979).

Even the briefest perusal of his sermons indicates that Sathya Sai Baba gives a special pride of place to Hindu scriptures. Here is only one example from many that could be selected:

> Of all the religions of the entire world, it appears to us that the Indian religion, the religion that has been at the back of the Indian mind, is the life breath and is the stream that is flowing through all the religions of this world. The religions of other countries are equally as sacred and sanctified but for only a certain limited time. On the other hand, the religion of this country is something which had no beginning and will have no end (Mc Martin 1982: 37–38).

For the devotee, in any case, such seeming contradictions merge ultimately into a wholeness: Sri Sathya Sai Baba is a human (Indian male) who is, on a more basic and important level, God Incarnate. All humans are equal particles of divinity, but it is his mission to lead all others to the full realization of their own divinity. All religions, he teaches, have as their purpose the leading of the devotees to unity with God (and thus are not only "true" but fundamentally "one") but Hinduism provides a clearer path—if by no means the only one.

The issue of "caste" is, as ever, a knotty one. If, as Hinduism teaches, all the misfortunes that occur in a person's lifetime are to be understood as the karmic consequences of the misdeeds of a previous incarnation (just as good fortune reflects "meritorious" previous behavior)—then may we not conclude that those humans at the bottom of the social ladder are there because they have corrosively wicked atmans? Is not a life of privation, characterized by the mistreatment and contempt of the majority of the human population—in other words, the life of an "untouchable"—a consequence of evil actions in a previous life?

This, of course, was a classic explanation and justification for the caste system. It was challenged by the Buddha more than twenty-five centuries ago, and by other teachers since. In this century particularly, Hindu teachers have avoided this explanation of social inequality, and many have forcefully rejected it. For such teachers, "caste" and other examples of human mistreatment of other humans have nothing to do with the "Law of Karma."

Thus, speaking as a Hindu to other Hindus, Sathya Sai Baba makes his own position on "caste" very clear:

> "When a Brahmin is born, he is just a Sudra. His birth does not confer on him the right to study the Scriptures, even though he might be the son of a great Vedic scholar. It is only when he has been formally initiated through a special ceremony, that he acquires a right to study the Sacred Scriptures. . . . The Lord does not weigh the status or caste of an individual before bestowing His Grace. He is all merciful and His Grace falls like rain or moonlight, on all the people. The Vedas have declared this and you should proceed and deserve to acquire His Grace" (quoted in Fanibunda 1976: 89).

To those of other societies, raised according to the tenets of other religions, Sathya Sai Baba recommends that they continue to follow the practices and customs of their people—and even, if they wish, their ancestral faiths:

> Let the children realise that prayer is universal and that prayer in any language addressed to any Name reaches the same God. Let them understand that God can be invoked through a picture or an idol to fulfil man's sincere desire provided it is helpful to others as well as to oneself [from an address to teachers in training—"Bala Vikas Gurus Training Camp" in 1978] (Kasturi 1981b: 149).

This makes it easier, of course, for people of very different faiths, who wish to be devotees but who who find much that is strange or disconcerting about him or his teachings, to find ways to come to him. Samuel Sandweiss, for example, records the conflict experienced by his wife in reconciling Sai Baba with "her Jewish upbringing":

Perhaps her greatest distress had come from observing the proliferation
of Baba's photographs throughout the house. Since in the Hebrew tradition
it is taboo to worship a human as divine, she was uncomfortable when
her Jewish friends and relatives came to our home and saw such an
array.

The conflict between Baba and Judaism was gradually resolved, however, as Sharon began to discover the universality in Baba's message
. . . when she learned that he encourages people to follow their own
familiar religion and teaches that since God is behind all names and
forms, everything is a manifestation of God (Sandweiss 1975: 219).

Christian devotees often focus on the similarities between Sathya
Sai Baba and Jesus:

After her first visit to Prasanti Nilayam a woman of Germany, a devout
and earnest seeker on the path, said, "Baba is the incarnation of purity
and love." Later, after spending more time with him, she wrote in a
letter: "I get more and more convinced from within that he is Jesus
Christ who has come again, in the fullness of Christ, as Satya Sai Baba"
(Murphet 1971: 206).

And Sathya Sai Baba responds to this—as we saw earlier—by urging
Christian devotees to pray to Jesus, by materializing representations of
Jesus, and even, in at least one case, by materializing what was accepted
as a piece of the "True Cross" by a Christian devotee (Sandweiss 1975:
174–177). Sandweiss adds:

To me, the most mind-blowing event of all regarding Baba's relationship
to Christ happened Christmas Day, 1972. He told a group of people:
*Christ said, "He who has sent Me will come again."* To my amazement
he said that he himself is the one to whom Christ was referring (Sandweiss
1975: 176).

Those who follow him are apparently at liberty to refer to him as
"Baba," as "Swami," as "Guru," as "Avatar," as "God"—and, presumably, by many other terms of respect which may in fact convey very
different attitudes or perspectives on authority or divinity in other
religions.

Is there then ambiguity in the perception of Sathya Sai Baba by
people deriving from different faiths? Perhaps. But a Hindu might well
argue that all the inconsistencies and seeming contradictions are simply
examples of *maya*—the cosmic illusion and confusion that serves to
misdirect a person and keep him or her from becoming a *sadhaka*, an
aspirant, who—through *sadhana* (proper exercises)—moves toward at-

tainment of *moksha* (release, or enlightenment, or salvation, or what you will). And Sathya Sai Baba is of course a Hindu and he too speaks of the "delusion" that must be overcome by the seeker after truth (see, for example, Kasturi 1981a: 90–91).

But there is of course much more to the teachings of Sathya Sai Baba. He is actively involved, for example, in the building of schools and hospitals and with relieving the plight of the impoverished and suffering. The purpose of these activities, however, would seem to be first to provide a source of "merit" for devotees obeying the commandment to engage in "seva"—and then to establish the proper conditions under which all people will be able, without distraction, to turn full attention to the thoughts and behavior that lead to good *karma* and to ultimate *moksha*:

> We have here 10,000 *Seva Dal* members, trained and dedicated for *seva*. I have doubts whether you are doing your duty to yourself and others which you have voluntarily taken upon yourselves. From the reports that you read, I understand that as part of rural service you go into the villages adopted by the *samithis,* and repair roads, clear drains, give some medicines, conduct *bhajans* and deliver lectures. Is this the work that the Sathya Sai Seva Dal has to do? Suppose you have a glass which you use to drink water from. Is it enough if the glass is cleaned on the outside? Inner cleanliness, inner health, inner illumination—these are far more important and the Sathya Sai Seva Dal has to take it up in a big way. . . . The government builds hospitals, provides roads, arranges for water supply and improves the outer forms of living. It is only a spiritual band of *sadhakas* like you that can succeed in reforming their habits and bring them on the path of peace, prosperity and harmony . . . . Lead them slowly and surely along the path of God, and these habits will drop off one by one (Kasturi 1981b: 205–206).

Like Shrdi Sai Baba before him, he advocates no rituals, no incantations—claiming that only "devotion" is required of devotees who gather in his name:

> pass your days in song. Let your whole life be a *bhajana*. Believe that God is everywhere at all times, and derive strength, comfort and joy by singing His Glory in His Presence. Let melody and harmony surge up from your hearts and let all take delight in the Love that you express through that song [from an address at Prasanthi Nilayam, 1976] (Kasturi 1981b: 69).

A Sai Baba "satsang"—a gathering for devotional purposes—therefore, is characterized almost entirely by the singing of bhajans (in

Sanskrit or Hindi, many written by Sai Baba himself, but hymns of any religion, in any language, are in principle acceptable) and the playing of accompanying music.

Devotees are urged by Sai Baba to turn to vegetarianism (subsumed under the value of "non-violence"), and to turn away from material pleasures and concerns. But they are not *required* to give up anything: one does the best one can, and strives to do better; to achieve as much as one can, in this lifetime. Sri Sathya Sai Baba asks no more than that, and turns no one away:

> I am always aware of the future, the past as well as the present of every one of you. So I am not moved by mercy. Since I know the past, the background, the reaction is different. It is your consequence of evil deliberately done in the previous birth, and so I allow your suffering to continue, often modified by some little compensation. I do not cause either joy or grief. You are the designer of both these chains that bind you. I am Full of Bliss—come and take Bliss from Me, dwell on that Bliss and be full of Peace (Mc Martin 1982: 6).

### The Hindu Renaissance

In no way is it my intent in this work to offer an explanation for the popularity of Sathya Sai Baba in India. Indeed, I depend, for such knowledge as I have on the subject, most particularly upon the writings of Charles S. J. White (1972), Agehananda Bharati (1970), D. A. Swallow (1976, 1982), and Lawrence A. Babb (1986).

Bharati's views on the "Hindu Renaissance" were referred to briefly in the last chapter, and I return to them now because they provide particularly important insights for those who would understand the attraction of Sathya Sai Baba to Hindus in India.

As Bharati sees it, this "Renaissance" reflected the transplantation of "the Western notion of the value and dignity of the individual into the language of Indian modernity":

> The interpretational focus was shifted from the canonical, monistic texts and their commentaries to noncanonical literature, particularly the *Bhagavadgita*. Here, the individual remained intact, its absorption into the brahman being presented as a secondary, and slightly inferior choice. . . . The modified Vedanta complex typifies the position of urban Hindu sermon: the individual approaches divinity, potentially to merge with It someday. For the time being, however, it is real in the ontological sense, hence amenable to social control. Most importantly, there is no longer the opprobrium of being an alien ideological import. . . (Bharati 1970: 287).

As a consequence, it would appear, there has been a coming together of contemporary urban Western-educated Indians with rural "village-saint" devotees in a joint rejection of traditional Sanskritic Vedic scholars (Bharati 1970: 281 *et passim*). And—in a comment that may be of particularly great significance for those of us who seek to understand the attraction of Sathya Sai Baba in Trinidad as well as India—Bharati observes:

> The Hindu Renaissance is indeed "all-embracing," to use a Renaissance phrase: Anyone who identifies with it shares its parlance, regardless of his religious background—Hindu, Muslim, Parsee, even Christian. "All religions are one" is a key notion of the Renaissance (Bharati 1970: 285).

"Key notion of the Renaissance" it may well be in India; in the Trinidad context, however, "all religions are one" stands as a remarkable contrast to West Indian calls for the obliteration of ethnic differences, usually couched as: "All of we is one"!

For India, Bharati argues, "The parlance of the Hindu Renaissance deemphasizes ritual, caste, and 'superstitions,' and it frequently plays down 'religion' " (Bharati 1970: 272). What then is left for the devotee? According to Bharati, an admiration for charismatic evangelical figures, and an emphasis in religious observance on *bhajan, kirtan,* and other forms of devotional songs, poems and hymns—frequently even sung to the music of film tunes (Bharati 1970: 270–271). With Bharati's analysis in mind, one can easily see how the personality, the teachings, the advocated forms of worship, of Sathya Sai Baba would attract both successful upper-class Indians caught up in Bharati's "Hindu Renaissance," as well as less sophisticated countryfolk.

There are, however, other views. Charles White argues, for example, that the "Sai Baba Movement" should be perceived as part of the continuous, continuing tradition of Indian "saints" going back before Kabir (who was born in the fifteenth century) to Hindu saints and Muslim sufis of earlier centuries in direct lines of influence (White 1972: 865–866). He points to reputed ties between Kabir and these earlier saints—and then to the links between Kabir and Shrdi Sai Baba—and finally to the links between Shrdi Sai Baba and Sathya Sai Baba (White 1972: 867–873; see also Daniel Gold's exploration of the role of North Indian *Sants* in the emergence of modern Hinduism [1987] and Charlotte Vaudeville's study of *Kabir* [1974]).

While White recognizes important differences between the two representatives (or incarnations) of what he terms the "Sai Baba Movement" (and between them and Kabir and the others he perceives as predecessors), the fact that he terms the sequence of "saints" a "movement" is significant. He sees common threads in their teachings, such as the "synthesis" of elements from religious sources other than (in addition to) Hinduism. He argues, further:

> One might say that they accomplish their work through "gesture" rather than through the spoken or written word. . . . From "gesture" and its impact on the observer, one can conclude that the attraction of these saints exists in the realm of what one might call "relationship." Those who are drawn to them . . . apprehend their "reality" in a very special way. This is the effect of *Darshan* whether proximate or distant. For a privileged few the living saints, and sometimes the departed as well in dreams and visions, bestow an initiation that creates an indissoluble bond between the Master and the disciple. This is described by Hindus as the closest of all human relationships. The followers of these saints declare that they direct all their devotion to the gods or God through the saint whose photograph takes the place of any other image in the domestic worship (White 1972: 874).

White therefore takes issue with Bharati on a number of points: he challenges Bharati's formulation of the "Hindu Renaissance"; he sees no conflict between the "saints" and the Indian traditional religion and religious scholarship; and—understandably, given his view of the antiquity of the "movement"—he sees little that is necessarily "Western" or even "modern" about it (White 1972: 876–678).

A third position is taken by D. A. Swallow, a scholar who has in fact lived among, and observed, followers of Sathya Sai Baba in India. She sees "guru cults" such as that of Sathya Sai Baba as, if not a new phenomenon, "an increasingly prominent feature of Indian religious life today, especially in the towns and cities, and among the urban middle classes" (Swallow 1982: 123). Thus, Swallow even cites Bharati in support of her own conclusion that: "Some of these godmen face criticism from the more reserved, scholarly ascetics and from obviously conservative laymen, who challenge their claim to divinity and deride their simplified and syncretic philosophical teaching" (Swallow 1982: 123–124).

Lawrence Babb suggests, however, that a major attraction of Sathya Sai Baba for "urban sophisticates" lies in the simplicity of his teachings, and, indeed, in his performance of miracles:

> the Sathya Sai Baba cult may be something of a Weberian reversal, an example of the reenchantment of the world. Here are urban sophisticates, who come from a class and background in which much of popular Hinduism is dismissed as mere "superstition," finding their religious selves at the feet of someone who is—to outward appearances at least—

a magician, and coming to live in a world in which the miraculous is a pervasive, significant fact (Babb 1986: 200).

Clearly, the issue is not a simple one, and I will leave it to scholars who are more familiar than I am with the wide body of Hindu religious literature to thrash it all out. I prefer to turn, as matters more pertinent for this work, to two questions raised by Swallow in her paper on Sai Baba and his "cult":

> How does a godman with an all-India following establish a claim to divinity, have it recognized and ratified and convince his followers that his spiritual resources are sufficient to encompass all their demands? Why do particular godmen attract extremely large followings, and why should the urban middle classes be so desperately in need of their miraculous power (Swallow 1982: 124)?

### Honey and Ashes—and Semen?

In her effort to answer the questions she has raised, Swallow constructs a complex, multi-dimensional approach. Though she sees the solution as one in which all the strands of her approach are interwoven, I have problems because some of her conclusions seem clearly applicable to Trinidad (and other overseas) devotees, but others do not.

Three analytic strategies are employed: the historical, the metaphorical and the sociological. Thus, she begins by noting, as White did, the "links" between Sathya Sai Baba and the "saintly and ascetic religious traditions" (Swallow 1982: 135) and draws attention to the efforts of both Sai Babas (in somewhat different ways) to forge an "ideological synthesis" (Swallow 1982: 132–134).

But this "saintly and ascetic" tradition, in her view, also represented an amalgam of *both* asceticism *and* sexual ecstasy, and she therefore draws our attention to the works in which Agehananda Bharati (1965) and Wendy O'Flaherty (1973) have wrestled with this aspect of Hinduism. Swallow is of the opinion that, while the "mediaeval Hindu Brahmanical reformation" emphasized the ascetic dimension and attempted to do away with the sexual and ecstatic elements, nevertheless: "[the] unreformed old ideas have persisted in popular belief until the present day, and are still an important element in the attractions of holy men. These are the traditional magical powers which Sathya Sai Baba claims today" (Swallow 1982: 131).

Thus, she argues, while Shrdi Sai Baba conveyed the image of the ascetic, Sathya Sai Baba (though he too follows an essentially ascetic regimen) "tends to dress in an erotic mode" (Swallow 1982: 138) and may be understood to be: "the thriving *lingam,* the living Siva, the supreme ascetic and the supremely controlled lover, who comprehends all the paradoxes facing men in the world, and offers a solution to them" (Swallow 1982: 152).[1]

For Swallow (deriving in large measure from O'Flaherty), the seeming paradox is resolved in the classic Hindu delineation of *Shiva* as both destroyer and creator, as both ascetic and sexual-ecstatic. To illustrate this, she points to the exudates for which Sathya Sai Baba is noted. It will be remembered that the Godman regularly produces quantities of *vibhuti* (sacred ashes) for his devotees, both personally and from many of his pictures (on which other substances are often said to appear, such as *kum-kum* or vermillion, and *amrita* or sacred honey), and he is said also to regurgitate *lingams*—phallic representations of *Shiva*—on certain occasions.

This congruence of honey and ashes is a particularly striking one for those anthropologists who are aware of Claude Lévi-Strauss' searching analysis of the symbolic inter-relationship of the two substances (1974). Swallow's metaphoric exploration, however, covers other ground—and encompasses seminal fluids, as well. Specifically, she argues that the ash once distributed by the earlier Shrdi Sai Baba and now produced by Sathya Sai Baba as an exudation of his own body has both a funereal dimension (the ashes of the funeral pyre) and a sexual one (what remains when *Shiva* "destroys the god of desire, *Kama*") (Swallow 1982: 138).

She goes on, therefore, to explore what she perceives as the underlying sexual imagery and metaphor of all the elements that relate to *Shiva* (and therefore to Sathya Sai Baba, who claims to be *Shiva* incarnate): the *vibhuti* as representing "seminal fluids," the annual regurgitation of a *lingam* by Sathya Sai Baba at the Mahasivaratri festival as a "metaphorical transformation of the castration idea," and so on (Swallow 1982: 148–149). *Shiva* "is the living *lingam* in the *yoni* (*yoni*: symbolic representation of the vulva), and the androgyne"—and so, therefore, is Sathya Sai Baba (Swallow 1982: 144–145). All this, she feels, contributes to the wide acceptance of Sathya Sai Baba:

> The devotees themselves, like the married sages in the Siva myths, suffer the conflict between erotic urges and ascetic ideals. At a more general level they are also torn by the conflicts between the temptations of the secular modern world and the traditional requirements of *dharma*. The message for his devotees that emerges from Sathya Sai Baba's double performance is that men and women should balance ascetic practices with the performance of their worldly duties (Swallow 1982: 152).

With the above passage, Swallow moves seamlessly from the metaphorical to the sociological, and she turns to the observations she herself made in Orissa while studying Sai Baba devotees in that state in 1972–73 (1976). During her research in Bhubaneswar and Cuttack, she observed many religious ceremonies and religious gatherings (satsangs), and interviewed at length many of the local Sai Baba devotees. "Running through almost all the accounts," she notes, "was one persistent thread—the concern with health—a concern which dominates the interest and conversation of middle-class India" (Swallow 1976: 99).

For, according to Swallow, the Sai Baba "cult" in India was a middle-class phenomenon, attracting followers of that class because it provided answers to middle-class problems:

Essentially Sathya Sai Baba is helping his "modern" middle-class followers to see the problems which cause them anxiety in terms of familiar traditional religious conflicts, without making them feel they are being old-fashioned. At the same time his versions cut out some of the earthy reality of the puranic tales and are thus acceptable to his rather puritanical followers (Swallow 1976: 289).

In her later article (1982) Swallow returns to this conclusion and expands upon it:

Most urban dwellers [in India] nominally accept the official ideology of secularism and egalitarianism, but are often unhappy with its practical consequences. . . . They continually have to make accommodations in every aspect of their social and religious life. In the new towns and the newer suburban sectors of older towns—areas where Sathya Sai Baba's following is most evident—it is often extremely difficult to maintain the cycle of religious observances, or to maintain a network of dependent ritual service caste families. . . . Traditional patterns of authority are threatened. The pattern of marriage alliances is gradually changing. Sisters and daughters have to be allowed greater freedom, with the result that their purity and modesty are more frequently suspect. There is much freer commensal interaction. So many people see the situation as one in which order has disappeared, controls have been lifted and self-indulgence is rife (Swallow 1982: 153).

Thus the conclusions of her dissertation—that Sathya Sai Baba is particularly attractive to middle-class Indians beset with contemporary socioeconomic problems—are incorporated, in her later article, into a more multi-faceted explanation. This is surely a legitimate and praiseworthy scholarly exercise, though it does raise problems—at least for me, in this work.

Her "sociological" level of analysis is one I can carry to Trinidad, where—though not uniformly applicable—it does provide helpful illumination. The "historical" level of analysis—the consideration of the continuities between Sathya Sai Baba and his "saintly" forerunners—might be open to challenge in Trinidad: how many Indo-Trinidadians know much if anything of the saintly holy men of India?

The "metaphorical" level of analysis is the most difficult to deal with, even when one is solely concerned with India. Swallow never tells us how or why her urban middle-class Indian Sai Baba devotees—described in her dissertation as "puritanical"—are at the same time attracted to a Godman who, in her view, is an embodiment of older, discredited, erotic-ecstatic elements in Hinduism.

For Trinidad, however, the problem is even greater: to what extent would Indo-Trinidadians share the visceral responses of Indians? I saw no evidence, during my research in 1958, of the use or awareness of *vibhuti* in village Hinduism. Indeed, though I gave great attention to religious belief and practice (see Klass 1961, 1978: 137–183), I noted little of the perceptions and orderings described by O'Flaherty and Swallow, nor have other students of Indo-Trinidadian religion referred to such features. This does not imply any attenuation of religious interest and activity, of course: it most likely reflects the aforementioned separation of Indo-Trinidadians from Hindu texts and the teachings of Indian holy men—and, perhaps, their long exposure to Western religious metaphors and orderings.

Nevertheless, given that separation, how likely are the Indians of Trinidad to recognize or otherwise to respond to the metaphors Swallow identifies for India—ash as "seminal fluid," ejection of *lingams* as "castration," and so on?

The problems become even more acute when we attempt to apply the foregoing explanations of Sai Baba's attraction to the question of *non*-Indian devotees. If we examine the writings of Western disciples, we find little mention of the "saintly" tradition (beyond the observation that Sathya Sai Baba is the reincarnation of a previous holy man, Shrdi Sai Baba), and hardly anything that reflects Swallow's "ecstatic" and sensual level of analysis. Instead, as we have seen, there is much interest in such things as the similarities between Sathya Sai Baba and Jesus Christ.

It may be that there is no one set of explanations for the attraction of Sathya Sai Baba that will serve for all his followers throughout the world—barring the one that is customarily offered by the devotees themselves: that each has been personally summoned to Baba by Baba himself.

Lawrence Babb, indeed, suggests something very much along these lines:

The point of devotion to Sathya Sai Baba is to evoke his presence in
one's life, to achieve intimacy with him (though the relationship may
seem to be very distant), and finally to achieve merger with him. When
he says he is "within" his devotees, as God is within them, this is more
than a metaphysical cliche, for Baba does indeed become an internal
presence in the lives, bodies and being of his true devotees (Babb 1986:
212).

But is this equally true for his "true devotees" outside of India? For
answers to that and related questions, obviously, we must explore the
emergence of a Sathya Sai movement within a particular cultural context, as Swallow did for India, and as I propose to do for Trinidad
and Tobago. And, even within what seems to be "one cultural context,"
we should be prepared for significant internal differences, for we are
not dealing with unstratified or homogeneous societies.

Thus, Samuel Sandweiss, we have seen, is an American devotee of
Sathya Sai Baba who reports on the purported relationship between
the Indian avatar and Jesus Christ. But Sandweiss, as it happens, was
born a Jew and is a practicing psychiatrist, and his passage to Sathya
Sai Baba, as he makes clear, reflects anxieties and concerns (and
metaphors?) deriving from both his religious heritage and his professional training:

> I was reared in the Jewish religion with the idea that God is formless
> and therefore one should not worship golden idols or the human form
> (Sandweiss 1975: 164).
> I used to think, before being awakened to the reality of the existence
> of God, that a state of being like this was available simply through
> suggestion, the use of our imagination and the psychological principles
> believed to govern conditioning in human behavior (Sandweiss 1975:
> 156).

Clearly, there are other "histories" and other "metaphors" that come
into play for overseas devotees of Sathya Sai Baba. In this work,
however, we can only be concerned with the nature of the attraction
of Sathya Sai Baba to people in the West Indian nation of Trinidad
and Tobago.

### Notes

1. Babb, too, perceives a phallic dimension to Sathya Sai Baba. He describes
a popular photograph of the Godman: "In this picture Baba stands erect with
his hands behind his back, a nearly featureless (and lingalike) saffron column"
(1986: 184).

# 8

# The Sathya Sai Movement
# in Trinidad

## *How It Began: The Official Version*

For devotees of any faith originating from a specific moment of divine revelation, it may well be that the circumstances of how the "Word" was actually first received are simply not amenable to the normal rules of history or staid record-keeping. After all, does not "divine revelation" imply a profound alteration of time and space, of ordinary human relationships as well as of the relationships between human and divinity? Are those who are receiving the revelation ordinary humans at that moment, or are they larger-than-life inhabitants of a liminal space-time? What have they to do with ordinary human concerns such as hunger, illness, lust, pride, fear, or jealousy?

And if such a moment of divine revelation is indeed outside of history and more the sort of thing the native Australians have termed "dream-time" (see Elkin 1964: 215 *et passim*)—would that not also be true, in some measure, for the particular moment when the "Word" was first reported to those living in some distant land? And what of the moment when an individual hears that God is presently walking the earth? In Trinidad, less than two decades after the news first arrived that a man in South India was claiming to be an avatar of *Shiva* and *Vishnu,* the account of the origins of the Satya Sai Seva Organization of Trinidad and Tobago was already murky and uncertain.[1] More than that: in its distortions of "actual" events and its presentation of miracles, ambiguities, and contradictions, it was being transformed into the stuff of legend before the very eyes of those who had in fact participated in those events.

Even the seemingly unyielding medium of the printed word has been affected by this process. In 1976, barely *two years* after the first formal satsang in Trinidad, Kamla Mahabir—an undergraduate student at the

University of the West Indies—reported, in an essay on the "Satya Sai Movement in Trinidad":

> Mr. Chilo Rooplalsingh, a resident of Marabella in South Trinidad, is the acknowledged founder of the Satya Sai Seva Organisation. He claims to have had his first knowledge of Sai Baba from a Moslem friend, Mr. Haniff Mohammed. Mr. Rooplalsingh was particularly interested in Baba after this as he had been suffering with a series of symptoms which doctors could not diagnose. . . . Mr. Rooplalsingh tried to collect all the information he could get from anyone who knew about or had heard or seen Sai Baba. Unfortunately there was no one to appease his relentless desire to know all there was to know about this man of miracles. Finally, he came into contact with one Mr. Melvin Gangapersad who had studied in India and who had visited Sai Baba at his ashram. From Mr. Gangapersad, Mr. Rooplalsingh got a bit more information (Mahabir 1976: 10).

Mahabir relates how Mr. Rooplalsingh was finally able to find books about Sai Baba (including Murphet's *Man of Miracles*) in Boston, how he wrote to Sai Baba soon after, in 1973, and how he actually visited Bangalore later that year and saw the Godman ("but did not find it possible to hold any discourse with him on that occasion"). There were, Mahabir notes, other people in Trinidad at about that time who also knew of Sathya Sai Baba (such as Mr. Roderick Noel, a government official who had learned of the Godman while visiting Guyana), but she concludes, as we see, that the credit for introducing the worship of Sathya Sai Baba to Trinidad must go to Chilo Rooplalsingh.

The official account of the birth of the movement in Trinidad appears in *Satya* (sic), the journal of the Sathya Sai Centres (sic) of Trinidad and Tobago, in the November 23, 1983, issue, in an article by Bickram Sawh entitled, "How it all Began":

> Sometime in 1973 Mr. Haniph Mohammed . . . who bereaved the SAI family by his passing away on April 3, 1980, in his normal literary pursuits chanced upon an article on "The Man of Miracles." Being close friends of the Rooplalsinghs of Marabella he immediately communicated with them since they were a noticeably religious family. This family decided to go to India to have the DARSHAN of the LORD.
>
> It was thus in November 1973 that they stood in amazement on the sands of PRASANTI NILAYAM looking at the flow of divinity (Sawh 1983: 29).

There is no mention, in Sawh's account, of Mr. Rooplalsingh's illness, or of his inability—during this first visit—to obtain an interview with

Sathya Sai Baba. Other elements of the original account have changed: Mr. Haniff (or Haniph) Mohammed is now given credit for discovering the first written account of Sai Baba, and Mr. Melvin Gangapersad has disappeared from the record.

When I interviewed Mr. Rooplalsingh—a wealthy hardware dealer of Marabella, a suburb of San Fernando in south Trinidad—he began the account of his worship of Sai Baba with a discussion of a series of fainting spells ("blackouts") he experienced from February 1972 onward. He seemed convinced that these illnesses, if not indeed of divine origin, were what led him ultimately to the feet of Sathya Sai Baba. He reported that a friend (presumably Mr. Mohammed) mentioned Sai Baba as someone who was reputed to have performed miracles, but the friend knew little else, he said. Seeking more information, Mr. Rooplalsingh heard of a "boy" in Trinidad who owned a record of Sai Baba singing and speaking, and the hardware dealer borrowed and copied the record.

The following year, having been unable to obtain satisfactory medical help in England, he and his wife (and his friend) decided to continue on to India. Together, they waited among the crowd in Puttaparthi, and when Sathya Sai Baba emerged from his ashram (tears came to Mr. Rooplalasingh's eyes and his voice choked with emotion as he reached this point in his account, as he says always happens) the three Trinidadians knew they were in the presence of God.

Mr. Rooplalsingh went into much detail, during the interview, about the illnesses that had been plaguing himself and his wife, and about his feelings upon first seeing Sai Baba. He also referred to many of the interviews he had had, over the years, with the Godman (during the most recent visit, in fact, Sathya Sai Baba had performed the marriage ceremony for Mr. Rooplalsingh's son), but he did not mention (possibly because he considered it inconsequential) that he had had no interview during his first visit to Puttaparthi.

And, as may be noted, he did not mention the role of Mr. Melvin Gangapersad (except perhaps as the unidentified "boy" who provided him with a record of Sai Baba's voice).

### Other Witnesses, Other Accounts

Mr. Melvin Gangapersad and his friends—many of them members of Sai Centres in the north—expressed in interviews the discomfort they experienced upon discovering that the account in *Satya* of the early days of the movement made no mention of his name and contribution, for they feel he certainly should be credited as the very first Trinidadian to hear of—*and to meet*—Sathya Sai Baba.

In 1965, he reports, he was a student living in India. He began his studies at Shantineketan University in West Bengal, and then moved on to Benares Hindu University. And it was at the latter institution he met a devotee of Sathya Sai Baba: a young man from Chile—not himself of South Asian descent—who was there to study Indian philosophy.

The young Chilean told Mr. Gangapersad of some of the teachings of Sathya Sai Baba, and gave the Trinidadian a picture, which he still treasures, of the holy man. During the ensuing two or three years the Trinidadian student read accounts of Sathya Sai Baba in Indian newspapers and began to attend weekly satsangs in Benares:

*The bhajans were really very touching and very catchy tunes. . . . I had my tape recorder and I recorded some of the bhajans, the devotee chant, and also the arati (*Int. Ref. # 04).

During this time, he reports, he did in fact travel to Bangalore, but did not manage to have even a glimpse of Sai Baba:

*The thing is, I didn't go to see him—probably, you know, Sathya Sai Baba says, "Not until the time is right can you come to me," and things like that. And although I went there—it was part of my education to go there . . . it entailed traveling a lot of places. And I had been to Bangalore, but at that time the "calling"—so to speak—was not there (*Int. Ref. # 05).

He returned to Trinidad in 1968, and began his career as a geography teacher at Naparima College (in southern Trinidad), and began to spread the word about Sathya Sai Baba, his miracles and his teachings, to his friends at the college. He was also attending regular Hindu religious services at the Gandhi Ashram in San Fernando, as part of a congregation that included many prominent Indians of south Trinidad, and he taught those congregants who were interested some of the "chants" he had recorded.

Other people became interested, and he told them what he knew or remembered of Sathya Sai Baba's teachings and distributed a few of the small pictures of the Godman he had brought home with him. One of the pictures was given to Mr. Rajanand Persad, a merchant of Chaguanas (a town in central Trinidad, in County Caroni).

When, on another occasion, I interviewed Mr. Persad himself, he also brought up the subject of that picture, but insisted he had no memory of who had given it to him: "someone," he said, had left the picture on the counter at his shop where he later found it—and he feels it was the first miracle Sai Baba performed for him, noting that while he put it away carefully and remembered where he put it, he was never able to find it again however hard he searched. Perhaps, he suggests, the picture disappeared because it had done its work of drawing his attention to Sathya Sai Baba (Mr. Persad eventually became Chairman of the Chaguanas Sai Centre)—or perhaps it disappeared because of his first negative reaction: he admits he was surprised and troubled by Sathya Sai Baba's hair, which at first glance seemed to him characteristic of someone of African, not Indian, descent.

Mr. Gangapersad, however, remembers introducing Mr. Persad and other Hindus of Chaguanas and other parts of Trinidad to the bhajans of Sai Baba during 1968 and 1969. In 1970, Mr. Gangapersad was able to return to India to resume his studies in geography at Benares Hindu University, and in January, 1971, he traveled to Bangalore to see Sathya Sai Baba for himself, at Whitefield, becoming—he believes—the first Trinidadian to meet with Sathya Sai Baba, and to experience at first hand an apparent example of Sathya Sai Baba's divine omniscience:

*The first thing he said to me was, "What have you done with yourself?" Because, before leaving here [Trinidad] I was about one hundred eighty pounds, and then in three months that I spent in India there I lost about fifty pounds, so I came out about one hundred thirty. . . . I couldn't answer because the tears just kept streaming down from my eyes. And he spoke to me, and he told me, "I know that you have completed your first degree—" (now, I didn't tell him; I couldn't even tell him anything) "—I know you have completed your first degree and you have come back here to do your Master's, and you will complete it." [Q: you had not said a word?] I could not speak at all! . . . And he asked me, after a couple of other things, he said, "Don't worry about anything. . . . I am taking care of everything for you" (Int. Ref. # 06).*

Mr. Gangapersad relates that he had further interviews with Sathya Sai Baba over the next few days, and received more gifts, including vibhuti, a necklace, and other items materialized in his presence by the holy man. He returned to Benares, where he continued his studies, now attending Sai Baba satsangs regularly, and occasionally returning to south India for additional visits to Sathya Sai Baba. In 1973, his studies completed, he returned to Trinidad, and it was in that year, he said, that he first began to talk of Sathya Sai Baba to Chilo Rooplalsingh of Marabella.

Mr. Gangapersad knew nothing of the phonograph record to which Mr. Rooplalsingh referred—for the young geographer had brought back only tapes from India—but the record was mentioned to me, in a different interview, by members of the Premsingh family, devotees of the village of Las Lomas in County Caroni in central Trinidad. In 1970, they claim, the eldest son, one Kimraj Premsingh, was working as a clerk in a department store in St. Augustine (a suburb of Port of Spain—site of the University of the West Indies) and was told of Sathya Sai Baba and his miracles by the then manager of the store, himself an immigrant from Sri Lanka. He also gave young Kimraj a record he had brought from India of Sathya Sai Baba singing and speaking, which, the family claims, Kimraj then loaned to Mr. Rooplalsingh.

That manager, incidentally, soon after went back to India specifically to see Sathya Sai Baba, who is reported to have told him, "I have special plans for you!" The manager returned to Trinidad and within a few weeks was killed in an automobile accident. Members of the Premsingh family consider this to be the miraculous sequel to Sai Baba's statement—particularly because it was discovered, after the accident, that all pictures of Sai Baba in the manager's car had turned milky white.

One reason the Premsingh family relates this story is because in their own home—now a Bhajan Mandali in which satsangs are held twice a month—they have a very special shrine to Sai Baba: a room filled with miraculous pictures (of both Sai Babas, of Hindu deities, of Jesus Christ) which continually and regularly exude *vibhuti,* "sindur" (the vermillion pigment used in Hindu rituals and known also as "kumkum") and a transparent sticky substance believed by devotees to be *amrita* or divine nectar.

### The Miraculous Moment

A number of devotees expressed to me their belief that the moment they each personally became aware that divinity walked the earth in the form of Sathya Sai Baba constituted a miraculous event: a moment when God called out directly to each one of them. Mr. Persad of Chaguanas, we have seen, prefers to remember his receipt of a picture of the Godman as an actual miracle. A devotee in Amity tells of his first visit to a satsang: because it was crowded he had to move to a room in the back of the house—where he observed a disembodied hand in the air, blue in color (the color associated with *Krishna,* he noted), distributing flowers. An elderly man in Fyzabad, in south Trinidad, told me he had resisted his wife's efforts to interest him in Sai Baba until, alone in his house one night, he observed *amrita* oozing down the glass covering a picture of Sai Baba's "Lotus Feet."

And for many devotees, the miracle came as Sai Baba responded to their prayers at a time of illness:

*You know I was non-vegetarian: I used to eat meat, I used to eat chicken, and so on. . . . And in early 1974 I started to develop this stomach pain. A friend of mine came and said, "There is a man from India, and he is doing a lot of miracles, and I have some of the ash. If you try it, it will help you." . . . So I tried it—not with any faith as such; I just took it because there wasn't any other thing to go to. And the first day, nothing doing—and the second, nothing—but the third day, when the pains became intense—and I took it . . . and I kneeled down [i.e., to pray after the fashion of Christians], because I tell you, we being lost we did not know, really, how to pray . . . and I kneeled down and I said, "Well, Lord, I am suffering with this pain, and my friend brought this vibhuti and I think it can help!" . . . On the following morning when I woke up I felt different, and since that pain left I never got that type of pain again. And, I started to devote myself, go around to satsangs, reading the books, listening to lectures, and so on (Int. Ref. # 07).*

The foregoing account is almost prototypic: what particularly attracted many Trinidadians (indeed, like the Orissans studied by Swallow) to Sathya Sai Baba—at least initially—was his reported ability to cure illness and to perform other miracles. Many people went to see him, as did Mr. Rooplalsingh, for a miraculous cure, or just to see a miracle performed before their eyes. However, like the hardware merchant, they came to the conclusion that they were actually in the presence of God Incarnate—something that came to mean more to them, as it did to Mr. Rooplalsingh, than any "miracles." Apparently, Shrdi Sai Baba's original technique for attracting devotees was still effective in Trinidad.

Again, though the account of the arrival of the "Word" of Sai Baba in Trinidad is clearly undergoing revision, some historical reference points may be noted. We observe, for example, that, in the early 1970s and even before, Trinidadians of Indian extraction were traveling to India regularly, for study and for religious pilgrimage, and it was through such people that knowledge of Sathya Sai Baba was brought to Trinidad. But not only through them: citizens of South Asian nations were in turn visiting Trinidad and taking up residence there, and their accounts of religion in India were listened to—as they had been for decades—with great respect.

It may not come as a surprise to the reader that Sai Baba's teachings came to Trinidad through the accounts of Hindus, but it should be remembered that considerably more than half the population of the island is non-Hindu—and is, instead, Christian or Muslim. Indeed, half the population is not even of Indian descent, and many non-Indian Trinidadians also travel abroad. One of the men present at the two founding meetings, we have learned, was Mr. Roderick Noel, a non-

Hindu and non-Indian Trinidadian, who had become interested in Sathya Sai Baba while in government service in Guyana, and another non-Indian, an important member of the government, Mr. Basil Pitt, also attended the early satsangs (Mahabir 1976: 27).

Why, then, in the years to come, did the movement attract primarily people of Indian descent? Why were the non-Indian founders almost forgotten? Why are the teachings of Sathya Sai Baba seen as "Hindu" today? Let us begin our approach to these questions with an examination of the development of the formal organization known as the Sri Sathya Sai Baba Centres of Trinidad and Tobago.

## Coming Together

### Why Organise?

> Do not fret against the rules and regulations which the Organisation imposes on you; they are laid down for your own good. Regulation is the very essence of Creation. The oceans observe their limits. Wind and fire respect their limits and bounds. . . . How then can this Organisation escape the prescription of certain rules and regulations? ("Excerpts from Divine Discourse"—Hyderabad 29/3/76; quoted in *Sai News Letter* [Ramdeen n.d.: 3], a publication of the Co-ordinating Committee of the Sri Sathya Sai Baba Centres of Trinidad and Tobago).

On Thursday (a day sacred to Sathya Sai Baba), April 18, 1974, a meeting was held in the Trinidad home of Dr. and Mrs. Krishna Pariag (or Prayaga) originally of Bangalore, India, and a second meeting was held on the following Thursday at the home of Mr. Rooplalsingh in Marabella (Sawh 1983: 29; Mahabir 1976: 11). These meetings are considered to have constituted the first formal gatherings of the Satya Sai Seva Organization in Trinidad, and from them derive not only all the recognized and acceptable satsangs[2]—but indeed that formal body now calling itself "The Sri Sathya Sai Baba Centres of Trinidad and Tobago."

Actually, the first meeting was not considered a satsang by those attending it (Dr. and Mrs. Pariag, Mr. and Mrs. Rooplalsingh, Mr. Roderick Noel, and Mr. Ramdath Leeladharsingh—according to both the Sawh and the Mahabir accounts). Essentially, those present agreed to meet again for prayer to Sathya Sai Baba, and to form a Trinidad branch of the Godman's world movement: "This was a meeting of hope and expectation—an ideal global set-up comprising citizens of East and West who accepted a challenge destined to change the face of the Caribbean" (Sawh 1983: 29).

At the second meeting, a week later, some twenty people assembled, listened to recordings of Sai Baba's bhajans and addresses, and began to sing with him. And, in addition, they agreed to continue meeting for prayer every Thursday thereafter, alternately in north and south Trinidad (Sawh 1983: 29).

The satsangs at the Marabella home of Chilo Rooplalsingh are the ones that most people remember best from the early days. People came from all over Trinidad to learn about the holy man of south India. Many report that they were particularly attracted by the music and singing. Soon, devotees who were gifted singers and musicians formed groups which traveled around the island playing and singing at Hindu temples and at religious gatherings everywhere. Among the early leaders of bhajans were Mr. Rajanand Persad of Chaguanas, who later withdrew from the "Mother Centre" at Marabella to found what was to become the Chaguanas Sai Centre, his son, Mr. Karo Persad, and Mr. Surujrattan Rambachan, a descendant of distinguished pandits of south Trinidad, and at the time a student (later, a member of the faculty) at the University of the West Indies.

Many devotees gathered for prayers at one another's homes, but within a few years there were three more or less formal "Sai Centres" in existence: Marabella in the south, Chaguanas in central Trinidad, and Tunapuna in the northern suburban belt just outside of Port of Spain. Each drew interested people from its respective region, and this led, as did the efforts of the peripatetic "bands" of bhajan singers and musicians, to the establishment of still more "Centres" in other communities.

It was not all simply peaceful growth and expansion, however. Sometimes the withdrawal of particular individuals or groups from one Sai Centre and the establishment of another Centre in the vicinity reflected conflict or personality clashes. Kamla Mahabir reports that by 1975 there were four distinct "Satya Sai Baba groups" in Trinidad, and that internal conflict played a role in their separation (1976: 21–22). According to Mahabir, conflict could frequently be traced to ruffled feelings on the part of those who led the singing of bhajans: "cases where certain singers are popular with the congregation so that whenever any new devotee sings, the crowd disregards him and does not sing the lines after him. . . . Therefore members are divided into rival groups competing for chances to sing or read the discourse" (Mahabir 1976: 22).

Though some devotees now jokingly dismiss the conflicts and arguments of the past as insignificant and possibly even "Baba's will" (since they did lead to the establishment of new Centres and thus to the spread of the movement!), others acknowledge that Sai Baba disapproves strongly of such conflict, and objects particularly to any jostling for the honor of leading the singing of bhajans. A satsang, however, consists primarily of such singing of bhajans, and it must be reported that disagreement over who shall lead the singing—and who shall not—continues to be a source of some stress.

Still, distressing though such disagreements may be to devotees and to Sai Baba, in all fairness it must be observed that the dissension, past and present, in the Sai Centres has really been very muted and orderly, particularly when one considers the turbulent histories of Trinidad religious movements, and of organizational fragmentation in general in that nation. There is, after all, only one Sathya Sai organization in Trinidad and it does receive the support and allegiance of almost all the devotees of Sathya Sai Baba in that nation—no small achievement.

Nor was it without effort. In September, 1975, "a devout follower of Sai Baba" (Mahabir 1976: 22), Mr. Rama Maharaj, assembled a group of leaders at the Gandhi Ashram in San Fernando for the purpose of ending differences and coming together in one formal body. They were apparently unable to reach accord at that time, however, and years of negotiation followed. New, and essentially independent, Sai Centres were formed, but if they had difficulty accepting a common leadership they never split into formally opposing bodies. The efforts at consolidation and accommodation finally bore fruit in July, 1983, with the establishment of the Co-ordinating Committee of The Sri Sathya Sai Baba Centres of Trinidad and Tobago.

The new body was formally commissioned by Mr. Indulal H. Shah, Chairman of the World Council of Sri Sathya Sai Organizations, at the Marabella Sai Centre on July 4, 1983. Mr. Tajmool Hosein—a prominent Trinidad jurist (born a Muslim, married to a Hindu—both now devotees of Sathya Sai Baba)—became, with the blessing of Sathya Sai Baba, the first Chairman of the new regional organization, and its representative to the world body.

### Rules and Regulations

Thirteen groups were recognized as official "Sai Centres." These were: Marabella, Gasparillo, San Fernando, Rio Claro, Rousillac and Clarke Road (in south Trinidad); Chaguanas, Cunupia and Carlson Field (in central Trinidad); and Tunapuna, El Dorado, Arouca and Valsayn (in north Trinidad). At the time, further, some twelve other groups were accorded the status of "Bhajan Mandalis"—centers for regular satsangs that were not as yet self-sustaining or able to carry out all the activities expected of a formal "Sai Centre." And, in the succeeding two years, two groups—St Helena in central Trinidad, and

Mayaro, the first Sai Centre in western Trinidad—succeeded to "Centre" status. New "Bhajan Mandalis" began to form everywhere; two of them in fact during the course of my research during the summer of 1985.

When I say "everywhere," however, I am referring only to Trinidad and there only to communities where people of Indian (and Hindu) derivation predominated. There were a few devotees (such as Mr. Hosein, the Chairman) who had been born Muslims, and an even smaller number of people—perhaps fewer than a dozen—who were not of Indian descent. In the early years, it was true, a group of devotees of primarily African descent had met for a while in a Baptist church in Port of Spain, but they had long since disbanded and those few who remained steadfast made their way—in 1985—to satsangs in the Indian communities. And, as far as I was able to determine, there were in 1985 only two devotees of Sathya Sai Baba in Tobago: a husband and wife—both non-Indian—who had no affiliation whatever with the Sathya Sai organization.

To be accepted as a full and formal "Sai Centre," a group of devotees must meet certain requirments. Though many are in permanent quarters, some Sai Centres—like most Bhajan Mandalis—do meet at the homes of members. They must, however, field a full slate of officers: a Chairman (who is responsible to the Co-ordinating Committee), a Secretary (who keeps records and is responsible for disseminating information and announcements at satsangs), and a Treasurer.

The latter office is an interesting one, given the universal and unbreakable principle of the Sathya Sai Baba movement that no dues or assessments ever be collected. The duties of the Treasurer, therefore, revolve around the dissemination of funds for "seva"—for good works. Even such funds are never solicited, but are voluntarily made available by members as the needs arise and to the amount a given devotee wishes. No record is kept of who gives (or does not give) what, but the treasurers are responsible, on their honor, for keeping the funds and disbursing them appropriately.

How, one might well inquire, are Sai Centres and the larger organization maintained, in the absence of dues and assessments? Solely, it is everywhere asserted, by the free and unsolicited actions of devotees who feel moved to reach into their pockets when bills arrive. The Chairman of the Chaguanas Sai Centre (Mr. Rajanand Persad), for example, insisted that this was the sole procedure followed for the erection of their building. On one occasion, he said, an enthusiastic but misguided devotee rose at the end of a satsang to note that the building still lacked a proper ceiling. The man proposed that each devotee present contribute enough to purchase one 4' x 8' ceiling panel, thereby solving the problem. Devotees eagerly crowded around him, money in hand.

The officers—not wishing to embarrass the good-intentioned devotee—waited until all the worshippers departed before pointing out his error to him: this constituted an assessment, and was therefore forbidden. The man returned the contributions, I was told, and when the ceiling panels finally arrived, one wealthy devotee—as was the custom—simply pocketed the bill and paid it later from his own account.

In the same way, all insist, all expenses of both Centre and parent organization are met. No one, devotees also insist, keeps track of who pays what bill or for how much: all that is left to the individual conscience. Still, only the wealthy may participate meaningfully in such an activity—and though Sai devotees insist that all are equal and have equal voice in the affairs of the Sai Centre, it is apparent that wealthy men predominate among those who run the organization, as well as the Sai Centres.

A Chairman who is sufficiently wealthy himself may conduct Centre business with comparatively little collaboration with other wealthy men; many Chairman, however, find it advisable to have an informal council of such devotees, with whom they can discuss matters involving large outlays of money.

Each Sai Centre, further, meets as a formal body—the "samiti"—at least once a month, to conduct the affairs of the Centre and to plan future events. The Chairman conducts the meeting and the Secretary keeps the minutes (both following procedures reminiscent of the old Arya Samaj meetings). Every member has an equal voice in the planning of activities: at one "samiti" meeting I attended, some teen-aged girls complained good-naturedly that they were expected to sweep the Centre while boys stood around doing nothing. The Chairman admonished the boys and instructed them to take their turns in the clean-up.

Most specifically, each Centre—to be accepted as such—must undertake "seva" projects in its neighborhood, and is responsible for the administering of its own program of religious education, in accordance with the nationwide program.

The Centres are also expected to maintain programs of bhajan-training, and to participate in the wider programs of the larger organization.

Bhajan Mandalis, on the other hand, are not subject to any of these formal requirements. They need only acknowledge the national organization as their parent body and observe the rules of satsang when they meet—and they are expected to turn to the parent body, and to nearby Sai Centres, for assistance in all other matters.

The Co-ordinating Committee, as originally constituted, was made up of representatives of all the Sai Centres (the Chairman of each Centre is almost invariably one of the representatives) and from it is drawn the Chairs of the official sub-committees: "Seva or Service" (charged with overseeing the requirement that all Centres devote the energies of their members to helping the needy and suffering); "Baal Vikas & Mahila Vibhag" (the first term refers to the educational program for children, the second to the formal activities of women, within the Organization); "Celebrations"; "Importation and Sale of Books, etc."; "Bhajan Training" (charged with dissemination of new hymns as well as formal training of individuals and entire Centres in singing and in the playing of instruments); "Sai News Magazine" (the sub-committee editing and publishing the journal *Satya,* and the occasional *Sai News Letter.*

Despite occasional grumbling, the new official organization and the subcommittees have pursued their tasks with vigor. Editions of *Satya* (itself an attractive, well-edited and professional-appearing publication) contain reports of the various sub-committees, and accounts of the activities of all the Sai Centres—as well as inspirational messages and excerpts from the sermons and sayings of Sathya Sai Baba, along with passages from the writings of devotees all over the world. And, in the May 1985 issue of *Satya* there was the following announcement:

> World Council has advised that until such time as the movement in other areas in the Caribbean has grown to warrant some degree of autonomy, the Co-ordinating Committee of Trinidad & Tobago will be responsible for the WEST INDIES region.
>
> We are pleased to advise that so far the SRI SATHYA SAI BABA CENTRE OF GEORGETOWN, GUYANA has applied to us and we are in the process of granting provisional affiliation.

### Notes

1. As I noted earlier, the spellings "Sathya" and "Satya" are used essentially interchangeably in Trinidad. In an attempt at some sort of consistency, I will prefer "Sathya"—spelling the name without the "h" only where the reference requires it.

2. During the late 1980s, according to Aisha Khan (*personal communication*), devotional gatherings, for the most part of Hindus but not always or necessarily of Sai Baba devotees—but nevertheless called "satsangs" or "sat sanghs"— have begun take place in a number of places in rural Trinidad.

# 9

# Singing with Sai Baba

## *A Satsang in Trinidad*

By 6:45 P.M. devotees are beginning to take their places, for services will begin at 7:15 sharp, as scheduled. We are in a typical upper-middle-class Trinidad Indian home in a neighborhood typical of the urban-suburban belt stretching westward from Port of Spain along the foothills of the Northern Range. To be even more specific, we are upstairs—where the family lives—above the lower floor where the family business is conducted, and we are on the veranda looking through the glass doors into the living/dining area which has been cleared of all furniture for the evening service.

This is a "Sai Centre"—one of the fifteen formal meeting places (as of 1985) at which Trinidad devotees of Sathya Sai Baba gathered regularly for communal prayers. Some of the Sai Centres had acquired or erected permanent quarters, but in 1985 about half still met in a home, usually that of the Chairman. One Centre was proudly peripatetic, meeting successively at one of four widely separated homes in central Trinidad so that all the scattered members shared both the burdens of travel and the pleasures of propinquity. The one we are visiting in this chapter, however, meets regularly at the home of the leader (and founder), though the members are beginning to discuss the possibility of the acquisition of new and permanent quarters.

Clean sheets have been spread over the entire floor area, perhaps to protect the carpeting, or perhaps to separate the devotees—all of whom will sit on the floor—from the lower surface on which, on other days, the inhabitants tread in shoes. For tonight, as at all satsangs everywhere, the devotees are in their bare or stockinged feet, having removed all footwear before entering the building.

A strip of cloth runs down the floor to the altar at the far end of the room, separating the floor space into two equal segments: only women will sit on the left, and only men on the right—an arrangement followed in most Sai Centres, though not an invariable one. The sep-

aration is what is important, and if local circumstances (the position
of doors, or of staircases, say) make advisable a reversal of the arrangement, no one comments on it.

The meeting room—normally the family living area—is large; perhaps eighteen feet wide by twenty-five feet deep. There are doors on
the left leading to corridors and other rooms, and at the far end is the
kitchen area, separated from the living room by a service counter. On
the walls are decorative plaques and other ornaments, but particularly
prominent among them are the representations in painting and photograph of Satya Sai Baba. On the walls of the more permanent quarters
of other Sai Centres there are often even more pictures of Sai Baba—
pictures of all sizes from full-length to snapshot—often interspersed
with quotations from his sermons. Similar pictures grace the walls of
every devotee's home, along with family pictures and oleographs of the
more traditional Hindu divinities.

The more permanent Sai Centres have permanent displays along the
wall that the congregation faces. In such places, a long, low, stepped
altar, covered with white cloth, takes up the center of the wall, and on
its two or three levels are arranged a number of large pictures. Representations of Sathya Sai Baba predominate, of course, but in addition
there is always at least one of Shrdi Sai Baba, along with pictures of
*Shiva, Vishnu, Krishna, Rama, Ganesha*—and, invariably, of some non-
Indian divinity or holy man. The "Bleeding Heart of Jesus" is a
particular favorite, but other representations of Christ may be seen in
different Centres, along with what are identified as portraits of Guru
Nanak (founder of the Sikh religion), of the Buddha and Mohammed,
and of others.[1]

In this Sai Centre there is room on the small (obviously portable)
altar for only three large pictures: Sathya Sai Baba in the center, with
Shrdi Sai Baba on his right and a very traditional oleographic representation of the elephant-headed *Ganesha* on his left. All three pictures
are decked with garlands of flowers and so is the single picture on the
altar step below them: the "Lotus Feet" of Sathya Sai Baba. And,
finally, on a low table just in front of the altar are lighted brass *diyas*
(oilcups), each resting on a tray of flowers.

Again, in the more permanent Sai Centres the array is much greater:
the congregation sees a chair to the side of the altar—a richly uphol-
stered armchair, usually, with a matching footstool. Draped on the
chair, or on the wall above it, is an orange or red robe—once actually
worn by Sathya Sai Baba—now the cherished property of the Sai Centre,
a sacred souvenir of a pilgrimage to Puttaparthi. Usually, too, the
permanent Sai Centres have more symbols of Hinduism, such as a
*lingam* on a pedestal, or an array of statuary representing *Krishna* and

*Vishnu* and other deities, or an enormous representation of the word
*Om* in devanagri script, studded with flickering colored lights. The Sai
Centres that meet only in people's homes rarely have room (as indeed
this one does not) for such displays, but those who gather for the
satsang feel that Sathya Sai Baba is fully present during the service,
despite the absence of his chair and footstool and robe.

And, *lingam* or no, the devotees consider this a Hindu service: not
only do they remove their footgear and segregate themselves according
to gender, but the women wear saris (or at minimum *orhinis* [veils]
over modest Western dresses) and some of the men wear *kurtas* (traditional Indian white shirts)—and a few have even set aside their
leather belts before the service begins.

It is close to 7:15 now, and devotees are crowding up the stairs. A
few of those who arrived very early sit very quietly in their places,
meditating, as the rules enjoin. Others whisper together about private
matters, though they know that socializing—before, during, and after
satsangs—is frowned upon. Most of the early arrivals, however, are
officials (the Chairman, in whose home we meet, plus the Secretary
and the Treasurer) or others concerned with the preparations for the
satsang. Women have arranged the pictures on the altar, and have
lighted the *diyas*. The Chairman and a male associate are connecting
and testing the complex and expensive bank of sound and recording
equipment of the kind that is to be found at every satsang of every
Sai Centre in Trinidad.

The musicians arrive and seat themselves in front of the men's
section: they are all males—as is usually, though not invariably, the
case. They assemble the instruments one always sees at satsangs, as
indeed at all Hindu religious events in Trinidad: the harmonium, the
*dhantal* (a long metal spike against which is struck a u-shaped metal
plectrum), the *tabla* (one-sided small drum), the *dholak* (larger, two-
sided drum), the *kirthal* (wooden frame set with small castanets, made
to fit over a musician's hand), and the *manjira* (two small brass cymbals,
attached by string, to be clashed together gently). These are the traditional instruments of Trinidad Indian music—but others are welcomed,
and one Sai Centre boasts a fine violinist.

The room is packed with people and the late-comers must sit out
on the veranda. Still, certain people—officials of the Centre along with
representatives of the Sai Organization and other distinguished guests—
work their way through the crowd to the front rows of the gathering.
On the other hand, some of the earliest arrivals had seated themselves
far to the rear, and even out on the veranda, long before space con-
straints made it necessary. In the very front row (of each gender side)
are respectively the man and woman who will lead the singing.

In all, perhaps fifty people are here, about equally divided between men and women. There are a few small children (the girls in saris) and one infant. Two or three of the women are elderly, and there is one old man, but most of the devotees seem between the ages of twenty and forty. One couple is "Afro-Trinidadian" and one woman might be of mixed Indian and African descent: all the rest are Indians. A few, by their dress, are clearly prosperous, and one or two seem comparatively poor—but most appear to be comfortably middle-class (the men are mostly shopkeepers, small businessmen, office workers, and civil servants).

### *The Service*

A hush falls as the lights are dimmed. The Chairman of the Centre—who in this case is both a musician and the lead singer—strikes a chord on the harmonium. He leads the congregation in a long, softly chanted, *Om.* Three times they chant, and then as he plays softly for a few moments they sit in silence, eyes fixed on the smiling face of Sathya Sai Baba lit by the flickering *diyas.*

As Sai Baba has requested, the services begin with the *gayatri mantra,* the traditional Vedic prayer that, in Trinidad once, only Brahmans recited. The members of the congregation who cannot read devanagri script have memorized a transliteration in Roman script provided by the Trinidad organization. Whatever its defects, this transliteration represents, at least for a Trindad Indian, a recognizable approximation of the original Sanskrit sounds:

"Om bhoorbhuvahasvaha thath Savithur varenyam
Bhargo devasya dheemahi dhiyo yonah prachodayath"
(Ramdeen *Sai News Letter* n.d.: 2).

Then the male lead singer, as at every satsang—again according to the rules laid down by Sathya Sai Baba himself—sings the first line of the prayer: "Ganesha Saranam Saranam Ganesha" (surrender, surrender, to *Ganesha*) and the congregation choruses the line after him. Again, devotees use the transliteration—and accept the translation—of this and all other bhajans provided for them in the official literature. After the fourth repetition, he leads them through four choruses of the second line: "Sayisha Saranam Saranam Sayisha" (surrender, surrender, to *Sai-Ganesa*). The tempo quickens as they repeat the sequence.

After that, and for the next hour, the congregation simply sings hymn after hymn:

"Krishna Krishna Jai Gopi Ramana
Bhaktha Vathsala Jivana
Hey, Radha Madhava Mohana."

For the most part, the hymns are mostly Hindu bhajans, but if the lead singer (or any singer who follows him) wishes, a Christian or Muslim devotional song may be introduced. The repertoire changes from week to week, and individuals and even Centres have their favorites—and the Sai Organization urges the members, as a most important act of piety, to devote time to the study of new bhajans.

The bhajans may be in Sanskrit or in Hindi; they may—as in the case of the one just given—be unchanged traditional Hindu hymns to traditional deities, or they may be modified to incorporate a reference to Sathya (and Shrdi) Sai Baba:

"Rama Rama Jai Rama Hari
Rama Krishna Shiva Sai Hari
Shirdi Puriswara Sai Hari
Parthipuri Sathya Sai Hari."

Sathya Sai Baba has composed many of the new bhajans, and has been taped leading devotees in song. Many Trinidad devotees, in fact, have copies of such tapes and play them over and over at home and while in their automobiles, singing along with the avatar.

The Chairman, like lead singers at all satsangs, introduces and leads the first few bhajans, and then gives way to the female lead singer. After she has led a few devotional songs, other devotees—usually alternately male and female—take up the microphone and begin new bhajans of their own choosing. In a few Centres, a book (a children's school notebook) is circulated before services begin, in which those who wish to lead the singing of a bhajan sign their names. In most Centres, however, as is the case here, the microphones circulate informally, beginning with the front ranks, to anyone who indicates an interest. No announcement is ever made of the singer's choice: he or she sings the first line of a bhajan *a cappella,* and by the time the congregation repeats it the musicians have picked up the melody.

At 8:15, quite promptly, the Chairman begins the series of bhajans and prayers that, in most Sai Centres, bring this part of the service to a close. These include the stirring bhajan that begins: "Subrahmanyam Subrahmanyam, Shanmukanatha Subrahmanyam (etc.)," in which the many names of *Shiva* are repeated at ever increasing tempo.

Then the congregation rises for the *arati:* the traditional Hindu adoration of the *murtis* (icons) representing all divine forms. At this satsang, the two or three men and women performing the adoration begin with the portrait of Sathya Sai Baba, gently waving their plates of burning camphor, and then move on to all the other pictures. In the Centres in which there are representations of Jesus Christ, or the Buddha or Mohammed or founders of other religions, the *arati* encompasses them as well. Standing, the rest of the devotees participate in the *arati* by chanting the verses of the traditional adoration of the "Lord of the Universe," now modified to include the name of Sathya Sai Baba. The song begins:

"Om Jai Jagadisha Hare
Swami Sathya Sai Hare
Bhaktanajana Samrakshaka Parthimaheshwara
Om Jai Jagadisha Hare."

As the arati comes to an end, the devotees reach the final, moving, verse:

"Narayana Narayana Om Sathya
Narayana Narayana Narayana Om
Narayana Narayana Om Sathya
Narayana Narayana Om Sathya
Narayana Narayana Om
Om Jai Sadguru Deva."

The songbook (*Songs of Sri Sathya Sai Baba* n.d.) translates this last verse as signifying:

"You have the form of Om, the radiant one,
You are Sathya Sai Mahadeva
(Supreme among the Devas).
Bearer of the Mandara Mountain
Accept this auspicious Arathi. . . ."

As the lights come on and the devotees settle back on the floor, one of the men comes forward, book and notes in hand, to deliver the "discourse." In most of the permanent Sai Centres, there is a lectern up front for the speaker, who is usually one or another of the more educated members of the congregation. At satsangs such as the one we are visiting—one held at the home of a devotee—the speaker simply stands and faces the other devotees.

The giver of the discourse opens a collection of Sai Baba's sermons (in English translation) and—without even bothering to identify the text—reads aloud Sathya Sai Baba's views on illness and the search for cures. The implication of the sermon, as the speaker notes approvingly, is that it is foolish to seek medical help solely from doctors, since only Sathya Sai Baba can effect true cures.

The discourse lasts about fifteen minutes, and is followed by announcements—from the Chairman, the Secretary, and a few others—of upcoming events. There will be a satsang at the home of a devotee celebrating his birthday, and all members are urged to attend. All are urged, too, to attend a class, at another Centre, where new bhajans are to be studied. The Secretary formally welcomes all newcomers, and all guests, including an important member of the Co-ordinating Committee who has been seated in the front row throughout the service.

The congregants rise again, and the services come to an end, as do all satsangs—as do all Hindu services in Trinidad—with the chanting of, "OM . . . SHANTI, SHANTI, SHANTI!"

Quietly, the devotees move to the staircase and down to where they have left their shoes and sandals. In principle, and according to the wishes of Sathya Sai Baba, there should be no "socializing" after the satsang: they have come together for prayer and for communion with the Lord of the Universe—not for gossip and casual conversation. Some devotees obey the rules, going off after the briefest of polite farewells, but here and there a knot of people gather briefly—women exchanging news about their families, and men discussing business matters. Upstairs, the officers confer on Centre affairs, as their wives straighten the room and put away the pictures of the Sai Babas and the other paraphernalia of the satsang.

### The Sai Centres

At every Sai Centre in Trinidad, such a group of people come together regularly once a week to hold a satsang. Thursday evening is the preferred and most common time for a satsang—it is the day sacred to the "Guru" (any guru, but for devotees Sathya Sai Baba is *the* guru) and the one on which many Hindu temples in Trinidad hold services. Other days are acceptable, however, and some Sai Centres have chosen to meet on Tuesday or Wednesday evenings, or at other times, most particularly in order to make it possible for devotees to attend more than one satsang during the week.

Indeed, many devotees spend as many hours as they can at satsangs, and they have plenty of opportunities: in a 1983 announcement in *Satya,* eight of thirteen Sai Centres gave Thursday (either 6:30 or 7 P.M.) as their satsang meeting time (two of them, Marabella and Chaguanas, listing an additional satsang on Sunday mornings at 7 A.M.); one Centre met on Saturday evening at 7 P.M., two on Tuesday evenings, one on Wednesday. The Arouca Sai Centre did not indicate a specific day of the week for satsangs in 1983, but in 1985 they were meeting on Monday evenings. Many Bhajan Mandalis meet once a week, though some assemble with less frequency. And, in addition to the formal meetings at Centre or Bhajan Mandali, many people invite fellow devotees to their homes at times of birthdays or other special occasions for still additional satsangs.

But devotees do not limit their attendance to times of prayer only. Members of Sai Centres are expected to participate in the education of children—usually on Sunday mornings—and many do; women, particularly, assemble weekly for "seva" (service) activities; there are discussion groups, and bhajan-study meetings, and Hindi-learning classes, and much more. All who wish—young and old—may attend the regular monthly samiti, the assembly of the whole body at which the affairs of the Centre are discussed and regulated, and future activities planned.

The Co-ordinating Committee has endeavored to establish some guidelines for all these activities, and particularly for the conducting of the satsang (which all agree is the most important activity of all). Nevertheless, there is considerable variation from Sai Centre to Sai Centre—and even more from Bhajan Mandali to Bhajan Mandali.

Most Centres begin their satsangs exactly at the time scheduled. Trinidad Indians, accustomed to the most casual adherence to time schedules in village Hindu temples, find this a most impressive demonstration of Sai Baba devotee discipline, as well as, for some, a reminder of Arya Samaj practices. The clock is watched, and Centres keep quite closely to the ideal of no more than an hour and a half for the total service. One hour is usually taken up with the singing of devotional songs and this is followed—again usually—by a "discourse"; a reading from the sermons of Sathya Sai Baba, or from one of the holy texts of Hinduism—or of any religion. On one occasion I heard a discourse involving a text drawn from the Koran, and on another a text from the New Testament. Some givers of the discourse simply read their passage without comment—others attempt briefly to interpret it, or to relate it (if it is not Sai Baba's own words) to the teachings of the avatar.

Kamla Mahabir reported, in 1976, that the satsang usually ended with the showing of one of the many films and videos available of Sai Baba—strolling in stately fashion among the people gathered on the grounds at Prasanti Nilayam, participating in Hindu festivals, and performing miracles (Mahabir 1976: 19). This was also the practice at the satsangs I attended in the spring of 1985 at the New York Sai Center.

In Trinidad, however, no films or videos were shown at any of the Sai Centre satsangs (some twenty in all) that I attended during the Summer of 1985. When I asked about the films, Sai Centre officials told me they were still available, and were very occasionally shown, but since the regular devotees had seen most of them over and over again, they were not in demand at satsangs. They were particularly useful, one official told me, for proselytizing, and had been (and would be) shown at inspirational open air meetings intended to attract possible converts. Even these meetings were occurring more sporadically, however, and only one was held during the summer of 1985. About half the Sai Centres had permanent quarters. In most cases this took the form of the vacant top floor of a building, usually commercial, belonging to a devotee, who carried on his business on the floor below. The Marabella Sai Centre introduced this pattern soon after its establishment, when Mr. Chilo Rooplalsingh moved from his apartment over his hardware store and converted it into a Sai Centre. The Rio Claro Sai Centre was also above a hardware store and the St. Helena Sai Centre occupied an enormous room above the offices of a trucking concern.

Hardware merchants were certainly well represented in the Sai Baba movement, suggesting an initial spread of information from Mr. Rooplalasingh through a network of business associates. Still, owners of transportation firms and supermarkets and other businesses that owe their prosperity to the oil boom were also among the leaders of the various Sai Centres, so the prevalence of hardware dealers may simply have been fortuitous.

One Sai Centre, that of Chaguanas, was occupying its own building— a temple designed and built for it alone, and almost completed by the Summer of 1985. The temple, surrounded by a wall enclosing a parking area, is larger than the Vishnu temple in nearby Amity, but smaller than the Hindu Temple in St. James, a wealthy suburb of Port of Spain, and much smaller than the new Divine Life Temple going up alongside the Princess Margaret Highway south of Chaguanas. They all resemble one another, however; like the others, the Chaguanas Sai Centre falls within what might be called the contemporary "Trinidad Hindu Temple" style—as distinct from the "Trinidad Mosque" or the various "Trinidad Church" architectural styles.

Until 1985, there was little interest in building temples to house the Sai Centres, but with the completion of the Chaguanas Centre attitudes began to change. Mr. Rooplalsingh, for example, owned a piece of land on a hill overlooking San Fernando and said that he dreamed of building a magnificent temple to Sai Baba there. He noted, however, that he must wait for permission from Sathya Sai Baba himself. Similarly, Mr.

Chandrasein Dookie, Chairman of the El Dorado Sai Centre, awaited a message from the avatar permitting him to activate a building program. Neither man chafed at the delay; both said their ambitions must give precedence to the divine plans of Sathya Sai Baba. Still, both felt that the necessary permission (or, perhaps, inspiration) would soon be forthcoming.

The arrangements within a Sai Centre must inevitably bow to the circumstances of the surrounding edifice: only the Chaguanas Sai Centre, for example, could be constructed so that the devotees would be facing what they believe is the shortest distance to India and to Sai Baba. Indo-Trinidadians are aware that the world is round, however, and note that it is possible to reach India by going in many different directions around the globe.

### Trinidad Hinduism and Sai Baba

One wall of a Sai Centre is chosen as the location of the altar, to which all devotees face. Somewhere in the room, usually over the altar, there will often be a large representation of the official emblem or symbol of the Sai Baba movement—a five-petaled lotus, with each petal in turn containing a symbol of one of five major world religions. These are, for followers of Sai Baba, Hinduism (represented by *Om* in devanagari script), Christianity (a cross), Islam (a star and crescent), Buddhism (a wheel), and the Parsi or Zoroastrian faith (a cup of fire). In the United States there is a sixth petal containing a Jewish Star of David, but this form of the emblem is not in use everywhere. Finally, in the center of the lotus there is a side-view of the symbol of Sathya Sai Baba: a lotus on a pedestal.

Prominently displayed in almost every Trinidad Sai Centre—in front of, or beside, the altar—is a *lingam* of *Shiva,* set in a *yoni,* and on a pedestal. Swallow, we noted earlier, emphasizes the sexual connotations of this symbol (the *lingam* representing a phallus and the *yoni* a vulva) and many Trinidad devotees of Hindu derivation are of course aware of these connotations. During my earlier study, in 1957–1958, the *lingam* was identified as phallic by some informants, but with an embarrassment they did not otherwise exhibit in discussing sexual matters; educated in Christian schools, they were uncomfortably aware of the shock such an identification might precipitate among Western observers.

In 1985, during discussions with Sai Baba devotees, the phallic nature of the *lingam* was never touched upon. Rather, most informants insisted quite earnestly that the *lingam* was to be understood as primarily a non-objective representation of *Shiva*—and thus, by extension, a graphic statement of the central mystery of the movement: Sathya Sai Baba as both a living human being and as an incarnation of God—in the form of the Hindu deity he first announced himself to be.

The seating arrangement at a satsang—all devotees sitting on the floor, with men and women sitting on separate sides—was characteristic of all Hindu temples in Trinidad during the time of my earlier study. Now, however, in temples from Amity to St. James Trinidad Hindus sit on benches or in pews, and there is no effort made to separate the sexes. Sai Baba devotees note the difference proudly: it is one example, for them, of the greater "purity" of their movement—of their view that worship of Sathya Sai Baba not only does not take them *from* Hinduism: it brings them *back* to an earlier, simpler Hinduism more in accord—they say proudly—with the religion in India.

Sitting on the floor or ground during a satsang is common practice at Sai Centres everywhere, but it is not rigidly enforced where people are not accustomed to the practice and would find it uncomfortable. In the New York Sai Center, for example, only the front rows of devotees sit on the floor; in the back there are rows of chairs for those who prefer such seating. Within the past couple of decades, Trinidadians of Indian descent have given up the practice of squatting or sitting on the ground: at home they eat sitting on chairs around the table, and almost every Indian house today boasts couches and armchairs. The seating arrangements in non-Sai Baba Trinidad Hindu temples, therefore, reflect the contemporary seating patterns—as well, perhaps, as emulation of non-Indian houses of worship.

Sai Baba devotees are certainly as accustomed to sitting on chairs as are any other Trinidadians, and many—particularly older men—experience as much discomfort from the unaccustomed position as any European would. In some Centres, therefore, a few chairs are scattered about for those who have become too stiff for the floor. Most devotees, however, refuse to use them. Some men, in every Sai Centre, manage to sit with their backs against the side or rear walls, a position which alleviates some of the discomfort, but many avoid even this modification, sitting cross-legged without support, shifting position occasionally to relieve the stiffness in their legs.

The Sai Baba movement does share with Trinidad Hinduism (and Islam) the practice of removing shoes before entering a place of worship. At some Centres (as at some Hindu temples) there are racks near the main entrances for the storage of shoes and sandals—and the footgear of men and women are kept carefully separate. This is also true at Hindu temples, although there the wearers of the footgear are then permitted to sit side by side!

## Conflict and Stress

There is another rule of seating at satsangs that, though never formally stated or invoked, was universally observed in Trinidad: the more important people sat up front, and those who considered themselves peripheral or who were newcomers, tended to stay to the rear. A number of people told me that, in the period before they decided to accept Sai Baba without reservation, they kept to the rear of the satsang, finally moving forward as an indication that they had become true devotees. One man, who had long occupied a forward position in the men's side, became incensed at some actions taken by the leadership of his Sai Centre, and expressed his anger by moving ostentatiously to the rear. When I mentioned this behavior to him after the service, he acknowledged it and affirmed that it was a conscious act.

Satsangs—and by extension Sai Centres—exist, in the minds of devotees, as places of worship only. If socialization is frowned upon— if hosts are urged *not* to provide refreshments—it will be understood that every effort is made to avoid contention and animosity.

Nevertheless, problems and disputes arise, and not infrequently there are bruised feelings. Ideally, it is understood, anyone who wishes to lead the group in song should have the opportunity, just as—people say—those with the best voices should occasionally humble themselves and do no more than join the choral responses. Still, some people do have beautiful voices; they love to sing, and others love to listen to them. And some have poorer voices, or do not know the newer bhajans—or are low in the pecking order that emerges despite the pious insistence that all devotees are equal in the sight of Sai Baba.

Some individuals (and some Sai Centres) took more seriously than others the injunctions of the Sathya Sai Organization and its Bhajan Sub-committee to learn more bhajans, and to practice regularly. At some Sai Centres—such as the one in El Dorado—there were many men and women who learned and practiced bhajans regularly, who alternated smoothly at their own satsangs and who offered to teach and coach the members of laggard Sai Centres . . . and who were astonished and saddened, they said, at the resistance and resentment they sometimes encountered. One such leader told me of a visit she had made to another Sai Centre with the wife of a senior official of the Sathya Sai organization. Both women were ignored during the satsang, she said, and were never offered the microphone, though the reputations of both as singers and as teachers of bhajans were known to all Sai Baba devotees in Trinidad.

The intensity of the conflict over who shall lead the singing of bhajans may seem amusing to outsiders, but it must be understood that singing of bhajans—with one devotee leading each hymn and the rest of the congregation responding—constitutes the body of Sai Baba devotional activity. There are of course other things that go on during a service, such as music and discourse, but it is clear that in the minds of devotees the singing of bhajans surpasses all else in importance. This may be because many of the hymns have been composed by Sathya Sai Baba himself (or are based upon his sayings)—or because he has instructed that devotion to him shall consist essentially of the singing of hymns—or because no one, however learned or however inspired—may properly interpret the teachings of, or otherwise speak for, Sai Baba.

This latter point means that *all* officials of the movement—from Centre Chairmen through members of the Co-ordinating Committee to member of the very World Council—are in principle solely administrators: their job is to see to it that the Movement runs smoothly . . . they have no right and no authority to say what Sathya Sai Baba *means*.

And yet, there is a formal organization—there are officers in every Sai Centre. There are decisions that must be made about rules of behavior, the conducting of satsangs, the lengths and topics of discourses, the priorities of activities to be performed. Occasionally, reprimands must be issued. The officers, who must take the lead in all this, find that they walk a kind of tightrope: they must set rules and standards and chastise those who are in violation of them—yet at the same time they must avoid the accusation that they are telling other devotees what God expects them to do or say or think.

For, from the persective of each devotee, God presently walks the earth—and so each may turn to him and receive instruction personally. Indeed, as all believe, Sathya Sai Baba can and will appear to each devotee during meditation, to provide instruction.

It might in fact be fair to say that during the satsang—indeed, whenever the devotee turns his or her mind to a contemplation of Sathya Sai Baba—that individual becomes what Victor Turner characterized as a "liminal entity": "neither here nor there," encompassed by "communitas" rather than "community," subject not to "structure" but rather to "anti-structure" (Turner 1969).

Whatever the problems inherent in such an interpretation (and I for one do see problems) it does help us to perceive the need to turn, in our inquiry into Sai Baba in Trinidad, from organization to individual. Who are the individual devotees? What does a devotee receive, directly from Sathya Sai Baba, to give meaning and fulfillment to the sense of discourse with divinity?

**Notes**

1. It need hardly be pointed out that such representations have been acquired without the approval of the other religious bodies. In any event, from the perspective of Sai Baba devotees, these are all manifestations of Sathya Sai Baba himself.

# 10

## "This Is My God"

### *The Devotee*

Nobody knows for sure how many devotees of Sathya Sai Baba there are in Trinidad, for they have never been counted and the keeping of membership roles—a practice occasionally embarked upon by a zealous Centre officer—is discouraged: Sathya Sai Baba, all believe, not only asks for neither dues nor contributions; he requires no formal declaration of membership.

As of 1985, however, there were fifteen formal Sai Centres, and at an average satsang at one of them one might note thirty to fifty people in attendance, and a slightly smaller number at a Bhajan Mandali satsang. The trouble is that, while on the one hand many people go to more than one satsang in a given week, on the other hand it is known that there are many devotees—and even "interested people"—who rarely come to satsangs, preferring to pray alone or with their families at home.

Estimates, it may therefore be easily understood, vary from the hundreds to the tens of thousands. There was a sort of consensus, nevertheless, among officials and other observant devotees, that—in all of Trinidad, in 1985—there were some six to eight thousand devoted followers of Sathya Sai Baba.

The ethnic composition of this body was easier to estimate than the total number. Though it is true that, in the early years, the Sai movement attracted some non-Indian Trinidadians to its ranks—and indeed still does—by 1985 such people constituted a truly tiny minority: hardly a dozen among the many thousands of Indo-Trinidadians.

Again, there were Indians of Christian and Muslim background among the early devotees, as there still are, but they too are in a very small minority—though the Muslim contingent included, in 1985, the leader of the organization in Trinidad, Mr. Tajmool Hosein. Overwhelmingly, Sai Baba devotees in 1985 were almost entirely of Indian Hindu background.

Some devotees were poor and uneducated, some lived in remote agricultural communities in the far south, but the main body of devotees—those regularly attending satsangs at Sai Centres and Bhajan Mandalis—derived largely from the more educated, the more urban (or suburban), and the more well-to-do segment of the Trinidad Indian population.

The Sai Centres, particularly, were attended by the families of businessmen, doctors, lawyers, teachers, officials and managers—and leadership ranks in Centres and in the larger organization reflected wealth and influence. All who sought Sai Baba were of course welcomed, but there was a clear (if unofficial and even unintended) socio-economic pattern in many Sai Centres: there were two or three composed almost exclusively of very wealthy people, and two or three where humbler folk were obviously more comfortable. The Sai Centres between those extremes exhibited more of a range, though the weighting was still obviously toward those of somewhat above-average income and education. Those who attended Bhajan Mandalis, however, did tend to be somewhat less wealthy and less educated than those who went to Sai Centres, but again there were many exceptions—as in the case of Bhajan Mandalis located in more remote districts but still comprised of the elite (merchants, teachers, etc.) of that district.

Those who come to Sai Baba are frequently seeking for something they feel is missing in their lives—very often, a sense of identification with the religion of their ancestors:

> *I being of Hindu family . . . you know, there wasn't much interest in spiritual matters, because, let us say, the Hindu religion became dormant. The older heads—whatever they knew, they used to tell you. . . . And the younger people were lost. Like, explaining what Lord Ganesh signifies, what Lord Siva signifies, and all those different things. Although we knew a little of it, the deeper knowledge was not there. And at that age—I was about twenty-six years [in 1974]—and you can imagine a young man at twenty-six—his life: no spiritual background, reckless life that he lived, you know, drinking and liming [Trinidad equivalent of "hanging out"]* (Int. Ref. # 08).

Again, a husband and wife recalling their life before they came to Sai Baba:

> *[H]: We were Hindus—brought up by Hindu parents and so—but not very religious. [W]: Not very religious. [H]: We never took it on as now. Now we are quite devoted. Before, I didn't accept the idea. ([Ques]: you mean you were a skeptic?) [H]: Yes, you might very well say that—that's true. An unbeliever. [W]: I used to believe there was a God! [H]: Well, she came*

*from a more religious background than me, you know. . . . And when I first listened to that tape, I said to myself, "Those people are crazy!" I couldn't understand a word they were saying. . . . But the turning point came when I went to a satsang for the first time, on the thirteenth of April, 1975. What I heard, by way of the bhajans, I couldn't understand most of it—but what I saw—there was a film show there of Sai Baba—and what I saw in that film, I was convinced* (Int. Ref. # 09).

Another man—an educated and devout Brahman—reported his first experience of the power of Sathya Sai Baba:

*In April 1974 I attended that first satsang. But like all Trinidadians, if you invite me for six, I could reach half-past six—"Trinidad Time"—nobody ain' hurry you, and nobody sticks to time—that's one of the bad diseases of our country. Except the Sai Baba movement! So, I reached there late, and there was no room in the hall—the living room—where the session was going on, so I got room in the bedroom. . . . Closing myself to myself, closing my eyes, I started meditating heavily. And the singing of these bhajans rang through me like a current. I could not believe myself what was going on with myself. I just felt the current rushing through me, like one who is standing in a storm, or going through in a broken wave in the ocean—I just felt something going through me. And without seeing the picture, I knew whomsoever there, is directed by—must have been—an avatar of the Lord—must! There can be nobody else—that can't be any falsity* (Int. Ref. # 10).

Some devotees commented on their initial surprise at the appearance of Sathya Sai Baba. Most particularly, his hair unsettled them at first, but the surprise was soon overcome, as when the above Brahman informant emerged from the bedroom:

*I inquired from a young lady who I know, "Which is Sai Baba's picture?" She said, "Over there." So I have to be very honest at this point, and I was looking for something like Krishna, or Rama, or you know—and then I was a little embarrassed because I couldn't make out who is the picture she was talking about. So I asked her a second time, so she showed me again in a manner as if: "You can't see? You don't see the picture here?" And when I looked at it, a drop of tears flew from my eye—I felt guilty, of disowning the picture: "Dear Lord, I am sorry, because the hair on your head really baffled me. . . . For whatever I have committed mentally, my Lord, please pardon me. I love you"* (Int. Ref. # 11).

### Under Sai Baba's Influence

With the acceptance of Sai Baba as God and guru, devotees report, their lives began to change. They found it easy to give up smoking, drinking, eating of meat—even movies and television. Most of all, many say, they felt their personalities undergo change. The following account, by a devotee who had little prior knowledge of or interest in Hinduism, is one example. It also exemplifies the marked tendency of Indo-Trinidadians (as against devotees in India, as we have seen) to accept Sathya Sai Baba as God:

*I feel more comfortable, more—inspired—than I—I look at human beings, and they are all one creation; they are God's creation. And we have to think about each individual as God's creation, and have that feeling of love towards everybody. It's hard, but it's still the practice, and someone may tell you something that may annoy you, but when you think of him as the creation of God and you also a creation of God, then it's only right to embrace that person with love, because Baba is the embodiment of love (Int. Ref. # 12).*

Many report that the lives of all their family members have been changed, and for the better, they feel:

*It make a big, big difference in our life. Before, we used to go to Carnival, and all that. Now, the children don't know anything about "party" or this or that. No outside life, except, well, when they used to go to school. Now they working, and satsangs, and so on. . . . We became vegetarian—six years now, we never even puts an egg in this house—and I, personally, could never believe that I was ever going to stop eating meat, because I would like it so much! I don't miss it—every day I would have fish or meat, and six years now I never tasted it and it don't worry me. . . . The love for Baba is more than the love for meat (Int. Ref. # 13).*

Devotees are eager to attempt to explain what the worship of Sai Baba has meant to them:

*I tell you, being a devotee—being one who is involved in bhajans—is something that you develop. Then there is the presence of Baba; actually, like when your eyes is closed and you are in concentration, and Baba gives his presence there—let us say, in spirit—it is something you will keep. It is nothing that someone will touch you and say, "Oh! I have a feeling!" No: you yourself will feel it, because there will be a difference. I have experienced it on many occasions, and you will feel there's a difference in the room—in peace, in quietness (Int. Ref. # 14).*

Still, Sai Baba expects more of his devotees than prayer and the relinquishment of bad habits. The devotee must give of himself to those in need:

"You must think about the gift you have to offer Swami on his birthday. You can feel that you have given Swami the proper gift only when you love your fellow man, take a share of his suffering, and engage yourself in fruitfully serving him. That is the only gift I wish for. Your present given to God is pure, steady, and selfless love" (from a discourse by Sathya Sai Baba entitled, *The Birthday Gift to Swami,* cited by Dr Michael Goldstein, Chairman of the North American Sai Organization, in a talk delivered July 27, 1985, at the Chaguanas Sai Centre).

To be fair to the Trinidad devotees, they did not really need this pep talk. In most Centres, a great deal of attention was given to seeking proper avenues for the performance of "seva." The following account, given by a woman who had been acclaimed by her fellow devotees for her seva efforts, could easily be duplicated by reports from other Sai Centres:

*What we used to do before, we used to go to the Homes—the different Homes, like Princess Elizabeth or Lady Hochoy, or several where they help handicapped children, and so on. But we found . . . they are sure to get a meal because the Homes are government-assisted. But these vagrants—you see them going into bins . . . I mean it is pathetic, it is really sad at times . . . and we suggested that they're the most deserving cases. So we started doing it once a week [helping those who run shelters for the homeless]. . . . They're sort of Christians, you know, they are doing it every day of life—we are the first set of people who started to help! From once a month, we've been doing it twice, and we've taken a third Thursday now. So what we'd like to do—as Baba says, we should dedicate at least four hours in seva per week. So, if we could cover four times a month I think we would be—because it takes from about six in the morning till about twelve to get through, so you see it covers that amount. . . . We do everything ourselves—we have some of the women from . . . three Centres that get together: Valsayn, El Dorado, and Arouca.*

*[Ques: What do the men do?] Well, in India they are supposed to do the delivery—in India the women cook and the men deliver—but we don't get them to do that. So we do it ourselves—we take it into town . . . east of the old cathedral, in Independence Square.*

*[Ques: How many vagrants do you feed?] They've got hundreds and hundreds of them, but we feed about two hundred fifty . . . a lot of roti [unleavened bread cooked on griddles]—and we do a curry—a vegetarian curry, and they eat it all—I think it is the only day they don't take meat,*

*because they love meat, you know . . . so we really do it nicely—it comes*
*out very nicely. We do a hundred pounds of flour (*Int. Ref. # 15).

Other women have been heard to complain, fairly good-naturedly,
that the burden of seva falls primarily upon them. Men say, in response,
that they do the best they can, but that the average Trinidad Sai Baba
male devotee is busy with good works, with study and prayer, with
formal devotions and with the preparations for periodic pilgrimages.
For many men, it may be understood, there is barely time for one's
business, and many talk of plans to retire, to turn mundane affairs
completely over to sons and to spend one's remaining years in contemplation of the living God and his teachings.

A few fortunate devotees are able to contemplate Sathya Sai Baba
while they work. A taxi driver, for example, plays a tape of Sai Baba
singing—and as he drives along, sings with him:

> *I wouldn't sing it for people to hear, but if my taxi is empty, then I'll*
> *sing loud! I have his picture in the taxi, and every day I answer questions*
> *about who this person really is. I tell them: "Well, you all wouldn't believe*
> *me—you all might say I'm crazy—but this is my God" (*Int. Ref. # 16).

### Sai Baba in Trinidad

To the devotee, Sathya Sai Baba is never far away. Will he ever
actually visit Trinidad? Devotees smile at the question: Swami is with
them whenever they pray to him, at home or at a satsang!

Many believe he visits them when they dream of him. That is, they
know they have been dreaming, but they also believe that the dream
was divinely inspired:

> *Every time I cannot find a way . . . Baba comes to me in a dream. And*
> *just before the service recently, for some reason I'd gone fall asleep at*
> *three o'clock in the evening [i.e., the afternoon] and I dreamed Sai Baba—*
> *you know?—coming, and walking on the altar of that very place there,*
> *laughing and so on, and I went there in that mood (*Int. Ref. # 17).

Two women, separately interviewed, told of dreams that suggested
(to the interviewer, not to the interviewees) something of the sexual
symbolism noted by Swallow. One woman said she had dreamed that
she was washing her underwear when a car drove by her house. As it
passed, she saw that it contained Sai Baba, who was waving to her.
The other woman mentioned a recurrent dream during which she was
troubled because something seemed to be cooking in her oven. Each

time, when she opened the oven door, she said, she would find "a fetal bag" inside the oven. When she would tear it open, an angel would emerge and fly toward heaven. After telling of the recurrent dream, she volunteered that she was convinced that it came from Sai Baba, though she could not imagine what its meaning might be.

Most of the dreams—or of the experiences of the materialization of Sai Baba in one's room during meditation—involve solutions to problems troubling the devotee:

*You know, many times I have a problem, I will pray to him, and ask him what to do. And before I built this house—we lived in a small house— a flat, downstairs—and for two years I had been looking, either for another house to buy, or if I should build in this spot. Because the family getting big and I need more space. So, one night I prayed to him, and I asked him, "Baba, what should I do? Should I keep on looking for a place to buy, or should I build? That is the question." And in a dream I had the same night, I saw myself pushing a wheelbarrow—a wheelbarrow of concrete mortar—which obviously would mean to me: "Build!" (*Int. Ref. # 18).

For many people, the most important dream is the one in which Sai Baba invites them to travel to India to visit with him:

*A friend of mine invited me to accompany him to India, to Sai Baba. So I told him, "Yes, I will go." So, they came here one evening to discuss plans, the costs, when we would be going, and so on. And by the time they left, I thought, "Okay, I will be going." That very night, I had a dream in which Sai Baba came to me. You see this gate here? The gateway was left open in the dream, and Baba walked through that gate. . . . And Baba came on the higher level, and I bowed to his feet there, and I kept saying, "Om Baba, Om Baba," bowing to his feet. Now that, there, gave me the idea that I should not go to Baba . . . because Baba came to me instead, meaning I should not go there. I did not go. . . .*

*Then, four years after, in 1981, I asked Baba, "Baba, can I come now?" And then I find myself at the airport in a dream! . . . So, I had passports and everything, but there was no ticket. So, I asked them: "Sir, where is my ticket?" And the old gentleman told the younger fellow, "Hey! Go bring him ticket!" . . . you know, Kenya-speaking English; that kind of accent. So that fellow went, but he didn't come back. Which means—I think he's telling me—"Okay, you can come now"* (Int. Ref. # 19).

The anxiety about his ticket experienced by this last devotee in his dream is certainly understandable: the cost of a round trip from Trinidad to Bangalore and back has rarely been less that four to six thousand (Trinidad and Tobago) dollars.

However, as we have just observed, the devotee believes that one travels to Sathya Sai Baba because the Godman has summoned one— and therefore most are convinced that if he summons you Sai Baba will see to it that funds for travel will be available for even the poorest pilgrim (and everyone knows of poor people who, seemingly miraculously, received money or tickets for the trip).

Most people, nevertheless, must raise the money themselves somehow—even when they have divine assistance. The cheapest way to travel is as a member of a tour group—it is even possible to reduce one's fare to almost nothing if one takes on the responsibility of organizing and leading such a group. Only a few men can manage such a feat, however, and most people must pay for their tickets, their accommodations, and their other travel expenses.

Wealthy people, of course, travel by themselves, sightseeing and shopping where and when they please. Even for the poorer devotee, on the organized and restricted tour, however, the trip to Bangalore to observe the darshan of Sathya Sai Baba at Whitefield or Prasanti Nilayam is both pilgrimage and excursion: it is a sacred trip to the feet of God, the most meaningful adventure a devotee can undertake— but it is almost invariably combined with sightseeing in India, shopping trips, and visits with relatives in Europe and the United states.

### Face to Face with God

Devotees are proud of the number of trips they have made—and the number of times they have had interviews with Sai Baba—and many even respond to questions about how long they have been devotees with accounts of their visits to Puttaparthi:

*We have been two times. The first trip was in October 1981. We left Trinidad on the first of October, and we returned back home the twenty-first of October: we spent the entire month outside. We had a wonderful time—very wonderful experiences. Twenty-one days we spent with Baba. . . . Before we went to Puttaparthi, we had a little tour—you know, it is nice to have a little tour of the city where you go—and we did in fact go to Hardwar to have a bath in the Ganges. We enjoyed it (Int. Ref. # 20).*

*I have been to Baba on four occasions. The first time I went there was in 1980, and I was selected to place a garland on Baba. At that time I was really surprised, because this thing is really rare. And in 1981, I took my wife and two kids. And Baba spoke with us—he spoke to my daughter, he spoke to my son, myself—he spoke to all of us, and he materialized*

*a silver pendant for my daughter. She wears it. And he materialized a*
*card for me—one of his calling cards—just waved his hand like this (*Int.
Ref. # 21*).*

The trip to India—particularly the organized tour—is not an easy
one: there are the usual conflicts between strangers who must live
together, and the discomforts of life in India for people not accustomed
to those conditions. One tour leader recounted, with some amusement,
the things that took place during the first trip he led to Bangalore:

*When we got there we didn't get our full amount of rooms—we got two*
*rooms for seventeen people! So I said, "Well, look, I will be sleeping in*
*the corridor." [A friend] said he will sleep in the corridor—that's two*
*couples. And then, so, everybody started sleeping in the corridor! So the*
*room was left for just two or three ladies. And then one of the fellows*
*. . . [Mr. R] . . . he started to quarrel and talk: "This kind of place!" I*
*said, "My dear friend . . . the guide spoke to you all and asked you—*
*twice, not once—to make up your mind that where you are going is not*
*a luxury place. . . . There's no hotel there—you are going by Baba! If*
*you don't want to go, stay here. And after he finished . . . I spoke to*
*you—I said, 'We are all about to leave—make up your mind . . . .' And*
*you all said, 'Yes!' Then why quarrel when you come to see God?" And*
*Mr. [R] said: "To hell with God!" (*Int. Ref. # 22*).*

The expenses and the discomforts are all worth it, say devotees. The
first sight of Sathya Sai Baba walking out of the ashram for his morning
darshan, many people say, repays them for the whole trip. Still, all
hope that the Godman will notice them personally, despite the size of
the crowd, and perhaps even smile or speak to them:

*The first time I went to India—it was in 1982. And the first morning that*
*I waked in Puttaparthi—in Prasanti Nilayam—and I went to darshan,*
*Baba left the ashram and came* direct *to me—and stand in front of me—*
*and speak to me. He ask me, "Where you came from?" Tears came in*
*my eyes, and my mouth open, and I look up at him, and I couldn't speak*
*for a couple minutes, and then I told him, "Trinidad." And he told me,*
*"I see, I see." That was the first* day *I was in Puttaparthi—when I awoke*
*there! (*Int. Ref. # 23*).*

And, of course, the pilgrim dreams of something even greater: of
being summoned to audience with the avatar:

*We had two interviews on that occasion. At the first interview, Sai Baba—*
*he spoke to a few of the devotees: there were thirty-two in that group at*
*that time, and I remember a few of the things that took place. For example,*

*he asked, "How many members in the group?" And we said, "Thirty-two." And Baba said, "Thirty-two? All right—I'll show you my card." And he did like this [circular motion of the hand] and produced thirty-two call cards with his picture—and he himself went and gave each person one. And as he gave the last one, he said, "See? Exact: thirty-two."*

*And there were other things materialized. He produced vibhuti, and gave it to a sick child. He materialized a pendant, and gave it to another little girl. . . . He materialized a ring—with his image—and gave it to a doctor. He's a plastic surgeon in Port of Spain. He was with us (Int. Ref. # 24).*

The fortunate pilgrim who is granted an interview thus believes himself to be in the very presence of God—who is performing miracles before the devotee's very eyes. It is understandable that the devotee remembers every word that Sai Baba says. Many try, in a spirit of devotion mixed with a bit of humor, to imitate the Godman's pronunciation and grammar: they feel his speech patterns are part of what they perceive as divine playfulness—since, they believe, if he wished he could easily speak in any language and command any accent.

Many have come away from interviews convinced that he was reading their minds—turning to them and answering questions they had not voiced aloud. Many ponder the nuances of every word, every gesture, of Sai Baba—for everything that happens in his presence, they feel, has profound meaning:

*Within our group, there was a lady—she had a bottle of ghee [clarified butter] from Trinidad taken to India to give Baba—she rushed in her room [when the summons to an interview came] to bring that, and it fell on the way coming out—it spilled right there. Baba don't want anything from you—he can't stop you from bringing it—all he can let you bring it and he can refuse it (Int. Ref. # 25).*

Pilgrimage, Victor Turner has demonstrated, is a liminal (or, at any rate, a "liminoid") experience: the participant moves out of the normal matrix of activity and relationship into a marginal and temporary betwixt-and-between social landscape until the return home (Turner 1978: 34–35). It might certainly be argued, however, that from the perspective of the Sai Baba devotee the ordinary world of job and family is the marginal one—and that the only true reality is sitting in the presence of Sai Baba. The devotee returns home and (seemingly) resumes his or her normal pattern of life—including attendance at satsangs, singing together with Sai Baba.

It may be that the rule against "socializing" at satsangs reflects the sense that the devotee—even at home, even in a Sai Centre—is really forever still back in Puttaparthi, ever alone at the feet of the living avatar:

*I went back for the "Third World Conference" in the same year—1980, again—and unfortunately I haven't been back until now and I'm looking forward to go this year for the World Conference—and the Birthday.*

*([Ques] Do you think there will be a big crowd?) Oh! Oh! But it is heavenly there! I don't think of the discomforts—because, just think what about what the yogis and the rishis went through in the Golden Age—in days gone by—and they never had darshan! (Int. Ref. # 26).*

# 11

## The Politics of Revitalization

### Revitalization in Trinidad

There is no one summary statement that can encompass all Trinidad Indian behavior and interest—but turned around that observation points to the absence of conformity, to the presence of multiple options. Furthermore, it is obvious, the wealthier the Indian—the more educated, the more removed from the traditional village matrix, the more cosmopolitan—the greater the number of options available to him and to her.

Trinidad is changing, we have observed, and the lives of the Indian people are undergoing particularly dramatic alteration. Within the space of a quarter-century, the horizons of the majority of Indo-Trinidadians have widened from the edge of their village to the total planet: they have television, they travel to far countries, they have full access to world issues and global culture.

And so we are reminded of—and must return to—Anthony Wallace's suggestions as to the circumstances that so frequently lead to the emergence of a "revitalization movement": when there are serious identity dilemmas, when there are too many cultural elements to choose among, when behavior is no longer even minimally predictable, and so on. Surely, the Trinidad Indian matrix is fertile soil for the emergence of a revitalization movement!

Swallow, it may be remembered, concluded that the Sai Baba movement in India could be approached—among other ways—as an example of revitalization. It seems to me, however, that *revitalization in Trinidad*—as represented by the Sai Baba movement there—has emerged as something quite different.

Clearly, of course, the Sai Baba movement in India constitutes a response to disorganization and a multiplicity of choices among a segment of the present population of India. Swallow discusses some of the reasons middle-class Indians—particularly those attempting to juggle Western education and values along with traditional Indian education and values—find the teachings of Sai Baba so attractive. My own observations of American men and women attending Sai Baba satsangs in New York point to "revitalization" dimensions of the movement there, as well.

Nevertheless, I would argue, there are significant differences between the movement in Trinidad, and the movement elsewhere. In India, as we have seen, the teachings of both Shrdi and Sathya Sai Baba are only minimally different from those of other Hindu gurus: the messages are the same about the nature of God, of the universe, of the human soul—about *moksha* and how to achieve it—and about most else. True, individuals may turn to Sathya Sai Baba because he—for them—cuts through the confusion and complexity and contradiction as no other guru can . . . and so, for them, he serves the functions Wallace has set forth for "revitalization." But for their neighbors, another guru—with essentially the same message—is more attractive. . . . And all this, we know, is intrinsic to Hinduism itself: the belief system revolves around Godmen who preach essentially the same message, and each attracts his own dedicated following. A Sai Baba devotee from India, we have seen, asserted only that she followed and accepted him because she could relate to him, and because she felt that listening to him had made her a better person.

Obviously, then, the teachings of Sai Baba in India do take on a "revitalization" dimension—but, equally obviously, to approach it on the subcontinent solely from that point of view is to distort it seriously: Swallow, White, Bharati, and Babb—despite their points of disagreement—all concur in seeing it as simply a variant of the ideological complexity that is Hinduism.

Again, for the United States and other countries where the followers are primarily of non-Indian and non-Hindu background, whatever "revitalization" may be occurring can hardly be interpreted as a "nativistic" form, as is clearly the case in Trinidad. I do not propose, however—at least in this work—to undertake such an analysis; it would take me too far afield. What is obvious is that there is no one simple explanation of Sai Baba's attraction that fits all cultural contexts (apart, that is, from the one offered by devotees: each has been personally summoned by the avatar).

In Trinidad, however, we observe that the movement has attracted a very specific set of devotees: people who are of Indian descent but whose cultural matrix is very different from those of people actually born in India. Even more specifically, the Sai Baba movement scores its greatest success among the segment of the Indian population that is wealthy, educated, and essentially cosmopolitan in outlook.

For Trinidad, then, the questions become: Why is the need for "revitalization" so pressing among this particular group? Why have they turned to the Sai Baba movement, over all the options available to them?

### Inside the Indian Community

It is important to note again that traditional Trinidad village Hinduism was in difficulty twenty-five years ago. The claim of Brahmans to sole right to religious leadership already troubled village Hindus, who were clearly affected by notions of universality and equality. Western education, along with pressures of Christian missionaries plus the social and ideological patterns of the dominant and prestigious, but non-Hindu, part of the Trinidad population, all conspired, even then, to make thoughtful Indo-Trinidadians critical of, and judgmental about, their Indian heritage and practices.

Which is not to say that the Indians were renouncing their traditional religion and other practices: most continued to subscribe to them, and from my most recent visits to Amity I have concluded that by and large they still do. But retention has been most selective: marriage rules and relations between the sexes and the age cohorts now approximate that of the larger Trinidad society;[1] dietary rules are still obeyed by some, but are increasingly being ignored, as are the traditional dress codes.

Even more significant for our concerns here, perhaps, is the almost total relinquishment of traditional caste restrictions—except for those maintained by Brahmans. In a way, therefore, the conflict between Brahman and non-Brahman has intensified: it is no longer some form of "We share the same values but we don't like the Brahmans lording it over us" but "We not only don't like Brahman assertions of superiority—we don't even share their values!"

And yet, the Brahman remains the cornerstone of Trinidad Hinduism; the only one entitled to conduct prayers, and usually the only one with the training to do so. Thus, before the coming of Sai Baba's teachings to Trinidad, though there were choices available to the cosmopolitan Indo-Trinidadian for cultural identification and religious expression, for many these choices were often perceived as unsatisfactory. For the most part, if one opted to be an "Indian" and a "Hindu" one was forced to subjugate one's education, knowledge of the world and of people, and one's sensitivities, to those of a Brahman pandit. This meant, usually, to a man whose sole claim to greater access to divinity was hereditary—whose knowledge of both ritual and theology had simply been acquired at his father's knee.

There are, of course, young Brahman men who are interested in, and who acquire, Western education. Almost invariably, however, such men move into other occupations, leaving the priestly practice to their more traditional brothers bounded by rural horizons, who for all practical purposes are literate only in Hindi or Sanskrit, and who are thus practitioners of what would be, for India, "village-level" religion (see, for example, Marriott 1955; Babb 1975; Klass 1978: 131–189; etc.).

In some societies, it may well be, a wealthy, educated, cosmopolitan class could, with reasonable ease, exercise significant control over the quality and practice of religion. This turned out not to be true for the Trinidad Hindus. As we have seen, the official organization of all Brahman priests is the Sanatan Dharma Maha Sabha. This body sets the standards for the practice of Hinduism in Trinidad and has successfully driven opposition groups such as the Arya Samaj out of existence. It even claims the right to pass on the admission to Trinidad of all itinerant swamis and gurus from India. The Maha Sabha has acquired, for reasons growing out of the history of Indians in Trinidad, almost sole authority over the social and educational concerns of Hindus in Trinidad. It has sponsored the creation of a network of schools, and has worked for the passage of laws—permitting cremation, Hindu marriage, etc.—desired by the Hindu community.

Nevertheless, the Maha Sabha has made little effective effort to monitor or improve the theological knowledge or practice of the Brahman priesthood. Most of all, it has resisted any effort by non-Brahmans, however educated, to participate meaningfully in the supervision of religion. Thus, when Maha Sabha officials, in 1985, spoke of the proposed establishment sometime in the future of a theological training school for young pandits, they referred only to instructors to be brought from India; there was no sense that anyone in Trinidad, particularly outside of the priestly community, could have anything useful to contribute to the plans or to the curriculum. In any event, no such training school had come into existence even five years later.

Distinguished non-Brahman Trinidadian Hindus are of course accorded respectful treatment by the Maha Sabha: jurists, businessmen, doctors and educators are frequently invited to address gatherings, to serve as judges in children's contests, and otherwise to contribute to the programs of the Maha Sabha. Unless they are also Brahmans, however, they are rarely made members of the Maha Sabha central leadership, and even Brahmans who are not also practicing pandits find themselves excluded from Maha Sabha decision-making: the claim is that, after all, it is primarily a priestly body.

Nor can those who chafe at the control of the Sanatan Dharma Maha Sabha do much to challenge it: the battles with opposing Hindu religious organizations are over, and the Maha Sabha has won. It controls (and in many cases owns) most rural Hindu temples and has the power to expel those who object to its proceedings or political positions. It even claims the power (rarely invoked) to deny the services of any Hindu pandit—to perform a marriage, to conduct prayers—to people whose beliefs and practices are offensive to the principles of the Maha Sabha.

Thus, those Trinidadians of education and wealth, of cosmopolitan interest and experience, who wished to continue to be Hindus, who often writhed in embarrassment at public meetings and private ceremonies at which Hinduism was represented and presented by men they perceived as narrow-minded, morally questionable, semi-literate, and speaking substandard English, found they had few options available to them.

They could, of course, opt out of Hinduism. The Canadian Mission to Trinidad in the nineteenth century gave rise to the present flourishing—largely Indian—Presbyterian community of Trinidad and Tobago, and the Indian component of Trinidad Roman Catholics and other Christian groups is also substantial. Another alternative might be Islam, which claims some 60,000 adherents in the nation, again mostly Indian. And, finally, one could of course give up all religious affiliation.

None of these are satisfactory alternatives for most Indo-Trinidadians. To become Christian is, in the eyes of Hindu (and Muslim) Trinidad Indians, to move away from the Indian ethnic group, to begin the immersion in non-Indian culture that may end with intermarriage and the obliteration of all distinctions. Some Christian Indians contest this view; there are families that have been Presbyterian or Roman Catholic for generations and that nevertheless have continued to marry within, and to identify with, the Indian community (or at least the Christian component of it) without great difficulty. On the other hand, those who convert to the evangelical or pentecostal sects find it almost impossible to maintain relationships with Hindu relatives and friends, even if they wish to. In any case, for Indians who were born Hindus the Christian alternative clearly appears to be unattractive.

And, whatever the attractions of Islam in India in past centuries, there seems to be little movement to that religion by Hindus in contemporary Trinidad. The Pakistan/India conflict and separation is probably a factor, but so are hostilities indigenous to Trinidad: many Hindus, for example, resent support by Trinidad Indian Muslims of "non-Indian" political groups. In addition, Islam in Trinidad is not without examples of conflicts similar to those of Trinidad Hinduism: the increasing insistence on orthodoxy of behavior—such as dietary restrictions and modest dress for women—is apparent even in urban areas.

Finally, religion has been, and remains, an important component of life in Trinidad, and the option of eschewing all religion is not a popular one, either. Most schools are still run by one religious body or another, though the government now controls the secular part of the curriculum. Radio and television stations broadcast religious services and messages; prayer meetings, revival tents, Ramayan yagnas, and a multitude of other religious events occur all the time in all parts of the island. If Trinidad has become cosmopolitan, it is still a church-going cosmopolitan island, and those who reject religion entirely find themselves in a small, and in certain ways socially-impoverished, minority.

## Universality and Equality

Into this stressful situation has come the movement inspired by the universalistic teachings of Sathya Sai Baba of India. I would suggest, to begin with, that the very fact that it comes directly from India is of crucial importance—and so is the fact that it is overtly universalistic.

In my earlier work on Amity, I referred to the cachet, the power of validation, to be found in anything that could be demonstrated to have come from India—such as wedding garments or behavior in wedding processions observed in movies (Klass 1961: 209). To non-Indians (in Trinidad, Europe, United States), to say that the teachings of Sai Baba come from India is perhaps equivalent to saying they come from Japan: that is, that they derive from an exotic but contemporary source. Trinidad Indians of course realize that Sai Baba lives in modern India, but they also respond to India as timeless—the land from which they derive—unchanging, authoritative, holy. A set of teachings from India, therefore, can be simultaneously perceived as something from a dearer, purer past—and something that is modern and in the forefront of world developments.

To Trinidadian Indians, Sai Baba's teachings awake echoes of childhood experiences: men and women sitting separately at religious services (the women modest in veils, and not in pantsuits); the musical instruments and the bhajans that were omnipresent in East Indian villages two or three decades ago. To attend a satsang, to become a devotee, is to eliminate choices—to return to devotional (and, usually, dietary) practices that one has given up, but somehow still longs for.

But, at the same time, one is not immersing one's educated Western cosmopolitan mind in a "primitive" religion that is the object of scorn to others of one's social matrix: this is a *universalistic* faith, subscribed to by wealthy and educated people of all nations. The visitor is continually told: "Supreme Court justices in India follow Baba!" "The brother of the [then] Prime Minister of Italy is also a devotee!" "The Prime Minister of Trinidad and Tobago is said to have a picture of Baba on his desk!"

Sai Baba has said that everyone in the world will soon accept him as God—but meanwhile a Trinidadian taxi-driver can go to India, the land of his ancestors and, after touring in Kashmir and shopping in Bombay, have an interview with God: a man who like himself was born a Hindu.

Further, the Sai Baba movement presents those Indians who felt alienated from traditional Hinduism, and yet tied to it, with an attractive alternative. A devotee of Sai Baba in Trinidad can be as much of a traditional Hindu—or as little!—as he or she wishes. Some devotees continue to invite their family pandits to perform marriages and conduct prayers exactly as they did in the past; others claim to have freed themselves completely from reliance on pandits—both meet happily in the Sai Centre and accept the other as fellow devotees of Sai Baba.

The Sai Centre itself has of course no need whatever of the Brahman pandit (though there are some who are devotees, and even some who are leaders). Any devotee, of any caste (or, indeed, of none) may play the instruments, join in the singing of bhajans, perform *arati,* and—best of all—lead the singing: there is nothing in the service that either requires or rejects the participation of the Brahman pandit. Those Brahmans who have moved to the fore within the movement have done so on the basis of their own individual knowledge of religion or philosophy and their own leadership traits. One may of course argue that Brahmans start with a certain advantage in matters of religion and leadership, but they cannot, in the Sai Centre, move to the fore solely on the basis of claimed hereditary right—nor can anyone be pushed to the rear solely on the grounds of low-caste membership, or even non-Indian heritage. In the Sai movement in Trinidad, caste inequality is totally obliterated.

Those devotees who wish to may continue to call upon orthodox Brahman pandits to perform marriages and other services—and many do. Those who do not wish to, however, need not: many Sai devotees have replaced most or all of their former prayers with regular home satsangs, with bhajan-singing instead of the pandit-administered rituals. There have been marriages among devotees without the services of pandits: the young couple is formally and legally married before a non-denominational government Registrar—then returns home for a satsang in which the young people declare themselves married in the name of Sathya Sai Baba.

Furthermore, there are Brahman pandits (upper-class, educated, cosmopolitan) among the devotees, and these can perform weddings and preside, if invited, at yagnas and prayer meetings—and, if they do, they accept no payment or gift for so presiding. They, and other devotees, point out that there is never a collection at a satsang, and that all devotees invariably contribute their services freely to other devotees.

## The Indo-Trinidadian Future

There is no question that all this has seriously disturbed the leaders of the Sanatan Dharma Maha Sabha, but they are divided about how to respond to the challenge. Shall they treat the Sai movement as a perversion of Hinduism—shall its members be excommunicated? There are some who have in fact proposed this: a communication to practicing pandits has been made, advising them not to permit pictures of Sathya Sai Baba at services over which they preside, and to refuse to officiate at such marriages or prayers. They are advised to object to bhajans that are revised to include the name of Sathya Sai Baba, and so on. In communities where there is strong interest in Sai Baba, such as Marabella, there have been incidents of pandits lecturing in the streets to passersby, claiming that Sathya Sai Baba is a charlatan and no avatar.

The difficulty, of course, is that Hinduism lacks the centricity of authority characteristic of many Western religions. Devotees express amusement at the charges against Sai Baba; they cite scriptural accounts of the rejection of *Rama* and *Krishna* by religious "authorities," and suggest mockingly that the pandits must be wise indeed if they know for certain who is and who is not an avatar.

It may be that some pandits are following the Maha Sabha instructions, but every devotee I questioned—who had recently engaged the services of a pandit—claimed that pictures and bhajans devoted to Sai Baba were used at their affairs without objection from the pandit. Indeed, if the pandit wishes to ignore the Maha Sabha directive, the organization cannot prevent him from practicing: his power to do so comes from his father, not from them. And, finally, the notion of "excommunication" is structurally contradictory to Hinduism—which is, after all, a body of faith built around the principle of *maya,* divine illusion precipitating confusion, error, and uncertainty.

Within the Sanatan Dharma Maha Sabha, therefore, there is another position advanced on the Sai movement: Do not oppose it. The proponents of this position argue that the Sai movement is not a threat to the Maha Sabha in the long run, even if it poses some immediate problems. They note that the movement attracts people who had dropped away from Hinduism—and brings them back: such people begin to observe the dietary laws they had given up, they study Hindi and the sacred books, they learn bhajans (even in doctored forms), and, most important, they raise their children to have a much deeper knowledge of, and interest in, Hinduism. Therefore, these leaders argue, the children of such devotees can be expected to return fully to the fold one day; their parents, the Sai devotees, are imperfect Hindus but they may well be perfect conduits for the return to orthodoxy of their children.

Sai devotees—many of them educated, worldly, and in many cases deeply involved, as teachers and lawyers and such, in the affairs of the Maha Sabha—are aware of all these arguments, and are not troubled by them. The view of some is that the Sanatan Dharma Maha Sabha is a provincial Trinidad organization; the Sathya Sai movement is a world-wide body and thus transcends local issues. Others, more interested in local affairs, foresee an eventual peaceful absorption of the Maha Sabha *into* the Sathya Sai movement—both because Sai Baba has predicted that all religions will eventually recognize him, and because they believe that more and more of the influential Indians of the island, including even officials of the Maha Sabha, are turning to Sai Baba . . . and so, they suggest, one day Sai Baba devotees will peacefully constitute the controlling element within that body.

Whatever the future may hold for the relationship between the Sathya Sai organization and the Sanatan Dharma Maha Sabha—both of Trinidad and Tobago—there can be no doubt that the coming of Sai Baba's teachings to that nation has effectively changed sociopolitical relations within the Indian community. There is now, for those who want it, a legitimate *Hindu* way around the Brahman/Maha Sabha authority structure: there is a respectable, India-sanctioned, tradition-observing place for the Western-educated world-oriented Indian. He is free to accept the village pandit or reject him and still remain an observant Hindu—work with the traditional religious organization on both religious and political matters or ignore it completely—without losing strength in battles over religion and politics.

Earlier, I asked how we might apply Louis Dumont's overarching categories—"Homo hierarchicus" in India, "Homo aequalis" in Europe—to the Indians of Trinidad. I now suggest that, after a century and a half in the West Indies, the Trinidad Indian is *both*—and *neither*. That is, he subscribes in some measure to both systems, but to neither completely.

It could be argued, for example, that the Trinidad Indian has given up such diagnostic (according to Dumont) features of "hierarchy" as caste ranking, marital restrictions, dietary rules, and untouchability. He has given them up—but we have seen that he has not yet *completely* given them up.

Within the Trinidad Indian community, some Brahmans still claim, *and are accorded,* front rank: in religion and in the major nationwide ethnic organization. Caste endogamy, occupation limitations, and diet restrictions have all seemingly disappeared (again, except for Brahmans), but they may in fact only have undergone a sea change. After my first Trinidad study, I suggested that the Indian community was beginning to perceive *itself* as a caste, as against all the other groups with which it was in contact (Klass 1961: 246). This perception, even if largely an unconscious one, may still be detected.

The Amity villager, we observe, still objects to association with the Afro-Trinidadian, whom he considers uncouth in manner and diet (traditional "untouchable" characteristics), and does his best to prevent marriage of his children with Afro-Trinidadians, expelling ("outcasteing"?) those who do. But, oddly, marriage of daughters with Europeans is accepted and approved, even though it almost invariably means the daughter will move far away: does this not hint of hypergamy (the practice, in many parts of India, of approving the marriage of a daughter to a man of higher caste)?

The Indian population of Trinidad and Tobago, we might say, is composed of representatives of both "Homo hierarchicus" and "Homo aequalis." More than that, Indian families are often composed of both types. And even more than that—individual Indians are often pulled both ways, sometimes simultaneously!

Thus, as we have seen, a non-Brahman family may attend services (as in Amity) at the "Vishnu Mandir" established by Basraj Bridglal as an alternative to Brahmanical control—yet refuse to accept the services of a non-Brahman pandit for the marriage of one of their children. Is this because the family of the in-marrying spouse objects— or because the head of the household himself, while resenting and in principle rejecting Brahmanical control of religion in practice finds himself unable to accept a non-Brahman as a "real" priest—or both?

Whatever the conflict between "Homo hierarchicus" and "Homo aequalis" in the mind of any given Indo-Trinidadian, politically there had existed a clear imbalance within the Indian *community:* authority and power was almost exclusively in the hands of "Homo hierarchicus"—the village pandit and the Sanatan Dharma Maha Sabha. "Homo aequalis" either acknowledged the leadership of "Homo hierarchicus" or withdrew (politically, if not physically) from the Indian community.

The teachings of Sathya Sai Baba, however, provided the Indo-Trinidadian "Homo aequalis" with an alternative: an egalitarian, universalistic, Western-acceptable but *India-derived* belief system—and *organization.* The Trinidad Indian value system had become bipolar, but the internal political structure was still unipolar—"hierarchical" organization versus "egalitarian" individuals—and the Sai movement fills the structural gap: I would argue that there are now signs of an emerging political bipolarity, in which "Homo aequalis"—Sai-inspired—will contend on equal organizational and ideological footing with "Homo hierarchicus," perhaps even within the Sanatan Dharma Maha Sabha itself.

## On the National Scene

The movement deriving from the teachings of Sathya Sai Baba, as we have just seen, affects relationships within the Trinidad Indian community. That Indian community, however, is of course very much part of the larger Trinidad society. In that context it becomes important to observe again that the message of Sathya Sai Baba is a universalistic one: all religions have merit, but now must be incorporated into the new faith that recognizes Sai Baba in all his incarnations as the living avatar of universal divinity.

The Sai Baba movement is therefore very much a proselytizing faith, and we have seen that it initially attracted Afro-Trinidadians as well as Indo-Trinidadians. Nevertheless, though the former are still welcome—indeed, are treated with every courtesy—their number has not grown at all, and hardly a dozen were attending satsangs in 1985. And, still further, while Afro-Trinidadians who found their ways to Sai Baba were welcomed, there was no discernible effort on the part of any Sai Centre or the Co-ordinating Council itself to proselytize among Afro-Trinidadians.

What emerges, therefore, is that while the message of Sathya Sai Baba may be everywhere else a universalistic and all-embracing one, in Trinidad and Tobago it is presented and received as a variety of Hinduism. Why should this have occurred?

The issue is clearly complex, containing as it does a number of seeming paradoxes, and I suspect the explanation I am about to offer is only one of many that can be made. In any case, I propose to approach the question—*Why has the Trinidad Sai movement failed to attract non-Indians?*—by leaning heavily upon some of the insights to be found in the work of Claude Lévi-Strauss. He has made us aware, particularly, of the importance, in human societies, of duality—of structural oppositions, congruences, contradictions.

For, surely, if there is opposition in the on-going relationship between Trinidadians of Indian and African derivation, there is also a recurrent contradiction, one that often irritates the Afro-Trinidadian and embarrasses the Indo-Trinidadian: the Indo-Trinidadian strongly resents being treated as an outsider and an alien, but then continually rejects all overtures from the Afro-Trinidadian to come together to end ethnic distinctiveness.

For example, we noted earlier that Dr. Eric Williams, in the mid-1950s, proposed an end to all divisions between East and West Indians; he promised that the People's National Movement would ignore ethnic, racial, cultural differences as irrelevant, and would, for example, treat rural Indians simply as poor rural people. And, as I observed in my original study, some Trinidad Indians, particularly from the Christian Indian sub-community, supported this position enthusiastically. The majority of Indians, however, rejected the PNM—much to Williams' surprise—and supported political parties dedicated to maintaining the ethnic divide (Klass 1961: 221).

This pattern of behavior seems to run through all areas of Trinidad Indian/African interaction. There are of course examples of Afro-Trinidadian rejection of Indians—of contempt and discrimination—just as there are examples of Indians who desire to see themselves and their ethnic group totally and indistinguishably merged within the Afro-Trinidadian population. Nevertheless, the cry most frequently heard from Afro-Trinidadians seems to be: "We are all one!"—to which the Indian response, if I may be flippant, is some form of: "Include us out!"

The examples of this are legion. The Afro-Trinidadian leaders of the "Black Power" Movement of the 1970s, for example, made what they clearly felt was a determined effort to incorporate the Trinidad Indian population. They attacked and attempted to root out all examples of hostility, discrimination, and contempt on the part of Afro-Trinidadians against Indo-Trinidadians, and at one point a horde of Afro-Trinidadian young people, mostly students, fanned out into the rural areas determined to convince what they sincerely perceived as their Black Indian brothers and sisters that they were indeed all "one." And again, as in the days of the formation of the PNM, only a numerically insignificant proportion of the Indian population responded favorably to the invitation; the majority either ignored the "Black Power" movement or formed opposition groups (Gosine 1986).

What was particularly puzzling for the "Black Power" advocates was that many Indians—particularly young intellectuals and radicals—expressed sympathy for both the underlying ideological position of "Black Power" (that the older political leadership of the nation had been corrupted and co-opted by European and North American values and interests) and the intent of the movement (the transference of power to a younger, less Western- and capitalist-influenced leadership). The Indian intellectuals were apparently eager to work with the "Black Power" movement, but only as a separate-but-equal "Black" organization—

something that was ideologically both incomprehensible and unacceptable to the "Black Power" leadership and following.

By the summer of 1985, "Black Power" had receded in importance
as a political movement, but it was by no means extinguished. On the
campus of UWI, particularly, it still had strong support among students
and faculty—and the efforts of the Afro-Trinidadian and Indo-Trinidadian intellectual leadership to effect some kind of jointure continued,
but still without success.

Many explanations have been advanced for this refusal of Indians
to accept African overtures. One of the earliest, as I have noted, was
the claim that pandits were forcing Hindus to swear on "Ganges water"
that they would not support non-Indian candidates. Scholars have proposed more likely explanations (cf. Klass 1961, Malik 1971, Singh 1974,
Gosine 1984, 1986 etc.), but here—without necessarily quarreling with
any of these latter—I would also point to the possibility of offence
caused by the (often unconscious) hegemonic implications of the offer
to absorb the Indo-Trinidadians.

As an example, let us return to the furor over the calypso "De
Caribbean Man"—something that has not been forgotten by either
group. Afro-Trinidadians were and are much moved by the song, and
it was sung with deep feeling by students at the UWI graduation
exercises in the year of its popularity. UWI Indo-Trinidadian faculty
members, on the other hand, led the opposition on the campus and in
the pages of national newspapers, insisting that "we" did *not* come
"from the same place, on the same boat"—and indeed by 1985 those
intellectuals who were intent on fostering awareness of Indo-Trinidadian
distinctiveness had succeeded in having "Indian Arrival Day" celebrated as a National Holiday for the first time. And, during the celebration, an important Indo-Trinidadian young political leader precipitated a new controversy (in the newspapers and in the halls of parliament)
by calling for more attention to "Indian culture" in Trinidad radio,
newspapers, and television.

To sum this point up: Afro-Trinidadians express in a number of
ways the high value they attribute to sociocultural unity—to ethnic
homogeneity. Integration is perceived as desirable at almost all levels:
marriage, politics, even in the rewriting of history. Note, however, that
I say *almost*: there is in fact one arena where such integration is clearly
not so welcome! And, further, while Indo-Trinidadians overwhelming
reject as threatening and unacceptable most overtures to integration
(marital, political and ethnic)—there is, again, one exception.

## The Structural Reversal

On the matter of *religion,* the positions of the two major ethnic components of Trinidad and Tobago are completely reversed. Afro-Trinidadians (primarily Christian) appear to resist and reject all efforts to amalgamate and integrate separate religious bodies, even Christian denominations. On the other hand, Hindu Indo-Trinidadians, like Hindus in South Asia, perceive a fundamental oneness in all religions, and prefer to focus on the similarities and ignore the differences. Agehananda Bharati, we have seen, concludes that the belief that "all religions are one" is fundamental to the Hindu Renaissance in India—and I have suggested that such a statement becomes, in Trinidad, the Indo-Trinidadian response to the Afro-Trinidadian's "All of we is one."

This difference is illustrated in the Census reports cited earlier. In 1980, the most recent year for which figures are presently available, out of a total population of slightly over one million people, some 654,000 identified themselves as members of Christian churches, while some 263,000 identified themselves as Hindu, and another 63,000 as Muslim (Central Statistical Office [*Annual Statistical Digest*] 1984: 15). As we saw, however, there was a striking difference between the Christian and Hindu religious categories in the Census: On the one hand, there is essentially only one Hindu category; on the other hand, the 654,000 "Christians" of Trinidad and Tobago are in fact neither listed nor counted as such. There are, it seems, eight separate denominations (Anglican, Roman Catholic, Seventh Day Adventist, Baptist, etc.)—all "Christian," but nowhere identified as such. In addition, indeed, the Census occasionally even lumps under one heading groups—such as "Baptists" and "Spiritual Baptists"—whose members are in reality quite antagonistic (Cent. Stat. 1984: 15).

None of this is surprising, of course. Ecumenism is a goal for Western religions that is rarely if ever achieved, and actual merger is even more difficult. Many of the denominations have traditionally denounced others as false or unacceptable as Christians, accusing them even of being agents of the devil. Most Christian groups in Trinidad insist that only by observing the teachings of their specific denomination can one achieve salvation; the teachings of other denominations are seen as leading to damnation. All the denominations proselytize, of course: they welcome anyone who will accept their teachings—but that means invariably the complete rejection of the recruit's original denomination or faith.

Hindus in Trinidad have always found this attitude on the part of Christians puzzling. In my earlier study I reported on the willingness of Amity parents to send their children to Christian religious services— "the 'Word of God' is always beneficial" (1961: 157)—and I noted how hurt and astonished they were when Christians referred to Hinduism as paganism.

This is in no way peculiar to Trinidad, of course: we have observed that the universalistic views of Sai Baba are common to all Hindus. Studying the teachings of other religions, therefore—singing their hymns and decorating one's home with their religious symbols—does not seem threatening to the Hindu. All those things are understood to have valid and intrinsic religious merit: a picture of Jesus next to a picture of *Krishna* next to a picture of Mohammed is neither an abomination nor an insult to a Hindu (whatever it may be to a Christian or a Muslim) but is, rather, an affirmation of religious universality.

What emerges from this analysis, I would argue, is something that almost impels us to turn to Claude Lévi-Strauss for guidance. In his paper, "The Bear and the Barber," for example, he contrasts "caste" and "clan" structurally in the following way: "castes naturalize fallaciously a true culture while totemic groups culturalize truly a false nature" (Lévi-Strauss 1963: 9).

In Trinidad, it seems to me, we may observe the presence of a remarkably analogous Lévi-Straussian type of parallelism-cum-opposition, one that might be expressed by the following formulation:

*Afro-Trinidadians place a high value on sociocultural and ethnic amalgamation but a low value on the blurring of boundaries between belief systems. Indo-Trinidadians place a high value on ideological amalgamation but a low value on the blurring of boundaries between sociocultural or ethnic groups.*

As we observed earlier in this chapter, in our examination of the Indo-Trinidadian community, there is again a bipolarity to be noted, and again it is a somewhat deceptive one.

The ideological opposition formulated above *seems* a balanced one, and the balance is seemingly reinforced by the almost equal representation of the two groups in the population. Nevertheless, there is a weakness, or lacuna, at one pole; in this case that of the Indo-Trinidadian population taken as a whole.

For, while Afro-Trinidadians have traditionally been puzzled by Indo-Trinidadian rejection of their overtures for amalgamation—just as Indo-Trinidadians have been puzzled by Afro-Trinidadian rejection of Hindu overtures—there has been a difference between the two sets of overtures.

The Afro-Trinidadian sociocultural overtures derive from prestigious, universalistic and *world-wide* intellectual movements. These movements reflect the teachings of world-renowned individuals—from Jacques Rousseau to Karl Marx to Martin Luther King to Franz Fanon and beyond—and Indo-Trinidadian intellectuals are well aware of that, considerably to their discomfort.

On the other hand, the Hindu overtures—in the past—were essentially those of illiterate villagers who adhered to what was (in Trinidad) a prestigeless religion of cane laborers, for the philosophical literature of Hinduism was unknown to the educated elements of both ethnic groups.

Though they found themselves somewhat at an intellectual disadvantage, the educated, elite stratum of the Trinidad Indian community nevertheless rejected the Afro-Trinidadian overtures. At the same time, however, such people, alienated from and equally embarrassed by village Hinduism as they were, made no effort to advance the universalism inherent in Hinduism.

## The Politics of Universalism

The coming of the Sai movement appears to have changed the situation quite radically. Those Indo-Trinidadians who subscribe to the teachings of Sathya Sai Baba believe they are part of a worldwide movement, dedicated to the amalgamation of all religions under the umbrella of a Hindu teacher. They have been introduced, through the movement, to the intellectual literature of Hinduism and to dimensions of Hindu thought, ritual, and music which not only transcend the Hinduism of rural Trinidad, but which in their view compete proudly with anything Christianity or Western philosophy can offer.

Given this, a new generation of Indo-Trinidadian leaders is maturing rapidly. Satsangs have been held on the campus of UWI and have attracted students. Intellectual leaders and political hopefuls are to be found in the Sai movement. Mr. Surujrattan Rambachan, for example, conducted what were unquestionably the most popular and prestigious Ramayan yagnas in Trinidad in 1985. Pictures of Sai Baba had pride of place at his yagnas, along with those of the traditional Hindu divinities, and so did the bhajans of Sai Baba. In his discourses, however, Mr. Rambachan—formerly a member of the UWI faculty (and as of 1989 a member of Trinidad's diplomatic corps)—drew upon Western philosophy and psychology, demonstrating, in almost classic Hindu fashion, their similarities to Hindu philosophy and theology.

The major effort of the Sai Baba movement, of course, is concentrated on spreading the word throughout the Indian population. The intellectual leadership of the Indian community appears to be swinging to the Sai movement. With the help of the teachings of Sathya Sai Baba and through the organized Sai movement now burgeoning in Trinidad, they hope to transmit, particularly to young Indo-Trinidadians, the understanding that Indian culture is at least the equal of anything emanating from the West.

What effect will this have on the political scene in Trinidad and Tobago? It is of course much too early to tell. I argued in an earlier part of this chapter that the emergence of the Sai Baba movement was precipitating changes within the Indo-Trinidadian community. Some of these changes could be noticed already; many, however, are still in only the most formative stage. The changes in the relations between Indo- and Afro-Trinidadian suggested by the foregoing analysis are of course even further in the future, if indeed they take place at all: political parties are formal organizations, often with impermeable structures and with rigidly ensconced leadership cadres.

Nevertheless, the political scene in Trinidad remains in flux: Kevin A. Yelvington reports that ethnic conflict continues to affect voting patterns and party structure in the island nation. The "ostensibly multi-ethnic National Alliance for Reconstruction (NAR)" (Yelvington: 1991) has lost ground as new, ethnically oriented parties have been formed— or, like the PNM, experienced a resurgence. Devotees of Sathya Sai Baba are to be found in many of the parties and may be expected, given their social and economic status, to play an increasing role in future elections.

\*     \*     \*

We have observed, let me conclude, that the teachings of Sathya Sai Baba appeal particularly to the educated, the worldly, the urbane among the Indian population of Trinidad and Tobago. For them, it is in the first instance a revitalization movement enabling them to cut through the bewildering array of alternatives clamoring for their attention and to return (as they see it) to a simpler and purer form of their ancestral faith, one from which they had become intellectually alienated, but to which they remained emotionally very much attached.

But with that return—with that revitalization—there have been dividends, potentially of great moment for these Sai devotees. Few people, of course, are consciously and totally aware of all the dividends—but I would argue that most devotees sense one or more of the advantages to be accrued:

*On the one hand, the movement provides a way in which devotees can evade the control of the Indian community by the village pandits and the Sanatan Dharma Maha Sabha—without themselves leaving Hinduism and the Indian community. Potentially, it is an avenue through which they may achieve the leadership of that community, and perhaps even of the Sanatan Dharma Maha Sabha.*

*And, on the other hand, it provides the devotees with what they perceive as an intellectually valid and respectable basis for maintaining Indian culture and ethnic separation. Even further, it has the potential to provide a source of political strength and even ideological strength, when viewed as a Hindu alternative to Western-derived philosophy and religion.*

Of course, none of the above was intended, as far as we can tell, by Sathya Sai Baba. As a living avatar, he offers a way to *moksha* for the individual in the future—and, in the present, a way to the enhancement of life through adherence to his teachings of love, peace, non-violence, truth, and good-works.

True, as his emissaries to Trinidad point out, these teachings are intended for people of *all* races and religions: why, some have asked, has the Sai Movement in Trinidad become restricted to people of Indian descent—why do the Sai Centres not go out actively and purposefully to proselytize the Afro-Trinidadians?

The Trinidad Sai devotees are distressed when these issues are raised: they explain that the Indian population seems more interested while the Afro-Trinidadians are more resistant; they note that the Sai movement *is* growing, and they need time to teach the present membership and put the organization on a firm footing. Then—they say, and clearly believe—they will reach out to the Afro-Trinidadians: they will broadcast Sai Baba's message of universal love and one all-embracing God. Just as they believe that one day the Pope will sit at the feet of Sathya Sai Baba, so too will Afro-Trinidadians become one with Indo-Trinidadians, united in the worship of the avatar.

However, universalistic messages, as we have noted in the case of Afro-Trinidadian overtures, can be seen or felt to have an imperialistic or hegemonic dimension. Christian missionaries—and not only in Trinidad—often in the past endeavored to do much more than simply spread the word that Christ had risen. Converts were expected to change their diets, their clothing, their marital and family patterns and much more, so as to conform not just to a belief system but to the culture of European societies.

Consider then the following words of Sathya Sai Baba (as cited by the devotee Fanibunda):

"Let the different faiths exist, let them flourish and let the glory of God be sung in all the languages and in a variety of tunes. That should be the Ideal. Respect the differences between the faiths and recognise them as valid *as long as they do not extinguish the flame of unity*" (Fanibunda 1976: 109; *italics mine*).

One may argue that, in that passage, Sai Baba was offering nothing but love and total ecumenism—but one may still understand how the part of the sentence I have italicized might offend and even frighten those who treasure their own religious teachings and see the "differences" as perhaps more important than the goal of "unity."

Whatever Sathya Sai Baba may or may not intend, in Trinidad the religion that has emerged from his teachings is understood by Indian and non-Indian alike to be a form of Hinduism, and the rules of dress and diet and behavior are those that derive from India. A few Afro-Trinidadians are willing to accept this, as a condition for becoming devotees—the overwhelming majority clearly can not.

In the West Indian nation of Trinidad and Tobago the Sai movement has become an (overseas) Indian revitalization movement, a new and intrusive element inside the Indian community, and a factor to be reckoned with in inter-ethnic relationships. Both Indo-Trinidadians and Afro-Trinidadians respond to it in these terms—Afro-Trinidadians, particularly, by exhibiting (after an initial degree of interest) little or no desire to join the movement.

Thus, it is true that Sathya Sai Baba, in his way, preaches that the "End of Time" is coming; that by the end of his lifetime, and certainly during the lifetime of his successor, Prema Sai Baba, *Peace* and *Love* will envelop the world. His followers in Trinidad believe this as fervently as devotees anywhere.

But, until then, it would seem, they find they must live in the world as it is presently constructed. Happily for them, the teachings of Sathya Sai Baba appear to be serviceable in that endeavor, as well.

### Notes

1. "Approximation" should not be interpreted as implying total "identity": in south Trinidad, according to Aisha Khan (*personal communication*), arranged marriages (known as "fix-ups") still occur under certain circumstances, and the rules of dating for Indo-Trinidadians are not exactly the same as those for Afro-Trinidadians.

# References

Alleyne, J. M. 1975 "The Creolization of Africans and Indians." In *East Indians in the Caribbean: A Symposium on Contemporary Economics and political Issues* (Faculty of Social Sciences and Institute of African and Asian Studies, U.W.I., sponsors). Trinidad and Tobago: University of the West Indies (Unpaginated volume).

Babb, Lawrence A. 1975 *The Divine Hierarchy: Popular Hinduism in Central India.* New York: Columbia University Press.

————. 1983 "Destiny and Responsibility: Karma in Popular Hinduism." In *Karma: An Anthropological Inquiry.* (C. F. Keyes and E. V. Daniel, eds). Berkeley: University of California Press, pp. 163–181.

————. 1986 *Redemptive Encounters: Three Modern Styles in the Hindu Tradition.* Berkeley: University of California Press.

Barth, Fredrik (ed.) 1969 *Ethnic Groups and Boundaries: The Social Organization of Cultural Differences.* Boston: Little, Brown and Company.

Bharati, Agehananda 1965 *The Tantric Tradition.* London: Rider.

————. 1970 "The Hindu Renaissance and its Apologetic Patterns." *Journal of Asian Studies.* 29,2: 267–287.

Boxill, Courtney 1975 "From East Indian to Indo Trinidadian." In *East Indians in the Caribbean: A Symposium on Contemporary Economics and Political Issues* (Faculty of Social Sciences and Institute of African and Asian Studies, U.W.I., sponsors). Trinidad and Tobago: University of the West Indies (Unpaginated volume).

Braithwaite, Lloyd 1953 "Social Stratification in Trinidad: A Preliminary Analysis." *Social and Economic Studies* 2: 1–175.

————. 1960 "Social Stratification and Cultural Pluralism." In *Social and Cultural Pluralism in the Caribbean* (V. Rubin, ed.). Annals of the New York Academy of Sciences 83, 5: 816–836. Reprinted in *Peoples and Cultures of the Caribbean: An Anthropological Reader* (M. M. Horowitz, ed.). 1971, Garden City, N.Y.: The Natural History Press, pp. 25–38.

Brent, Peter 1972 *Godmen of India.* London: Allen Lane The Penguin Press.

Brereton, Bridget 1974 "The Experience of Indentureship: 1845–1917." In *Calcutta to Caroni: The East Indians of Trinidad* (J. F. La Guerre, ed.). Trinidad and Jamaica: Longman Caribbean Limited, pp. 25–38.

Brooke, Tal 1979 *Sai Baba: Lord of the Air.* New Delhi: Vikas Publishing House Pvt Ltd.

Central Statistical Office (Trinidad & Tobago) 1958 *Annual Statistical Digest* No. 6 (1956). Trinidad: Government Printing Office.

———. 1984 *Annual Statistical Digest* No. 29 (1982). Trinidad and Tobago: The Central Statistical Office Printing Unit.

Clarke, Colin G. 1967 "Caste among Hindus in a Town in Trinidad: San Fernando." In *Caste in Overseas Indian Communities* (B. M. Schwartz, ed.). San Francisco: Chandler Publishing Company, pp. 165–169.

———. 1986 *East Indians in a West Indian Town: San Fernando, Trinidad, 1930–70.* London: Allen & Unwin.

Cross, Malcolm 1980 *The East Indians of Guyana and Trinidad.* Report No. 13. London: Minority Rights Group Ltd.

Crowley, Daniel J. 1957 "Plural and Differential Acculturation in Trinidad." *American Anthropologist* 59: 817–819.

———. 1960 "Cultural Assimilation in a Multiracial Society." In *Social and Cultural Pluralism in the Caribbean* (V. Rubin, ed.). Annals of the New York Academy of Sciences 83, 5: 850–854. Reprinted in *Slaves, Free Men, Citizens: West Indian Perspectives* (D. Lowenthal, L. Comitas, eds.). Garden City, N.Y.: Doubleday/Anchor Press, pp. 277–285).

Deosaran, Ramesh 1979 " 'The Caribbean Man': A Study of the Psychology of Perception and the Media." In *East Indians in the Caribbean: A Symposium on Contemporary Economics and political Issues.* (Faculty of Social Sciences and Institute of African and Asian Studies, U.W.I., sponsors). Trinidad and Tobago: University of the West Indies (Unpaginated volume).

Dookeran, Winston 1974 "East Indians and the Economy of Trinidad and Tobago." In *Calcutta to Caroni: The East Indians of Trinidad* (J. G. La Guerre, ed.). Trinidad and Jamaica: Longman Caribbean Limited, pp. 69–83.

Dumont, Louis 1970 *Homo Hierarchicus: An Essay on the Caste System.* Chicago: The University of Chicago press.

Durkheim, Émile 1965 *The Elementary Forms of Religious Life.* (Originally published 1915) New York: The Free Press (Translated by Joseph Ward Swain).

Elkin, A. P. 1964 *The Australian Aborigines.* Garden City, N.Y.: Doubleday & Company (The Natural History Library, Anchor Books) (originally published 1938, Angus & Robertson Ltd.).

Faculty of Social Sciences and Institute of African and Asian Studies, U.W.I. (sponsors) 1975 *East Indians in the Caribbean: A Symposium on Contemporary Economics and Political Issues.* Trinidad and Tobago: University of the West Indies (Volume of bound papers, first symposium).

Fanibunda, Eruch B. 1976 *Vision of the Divine* (Reprinted 1981). Prashanti Nilayam: Shri Satya Sai Books and Publications.

Forbes, Richard Huntington 1979 "Arya Samaj as Catalyst: The Impact of a Modern Hindu Reform Movement on the Indian Community of Trinidad between 1917 and 1939." In *The East Indians in the Caribbean: A Symposium on Contemporary Economics and Political Issues.* (Faculty of Social Sciences and Institute of African and Asian Studies, sponsors). Trinidad and Tobago: University of the West Indies (Unpaginated volume).

Frazier, E. Franklin 1948 *The Negro Family in the United States.* (Revised Edition) N.Y.: Holt, Rinehart and Winston, Inc.

Freyre, Gilberto 1964 *The Masters and the Slaves: A Study in the Development of Modern Brazil* (Revised Edition) N.Y.: Knopf.

Gangulee, N. 1947 *Indians in the Empire Overseas.* London: The New India Publishing House.

Glazier, Stephen (ed.) 1985 *Caribbean Ethnicity Revisited* (A Special Issue of *Ethnic Groups: International Periodical of Ethnic Studies*). New York: Gordon and Breach Science Publishers.

Gold, Daniel 1987 *The Lord as Guru: Hindu Sants in North Indian Tradition.* New York (Oxford): Oxford University Press.

Gosine, Mahin 1984 "Culture and Ethnic Participation in a Social Movement: The Case of the East Indians and the Black Power Movement." In *Collected Papers, third Conference on East Indians in the Caribbean, August 28– September 5, 1984.* St. Augustine: University of the West Indies (Unpaginated volume).

———. 1986 *East Indians and Black Power in the Caribbean: the case of Trinidad.* New York: African Research Publications.

Greenfield, Sidney M. 1966 *English Rustics in Black Skin: A Study of Modern Family Forms in a Post-Industrialized Society.* New Haven, Conn.: College & University Press.

Haraksingh, Kusha R. 1984 "The Hindu Experience in Trinidad." In *Collected Papers, third Conference on East Indians in the Caribbean, August 28— September 5, 1984.* St. Augustine: University of the West Indies (Unpaginated volume).

Herskovits, Melville J. 1941 *The Myth of the Negro Past.* New York: Harper & Brothers.

———. 1966 *The New World Negro: Selected Papers in Afroamerican Studies.* (F. S. Herskovits, ed.) Bloomington: Indiana University Press.

Herskovits, Melville J. and Frances S. Herskovits 1934 *Rebel Destiny: Among the Bush Negroes of Dutch Guiana.* New York: McGraw-Hill.

———. 1947 *Trinidad Village.* New York: Knopf.

Horowitz, Michael M. (ed.) 1971 *Peoples and Cultures of the Caribbean: An Anthropological Reader.* Garden City, N.Y.: The Natural History Press.

Jayawardena, Chandra 1963 *Conflict and Solidarity in a Guianese Plantation.* London: London School of Economics Monographs on Social Anthropology, No. 25.

Jenkins, E. 1871 *The Coolie, His Rights and Wrongs.* New York: George Routledge and Sons.

Kasturi, N. 1969 *The Life of Bhagavan Sri Sathya Sai Baba.* Bombay: Dolton Printers.

———. 1981a *Sathya Sai Speaks: Discourses of Bhagavan Sri Sathya Sai Baba* (Vol. 4). Bangalore: Sri Sathya Sai Books and Publications.

———. 1981b *Sathya Sai Baba Speaks: More Discourses given by Bhagavan Sri Sathya Sai Baba* (Vol. 10). Prasanti Nilayam: Sri Sathya Sai Books and Publications.

Keyes, Charles F. 1983 "Introduction: The Study of Popular Ideas of Karma." In *Karma: An Anthropological Inquiry.* (C. F. Keyes and E. V. Daniel, eds.). Berkeley: University of California Press, pp. 1–23.

Keyes, Charles F. and E. Valentine Daniel (eds.) 1983 *Karma: An Anthropological Inquiry.* Berkeley: University of California Press.

Klass, Morton 1959 *Cultural Persistence in a Trinidad East Indian Community.* Department of Anthropology, Columbia University (Ph.D. dissertation).

————. 1960 "East and West Indian: Cultural Complexity in Trinidad." In *Social and Cultural Pluralism in the Caribbean* (V. Rubin, ed.). Annals of the New York Academy of Sciences, 83, 5: 855–861. Reprinted in *Slaves, Free Men, Citizens: West Indian Perspectives* (D. Lowenthal, L. Comitas, eds.). Garden City, N.Y.: Doubleday/Anchor Press 1973, pp. 287–298.

————. 1961 *East Indians in Trinidad: A Study of Cultural Persistence.* New York: Columbia University Press. (Reprinted 1988 Waveland Press)

————. 1978 *From Field to Factory: Community Structure and Industrialization in West Bengal.* Philadelphia: Institute for the Study of Human Issues.

————. 1980a *Caste: The Emergence of the South Asian Social System.* Philadelphia: Institute for the Study of Human Issues.

————. 1980b "Ecology and Family in Two Caribbean East Indian Communities." In *New Ethnics: The Case of the East Indians.* (P. Saran and E. Eames, eds.) New York: Praeger, pp. 48–60.

Kolenda, Pauline Mahar 1963 "Toward a Model of the Hindu Jajmani System." *Human Organization* 22: 11–31.

La Guerre, John Gaffar (ed.) 1974 *Calcutta to Caroni: The East Indians of Trinidad.* Trinidad and Jamaica: Longman Caribbean Limited.

Lévi-Strauss, Claude 1963 "The Bear and the Barber." *The Journal of the Royal Anthropological Institute of Great Britain and Ireland* 93, 1: 1–11.

Lowenthal, David and Lambros Comitas (eds.) 1973 *West Indian Perspectives: (1)Slaves, Free Men, Citizens; (2)Work and Family Life; (3)Consequences of Class and Color; (4)The Aftermath of Sovereignty.* Garden City, N. Y.: Anchor Press/Doubleday.

Mahabir, Kamla 1976 "Satya Sai Movement in Trinidad" (Unpublished thesis) *Caribbean Studies Project,* Faculty of Arts and General Sciences, University of the West Indies, St. Augustine, Trinidad and Tobago.

Malik, Yogendra K. 1971 *East Indians in Trinidad: A Study in Minority Politics.* London: Oxford University Press.

Maring, N. H. 1979 "Cult." In *Encyclopedic Dictionary of Religion* (Vol. 1) (P. K. Meagher, T. C. O'Brian, C. M. Aherne, eds.). Washington, D. C.: Corpus Publications, p. 958.

Marriott, McKim 1955 "Little Communities in an Indigenous Civilization." In *Village India: Studies in the Little Community,* (M. Marriott, ed.). American Anthropological Association Memoir 83.

Mc Martin, Grace J. (ed.) 1982 *A Recapitulation of Satya Sai Baba's Divine Teaching.* Hyderabad: Avon Printing Works.

Mintz, Sidney W. 1985 *Sweetness and Power: The Political, Social and Economic Effects of Sugar in the Modern World.* New York: Viking.

Murphet, Howard 1971 *Sai Baba: Man of Miracles.* Delhi: The Macmillan Company of India Limited.

Neale, Walter C. 1957 "Reciprocity and Redistribution in the Indian Village: Sequel to some Notable Discussions." In *Trade and Market in the Early*

*Empires: Economies in History and Theory* (K. Polanyi, C. M. Arensberg, H. C. Pearson, eds.). Glencoe: Free Press, pp. 218–236.

Neufeldt, Ronald W. (ed.) 1986 *Karma and Rebirth: Post Classical developments.* State University of New York Press.

Nevadomsky, Joseph 1977 *The Changing Family Structure of the East Indians in Rural Trinidad.* Anthropology Department, University of California, Berkeley (Ph.D. dissertation).

――――. 1983a "Changes over Time and Space in the East Indian Family in Rural Trinidad." In *Overseas Indians: A Study in Adaptation* (G. Kurian, R. P. Srivastava, eds.). New Delhi: Vikas Publishing House Pvt Ltd., pp. 180–214.

――――. 1983b "Economic Organization, Social Mobility, and Changing Social Status among East Indians in Rural Trinidad." *Ethnology* 22,1: 63–79.

Niehoff, Arthur 1967 "The Function of Caste among the Indians of the Oropuche Lagoon, Trinidad." In *Caste in Overseas Indian Communities,* B. M. Schwartz, ed). San Francisco: Chandler Publishing Company, pp. 149–163.

Neihoff, Arthur and Juanita Niehoff 1960 *East Indians in the West Indies.* Milwaukee: Milwaukee Public Museum Publications in Anthropology, No. 6.

O'Flaherty, Wendy Doniger 1973 *Asceticism and Eroticism in the Mystery of Siva.* London: Oxford University Press.

O'Flaherty, Wendy Doniger (ed.) 1980 *Karma and Rebirth in Classical Indian Traditions.* Berkeley: University of California Press.

Osborne, Arthur 1957 *The Incredible Sai Baba: The Life and Miracles of a Modern-day Saint.* Bombay: Orient Longman Ltd.

Patterson, Orlando 1967 *The Sociology of Slavery.* London: McGibbon and Kee.

Penelhum, Terence 1986 "Critical Response." In *Karma and Rebirth: Post Classical Developments.* (R. W. Neufeldt, ed.). State University of New York Press, pp. 339–345.

Radhakrishnan, Sarvapalli 1939 *Eastern Religions and Western Thought.* Oxford: The Clarendon Press.

Ramadhar, Koonj (ed.) 1983 "The Birth Anniversary of our Lord." (Editorial) *Satya* (11–23–1983), p. 5.

Ramdeen, Ramadhar (ed.) n.d. *Sai News Letter.* Published by the Co-ordinating Committee, West Indies, 27 Grove Road, Valsayn, Trinidad.

Sahukar, Mani 1971 *Sai Baba: The Saint of Shirdi.* Bombay: Somaiya Publications Pvt Ltd.

Sandweiss, Samuel H. 1975 *Sai Baba: The Holy Man . . . And the Psychiatrist.* New Delhi: M. Gulab Singh & Sons (P) Ltd.

Sawn, Bickram 1983 "How it all Began." *Satya* (11–23–1983), pp. 29–30.

Schwartz, Barton M. 1967 "The Failure of Caste in Trinidad." In *Caste in Overseas Indian Communities* (B. M. Schwartz, ed). San Francisco: Chandler Publishing Company, pp. 117–147.

Schwartz, Barton M. (ed.) 1967 *Caste in Overseas Indian Communities.* San Francisco: Chandler Publishing Company.

Singh, Kelvin 1974 "East Indians and the Larger Society." In *Calcutta to Caroni: The East Indians of Trinidad* (J. G. La Guerre, ed.). Trinidad and Jamaica: Longman Caribbean Limited, pp. 39–68.

Skinner, Elliot P. 1971 "Social Stratification and Ethnic Identification." In *Peoples and Cultures of the Caribbean: An Anthropological Reader* (M.M. Horowitz, ed.). Garden City, N.Y.: The Natural History Press, pp. 117–132.

Smart, Ninian 1984 *The Religious Experience of Mankind* (3rd Edition). New York: Charles Scribner's Sons.

Smith, Abbot Emerson 1947 *Colonists in Bondage: White Servitude and Convict Labor in America 1607–1776*. Chapel Hill, N.C.: The University of North Carolina Press.

Smith, M. G. 1955 *A Framework for Caribbean Studies*. Jamaica: Extra-Mural Department, University College of the West Indies.

———. 1965 *The Plural Society in the British West Indies*. Berkeley: University of California Press.

Songs of Sri Sathya Sai Baba [no editor] n.d. Tustin, California: Sri Sathya Sai Book Center of America.

Spiro, Melford E. 1968 "Religion: Problems of Definition and Explanation." In *Anthropological Approaches to the Study of Religion* (M. Banton, ed.). A.S.A. Monographs No. 3. London: Tavistock Publications, pp. 85–126.

Swallow, D. A. 1976 *Living Saints and their Devotees: A Study of Guru Cults and their Devotees in Western Orissa*. Cambridge University (Ph.D. dissertation).

———. 1982 "Ashes and Powers: Myth, Rite and Miracle in an Indian God-Man's Cult." *Modern Asian Studies* 16: 123–158.

Turner, Victor 1969 *The Ritual Process: Structure and Anti-Structure*. Chicago: Aldine Publishing Company.

Turner, Victor and Edith Turner 1978 *Image and Pilgrimage in Christian Culture: Anthropological Perspectives*. New York: Columbia University Press.

Van Der Zee, John 1985 *Bound Over: Indentured Servitude and American Conscience*. New York: Simon and Schuster.

Vaudeville, Charlotte 1974 *Kabir*. Oxford: Oxford University Press.

Vertovec, Stephen 1985 "Ethnic Identiy, Religious Pluralism and Socio-Cultural Change in Village Trinidad" (Unpublished paper, read at the XVth Congress of the International Association for the History of Religions, University of Sydney, Australia, 18–23 August 1985).

———. 1987 *Hinduism and Social Change in Village Trinidad*. Oxford University (Ph.D. dissertation).

Wallace, Anthony F. C. 1966 *Religion: An Anthropological View*. New York: Random House.

White, Charles S. J. 1972 "The Sai Baba Movement: Approaches to the Study of Indian Saints." *Journal of Asian Studies*. 31,4: 863–878.

Williams, Eric 1944 *Capitalism and Slavery*. Chapel Hill: The University of North Carolina Press.

Wiser, William H. 1936 *The Hindu Jajmani System: A System Inter-relating Members of a Hindu Village Community in Service*. Lucknow: Lucknow Publishing Company.

Yelvington, Kevin A. 1991 (scheduled) "Trinidad and Tobago, 1988–89" In *The Latin American and Caribbean Contemporary Record,* Vol. 8. New York: Holmes and Maier.

Yinger, J. Milton 1970 *The Scientific Study of Religion.* London: The Macmillan Company.

# Index